CW00689132

RACIAL RECONCILIATION
AND PRIVILEGE

RACIAL RECONCILIATION AND PRIVILEGE

THE DEBATE WITHIN THE SEVENTH-DAY ADVENTIST CHURCH ON REGIONAL CONFERENCES

Winsley B. Hector

CLAREMONT DISSERTATIONS OF DISTINCTION 2

Racial Reconciliation and Privilege
The Debate within the Seventh-day Adventist Church on
Regional Conferences
Claremont Press
Claremont, California
Claremont Press, Claremont 91711
Imprint of Claremont School of Theology
© 2017 by Claremont School of Theology
All rights reserved, Published 2017
Printed in the United States of America

ISBN 978-1-946230-36-2

Library of Congress Cataloging-in-Publication Data

Racial Reconciliation and Privilege
The Debate within the Seventh-day Adventist Church on
Regional Conferences / Winsley B. Hector
    xvii + *320* pp. 22 x 15 cm. –(Claremont Dissertations of
           Distinction 2)
Includes bibliographical references and indices.
ISBN 978-1-946230-36-2
    1.   Christian denominations — Other Protestant
    denominations — Adventists. 2. General Conference of
    Seventh-Day Adventists 3. African American Seventh Day
    Adventists
    BX 6153.2 .H44
Cover: Selected works of Ellen White and W. E. B. du Bois. Note
how early to mid-twentieth century editions of Ellen White's core
works prominently featured white families.

This book is dedicated to

my wife,
Cleo Hector,

and my son,
Joseph Hector,

who have had to endure
an inordinate amount of my
absence in order that this project
could arrive at its long-awaited conclusion.

Contents

Foreword

Seeking to quell the Los Angeles riots in 1992, Rodney King is reported to have asked the profound, searching and fundamental question: "Can we all get along?" Essentially, this is the question Winsley Hector addresses in his new book, emanating from his detailed and thought-provoking 2012 doctoral dissertation, entitled *Racial Reconciliation, Privilege and the Debate within the Seventh-day Adventist Church in the United States on the future of Regional [Black] Conferences.* Hector is to be commended for his willingness to tackle this emotive subject referred to in his study as the "vexed terrain."

In Jud Lake's new book telling the story of race relations and American Civil War from the unique perspective of Seventh-day Adventist Church pioneer Ellen G. White, two significant comments are made: (1) Seventh-day Adventist history cannot be correctly understood without seeing the interactions between Adventist history, American history, and even world history; and (2) Lake's book shows the relevance of White's essays to contemporary the Civil War discussion. Similar comments may be made about Hector's new book, telling the story of race relations and the establishment of a unique African American administrative structure within the Seventh-day Adventist Church. It is clear that (1) Seventh-day Adventist race relations cannot be correctly understood without seeing the interactions between Adventist history, American history, and even world history; and (2) Hector's work shows the relevance of Seventhday Adventist race relations to both historic and contemporary discussions on racial reconciliation, within and beyond ecclesiastical circles.[1]

---

[1] Alita Byrd, "New Book Puts Ellen White against Civil War Backdrop," *Spectrum Magazine* 45.1 (Spring, 2017): http://spectrummagazine.org/article/2017/06/22/new-book-puts-ellen-

Hector's work is anchored in the discipline of spiritual care and pastoral counseling (SCPC), and it challenges the organizational leadership of the North American Division of the Seventh-day Adventist Church (NAD) to follow the north star of the ministry of reconciliation, which he describes as "restoring fractured relationships and ending estrangement." He expertly provides the historical background and outlines the arguments both for the continuance and the closure of Regional Conferences as advocated by those he identifies as the Pragmatists and the Idealists respectively. The Pragmatists, championed over the years by such persons as former world Church Vice President Dr. Calvin Rock, Oakwood University President, Dr. Les Pollard, and Regional Conference leaders, argue for this structural accommodation on the basis of cultural solidarity, "mission particularity" and the development of black leadership. On the other hand, former *Adventist Review* editor Dr. William Johnson, Harvard professor, and Adventist thought leader, Dr. David Williams and Andrews University Pastor Dwight Nelson proffer the "unity defense" for dissolving Regional Conferences. Idealists are of the opinion that Regional Conferences represent a visible sign of the church's racial legacy and current divisions. Interestingly, Hector posits that Idealists say little about a process of reconciliation, the assimilation of black members and administrators into the general church structure, or the resultant effect of abolishing Regional Conferences on both black and white members.

Of course, as is well argued, it is quite difficult to talk about racial reconciliation in the NAD without addressing the specter of white privilege. It is the unspoken behemoth that is central to any discussion of the subject. A failure to confront the historical legacy of white privilege, which McIntosh defines as "an invisible package of unearned assets," will frustrate any efforts at racial reconciliation, no matter how magnanimous the intent.

---

whiteagainst-civil-war-backdrop (accessed 6/28/17). Judson S. Lake, *A Nation in God's Hands: Ellen White and the Civil War* (Nampa, ID: Pacific Press Publishing Association, 2017).

I applaud Hector for his hopeful stance in this study and his desire to see the implementation of the Yamamoto's four stage model of racial reconciliation (Recognition, Responsibility, Reconstruction, and Reparation) to bring about the desired racial reconciliation within the NAD. Hector believes that, with some adaptation, this model can serve as a constructive approach to this complex but necessary work of racial healing. He goes further by advancing the position that any signal from church leaders at the NAD to engage in overcoming past alienation must be met with support from all black leaders of Regional Conferences, as well as the other conference and union administrators in a national, racial reconciliation process. Theoretical and research support should also be forthcoming from the Church's academic community as they lend their influence to this endeavor. Hector has spent years of arduous research on this vital subject, and it is hoped that his book can indeed be a catalyst for the deliberations he advocates.

Some may argue that his approach is unrealistic, too "aspirational" given our fallen human nature. But as a people of faith, challenged by the unerring Biblical message of unity in John 17, I fully support his laudable intellectual pursuit and corrective. This book represents an important contribution to the debate within Adventism, particularly within the NAD, and it is illustrative of Hector's ability to express his honest convictions with academic vigor and professionalism. The growing national interest in the issues of diversity, inclusion and equity as evidenced recently by the outbursts and the resultant #ItIsTimeAU video by students at Andrews University – the Church's flagship training institution – as well as the graying of the white members in the NAD, and the continued growth and influence of visible minorities in the Church, all demonstrate the wisdom of engaging in a process as Hector outlines. Too much is at stake to do otherwise.

Clinton A. Valley, MBA, Ed.D
Former President
University of the Southern Caribbean

PREFACE

The Seventh-day Adventist Church (SDA) in the United States established a unique governance structure called Regional [Black] Conferences in 1944, to accommodate its black members. This reluctant decision of church leaders at the time was significantly informed by the church's discriminatory practices. In the intervening period, these largely black-constituted and black-operated conferences have facilitated a significant expansion of black membership, leadership, financial resources, and political and social capital for blacks within Seventh-day Adventism. Despite these achievements, Regional Conferences present a dilemma for some black and white church leaders and laypeople, and a debate has ensued. "Idealists" question whether these institutions represent the best in Christian ethics of inclusion and equality; "Pragmatists" counter that their viability is justified by the productivity they facilitate and the need for cultural solidarity among blacks. This debate comes at a time when racial barriers in U.S. society are being challenged. However, a critical examination of the arguments for the closure or continuance of Regional Conferences reveals impediments to resolution–especially white privilege–that could be ameliorated by adapting Eric K. Yamamoto's "Interracial Justice" model as a means of working toward racial reconciliation in the SDA Church.

I was motivated to research this topic for my doctoral dissertation because of the SDA Church's racial past, in the hope that this re-examination might establish both a mandate and possible methods for engaging in the essential Christian practice of reconciliation, leading to a resolution on a dark chapter that the SDA church shares with the wider United States society. Since reconciliation is a complex process that extends beyond the spiritual care and pastoral counseling field, a multidisciplinary approach was adopted, including insights from ethics, social psychology, and the peace and justice movement to arrive at the most salutary model. In this regard, Eric K. Yamamoto's

"Interracial Justice" model of racial reconciliation, with its four stages of Recognition, Responsibility, Reconstruction, and Reparation, could serve as a basic framework for the SDA Church if it is to contend with this most "vexing" problem. I am indebted to Claremont Press for making this text readily available to a wider audience since it can serve to illuminate and motivate, then investigate and finally judiciously effectuate a more authentic way of being within the SDA Church in the United States around the issue of race relations.

I would also like to acknowledge members of my dissertation committee Kathleen Greider, Duane Bidwell and Phil Zuckerman for their guidance and mentoring, without them this publication would have been impossible. I am also grateful to the following friends and colleagues who have provided invaluable support and encouragement as conversational partners; they include Josh Anguiano, Charles Bradford, Jeffrey Brown, Curtis Fox, Joseph McCoy, Calvin Rock, Dan Smith, and Clinton Valley. I would like to thank G. Alexander Bryant, Secretary of the North American Division of the SDA Church, who offered valuable insights into the thinking of church leaders on this subject. I have also appreciated the assistance from reference librarians at Claremont School of Theology, Claremont Graduate University, and La Sierra University. Importantly, I would like to thank my Lord and Savior Jesus Christ, who as Comforter and Counselor sustained me during what at times was a most grueling, but enchanting process.

Winsley B. Hector

Introduction

> What should be done for the colored race has long been a *vexed question*, because professed Christians have not had the Spirit of Christ. They have been called by His name but they have not imitated His example. Men have thought it necessary to plan in such a way as to meet the prejudice of the white people; and a wall of separation in religious worship has been built up between the colored people and the white people.[1]

To most outsiders, the Seventh-day Adventist (SDA) Church in the United States may have the appearance of a religious organization at peace with itself regarding the issue of race relations. From the time of its formal organization in 1863, in the midst of the U.S. Civil War, the SDA Church has avoided the fate of other denominations such as the Methodists, Baptists, and Presbyterians, with their North–South divide due to slavery and post-Civil War racial hostilities. The intact nature of the denomination over the intervening period has, however, masked the fact that the SDA church has not been immune from racial tensions between blacks and whites.

White Adventist historians Richard W. Schwarz and Floyd Greenleaf, in their authorized history of the SDA church, confirm that "One of the knotty social issues that haunted the church from its early days was the question of ethnic diversity. Its most virulent manifestation erupted in relations between Black and White Adventists."[2] Just a generation ago, some blacks were not permitted

---

[1] Ellen G. White. *The Southern Work* (Washington, DC: Review and Herald Publishing Association, 1966), 20; italics mine.

[2] They mentioned three countries where racial tensions flared up, in the US, the UK, and South Africa, only the first two will be addressed in this dissertation. The primary focus of this study is the racial tensions between blacks and whites in the US and the UK since they lend themselves to a useful comparison. Richard W. Schwarz and Floyd Greenleaf, *Light Bearers: A History of the Seventh-day Adventist Church* (Nampa, ID: Pacific Press Publishing Association, 2000), 499.

1

to worship in white congregations, and black leaders were excluded from eating in the General Conference (GC) cafeteria;[3] such has been the nature of discrimination meted out to blacks. Yet these discriminatory practices are not surprising given the observations of Adventist scholars Malcolm Bull and Keith Lockhart that as a nascent denomination, Adventists were an "all-white movement that embodied the prejudiced attitudes and experienced the racial problems of America as a whole."[4] It should be noted that Bull is white and Lockhart is black.[5]

Ongoing racial discrimination brought Adventism to a crossroads in 1944, when the church finally acquiesced to blacks' request for their own governance structure called Regional [Black] Conferences. They were given the name Regional Conferences because their territory was not limited to states, as were most of the traditional conferences, and they were viewed as a structural accommodation to blacks in order to achieve self-determination and growth within the wider black community. These largely black-constituted and black-operated organizational tiers have facilitated a significant expansion of black membership, leadership, and financial resources, as well as political and social capital for blacks within Adventism.[6] More recently, this structural accommodation presents a dilemma for church leaders, some of whom question whether these Regional Conferences represent the best in Christian ethics of inclusion and equality, and others of whom argue that their viability is justified by their productivity and need for cultural solidarity. Decades after their formulation, Regional Conferences are at the center of a debate inside Adventism. The debate highlights an

---

[3] William G. Johnsson, "Four Big Questions." *Adventist Review* (May 25, 2006): http://www.adventistreview.org/issue.php?issue=2006-1515&page=8 (accessed 8/17/10). The GC is the world headquarters of the Seventh-day Adventist Church.

[4] Malcolm Bull and Keith Lockhart, *Seeking a Sanctuary: Seventh-day Adventism and the American Dream* (San Francisco: Harper & Row, 1989), 193.

[5] I will attempt to identify the ethnicity of all Adventists referenced to in this dissertation, given the relevance of ethnicity to the issue of racial reconciliation in the SDA Church.

[6] Though mainly established to expand Adventism among blacks, Regional Conferences are comprised of ethnic minorities including Latinos.

understandable ambivalence over the prevailing governance structure at a time when racial barriers in the wider society are being challenged. But does this debate also underscore the anomaly that a religious institution with an underlying premise of deconstructing barriers may inadvertently contribute to the perpetuation of the historical racial injury?

Opponents of Regional Conferences span the ethnic spectrum, and they view the demise of these conferences as evidence of the church turning its back on its troubled racial past. Their theological basis for the dismantling of Regional Conferences coalesces around the Christian mandate of unity and mutual love. Illustrative of this perspective is the position of Dwight Nelson, the white senior pastor of Pioneer Memorial SDA Church on the campus of Andrews University. Nelson writes, "Isn't it clear that God isn't looking for a White church or Black church? He waits for the remnant church. 'By this will the world know that you are My people if you have love for one another.'"[7] Nelson views Regional Conferences as anomalous and anachronistic since the separate but equal paradigm of decades past in American society is no longer valid.[8] On the other hand, proponents of Regional Conferences affirm the idiom, "If it ain't broke, don't fix it," and central to their argument is the need for cultural solidarity. Prominent amongst this group is black administrator Calvin Rock who posits that "Cultural pluralism neither prevents fraternity nor discourages contact. It simply organizes what already exists — 'grassroots' diversity — for the sake of gospel proclamation."[9] Furthermore, Rock believes that dissolution of Regional Conferences will do more to rupture than

---

[7] Dwight K. Nelson, *The Eleventh Commandment: A Fresh Look at Loving Your Neighbor as Yourself* (Nampa, ID: Pacific Press Publishing Association, 2001), 62.

[8] Nelson advances this idea in a sermon. Nelson, "The Truth in Black and White," *Pioneer Memorial SDA Church* (Jan. 16, 2010): http://www.pmchurch.tv/article.php?id=30 (accessed 9/6/10).

[9] Calvin B. Rock, "Black Seventh-day Adventists and Structural Accommodations," *Perspectives: Black Seventh-day Adventists Face the Twenty-first Century* (ed. Calvin B. Rock; Hagerstown, MD: Review and Herald Publishing Association, 1996), 119-26.

repair relationships among blacks and whites, because of the black disempowerment that would result.[10]

As a result of the ongoing dialogue in Adventism on the future of Regional Conferences, the status quo is maintained and racial reconciliation is sidelined as, metaphorically speaking, radio silence is assumed by prominent national and international church leaders.[11] Responding to questions from young adults during a forum, former GC president Jan Paulsen elevated the conversation on the future of Regional Conferences when he articulated his concerns about the status quo. Paulsen admonished his audience to: "Tell leaders you think the reasoning behind regional conferences is no longer valid. I also tell them, but it is good if they hear it from you as well."[12] There appears to be a sense of resignation in Paulsen's response since his solicitation on the matter had been ineffectual – and so for many, the "vexed question" remains.

Given the nature of racism in the United States due to the historic injury of slavery, to preserve their dignity and humanity blacks have sought refuge in black institutions, be they educational, religious or economic — what Roy Brooks calls "limited separation."[13] This coping strategy, which is an understandable defense against the destruction of the black self by racism and white supremacy, is deemed by some to be inconsistent with a denomination whose self-

---

[10] Calvin B. Rock, "Adventist Review: Readers Respond to Four Big Questions." *Adventist Review* (Aug. 10, 2006): http://www. adventistreview.org/issue.php?issue=2006-1522&page=13 (accessed 8/17/10).

[11] See pages 11-12 for a definition of racial reconciliation.

[12] "Let's Talk Encore: D.C. Young Professionals Talk Change with Adventist Church President," *Adventist News Network* (Sept. 29, 2009): http://news.adventist.org/2009/09/lets-talk-encore-dc.html (accessed 8/25/10).

[13] This civil rights theory "envisions voluntary racial isolation that is racially nonexclusive and available to all racial groups, not just to blacks. Thus, limited separation is not total separation or racial segregation." Roy L. Brooks, *Racial Justice in the Age of Obama* (Princeton, NJ: Princeton University Press, 2009), 63-64.

understanding is that of "the Remnant Church."[14] As the record will show, since the SDA Church failed to adhere to its own ideal of equality and justice for all, some form of structural accommodation became necessary to enable blacks to survive in the SDA Church during the heights of pre-civil rights racial discrimination and in light of contemporary racial disparity. Whether such structures should remain, is secondary to the more important issue of causation, chief among which are racism and embedded privilege. This focus on racism and privilege is obligatory, given what most race relations scholars, such as Houston A. Baker, assert, "the undeniable national truth is that thoroughgoing, redemptive victory over race in America — at least with respect to the black majority — is still a dream."[15]

Is the fact that a system of structural accommodation remains in the twenty-first century, with minimal effort on the part of Adventist leaders to explore alternatives, evidence of the underappreciated concept of privilege? Privilege is typically

---

[14] The Remnant church doctrine, based upon an understanding of Revelation 12:17, is the belief that the SDA church has a unique message of faith in Jesus and confidence in God's word, including adherence to God's commandments, which must be shared with the world before the Second Coming of Christ. These references include Michael Pearson, points to "the moral dilemmas within contemporary Seventh-day Adventism," dilemmas that essentially stem from the church's theological past. Michael Pearson, *Millennial Dreams and Moral Dilemmas: Seventh-day Adventism and Contemporary Ethics* (Cambridge: Cambridge University Press, 1990), 5-6. See also Zdravko Plantak, who observes "inconsistencies in the church's approach to human rights." Zdravko Plantak, *The Silent Church: Human Rights and Adventist Social Ethics* (Basingstoke, Hampshire: Macmillan, 1998), 3. Both Pearson and Plantak highlight beliefs in the Advent, the Remnant, and Church Unity as profoundly shaping Adventist ethics and Adventists perception of themselves in the world. By "Advent" is meant the Second Coming of Christ to the earth to reward the faithful with eternal life and the unfaithful with damnation; the Remnant concept as stated is one of religious exclusivity, doctrinal purity, and Church Unity. Pearson, 17-42.

[15] Houston A. Baker, Jr., *Betrayal: How Black Intellectuals Have Abandoned the Ideals of the Civil Rights Era* (New York: Columbia University Press, 2008), 213.

addressed as a white, often male phenomenon, but it affects all those in positions of power. In her landmark article, Peggy McIntosh reflects on how she was taught to see "racism as something that puts others at a disadvantage," but what was overlooked was the corollary: that privilege advantages whites. McIntosh defines white privilege as "an invisible package of unearned assets" that whites can access and utilize daily, but its presence is obscured.[16] Furthermore, Frances E. Kendall argues that the hidden nature of white privilege makes it difficult for most whites to understand the "complexities of white privilege and how it affects their daily lives. [On the other hand] people of color in all organizations are very clear that primary access to power and influence lies in white hands."[17] Consequently, any effort to mitigate the forces of racism must at a minimum include making visible the privilege of whiteness, argues psychologist Derald Wing Sue: "As long as Whiteness remains invisible and is equated with normality and superiority, People of Color will continue to suffer from its oppressive qualities."[18] Similarly, so long as the debate within the SDA Church revolves around the future of Regional Conferences, the privileges whiteness confers in the SDA Church will remain hidden and ascendant, and the disenfranchisement and oppression of blacks will remain covert and constant.

This debate about the Regional Conferences underscores the anomaly that a religious institution with the stated premise of deconstructing barriers may inadvertently contribute to the perpetuation of historical racial injury and embedded privilege, thus impacting how black and white Adventists relate. As a black Adventist clergyperson in the field of spiritual care and pastoral

---

[16] Peggy McIntosh, "White Privilege: Unpacking the Invisible Knapsack," (1988): http://www.case.edu/president/aaction/unpacking TheKnapsack.pdf (accessed 7/6/10).

[17] France E. Kendall, *Understanding White Privilege: Creating Pathways to Authentic Relationships across Race* (New York: Routledge, 2006), xii.

[18] Derald Wing Sue, "The Invisible Whiteness of Being," *Addressing Racism: Facilitating Cultural Competence in Mental Health and Educational Settings* (ed. Madonna G. Constantine and Derald Wing Su; Hoboken, NJ: John Wiley & Sons, 2006), 28; Derald Wing Sue, *Overcoming Our Racism: The Journey to Liberation* (Hoboken: John Wiley & Sons, 2003), 138.

counseling (SCPC), I aim to provide a nuanced perspective regarding this ongoing dispute.[19] My experience with racism in the SDA Church comes primarily from my home in England. I was one of over fifty black British students who was encouraged to attend Oakwood University (a historically black Adventist institution), because Newbold College of Higher Education, the Adventist school we should have been able to attend, discriminated against British blacks in its admissions policy. However, I have first-hand accounts of racism in Adventism in the United States from my black relatives and friends as well as stories from some of my Oakwood University professors. I personally recall hearing one black professor, Elder E. E. Cleveland (the most successful Adventist evangelist) share the experience of himself and other blacks being denied entrance into the cafeteria of the SDA General Conference because of their color, this despite his position there as the associate secretary for the Ministerial Association in the late 1950s and 60s. As a civil rights leader in his own right, he was fond of reminding his students that he became the first black man to integrate a GC department. Many of my Caribbean relatives who came to study medicine or to pursue other professions in the United States recall being redirected to the nearest black SDA church because they were not welcomed by many of the white churches in Southern California in the 1960s. These anecdotal experiences serve to illustrate the degree of racial discrimination which many black Adventists have encountered. They also serve to illuminate why, in the end, blacks sought to establish their own conferences as a means of solidarity rather than walk away from the church they adored to establish their own denomination. I believe that it is this deep sense of commitment to the theological tenants of the SDA Church by blacks, despite the racial inequities they have encountered, that can act as one of the drivers for racial reconciliation.

The Regional Conference debate tends to unfairly but understandably situate the future of Regional Conferences at the center of the conversation, while minimizing impediments to racial reconciliation, including the issue of privilege. In contrast, in this

---

[19] Spiritual care is used in preference to pastoral care simply because of the more inclusive nature of the term.

book, I argue that only after serious consideration is given to the process of racial reconciliation should any calculation about the future of Regional Conferences be deemed necessary. Since reconciling — restoring fractured relationships and ending estrangement — is one of the core functions within the pastoral care tradition (the others being healing, sustaining, guiding, prophesying and liberation) the relevance of the field for bringing clarity and insight to issues of racism and racial reconciliation is apparent.

Reconciling is viewed by pastoral care historians William Clebsch and Charles Jaekle as having the most promise of all the pastoral functions. They argue that the theological basis for reconciliation is rooted in the fact that breaches in interpersonal relationships are, at their core, alienation from God.[20] Given its importance, "reconciling" is surprisingly underdeveloped within the SCPC field, as evidenced by its inconsequential entry in the *Dictionary of Pastoral Care and Counseling* (DPCC), and the fact that few leaders in the field have deemed it important enough to emphasize.[21] Both the underrepresentation and the importance of reconciling will be explored later in the book as I examine the debate inside Adventism over the future of Regional Conferences.

It is hoped that a formulation for attempting racial reconciliation will emerge from this study, building on the work of others in the field of SCPC. To achieve such a formulation, it will be necessary to expand the horizon of pastoral theology and care to include insights from clergy practitioners, as well as scholars in the field of ethics, systematic theology, social psychology, and the peace and justice movement. It should be stated, however, that reconciliation is a complex undertaking, as professor of peace studies Johan Galtung acknowledges when he writes, "Reconciliation is a theme with deep psychological, sociological, theological,

---

[20] They observe that, "Partly by virtue of insisting that broken human relationships involve a breach in man's ultimate relationship with his Creator, pastoral care takes the human need for reconciliation with a seriousness unsurpassed by that of other healing arts." William A. Clebsch and Charles R. Jaekle, *Pastoral Care in Historical Perspective: An Essay with Exhibits* (Englewood, NJ: Prentice-Hall, 1964), 81.

[21] The three prominent leaders in the field addressing reconciling to any significant degree are Anton T. Boisen, Wayne E. Oates, and Charles V. Gerkin.

8

philosophical, and profoundly human roots—and nobody really knows how to successfully achieve it."[22] Questions that can serve as a compass in navigating this "vexed" terrain include the following: Is doing nothing but debate the anachronism or relevance of Regional Conferences a viable option? Why has racial reconciliation never been a part of this ongoing dialogue? Is it realistic to burden the Christian gospel with finding solutions to the self-perpetuating scourge of racism? Does Christian unity demand multicultural union? Is what H. Richard Niebuhr considered to be the "basic moral issue"[23]—namely, Christ transforming culture–practicable in an increasingly nativistic, tribalistic, and parochial era? This latter question provides a sobering reality that the subject of this book may be too aspirational, given the unjust nature of humanity; but should we not strive to restore to wholeness our common humanity?

The thesis of this book is that a critical examination of the arguments for the closure or continuance of Regional Conferences reveals impediments to resolution—especially white privilege—that can be ameliorated by adapting Eric K. Yamamoto's "Interracial Justice" model as a means of working toward racial reconciliation in the SDA Church. The methodological approach employed in addressing this thesis is that of a literature research and analysis on the subjects of racial reconciliation, white privilege, and racism, particularly as it relates to the SDA Church in the United States. Finding scholarly material addressing racial reconciliation from an SCPC and an Adventist perspective has been difficult. It has been interesting to note that, for most authors, a definition of racial reconciliation is rarely articulated, with most perhaps assuming the reader comes to the subject with a preconceived definition. This assumption is clearly problematic since racial reconciliation means different things to individuals and groups, according to their

---

[22] Johan Galtung, "After Violence, Reconstruction, Reconciliation, and Resolution: Coping with Visible and Invisible Effects of War and Violence," *Reconciliation, Justice, and Coexistence: Theory and Practice* (ed. Mohammed Abu-Nimer; Lanham, MD: Lexington Books, 2001), 4.

[23] Niebuhr believed that cultural values could be transformed for Christian purposes. Glen H. Stassen, D. M. Yeager and John Howard Yoder, *Authentic Transformation: A New Vision of Christ and Culture* (Nashville: Abingdon Press, 1996), 32.

respective contexts.[24] The working definition for racial reconciliation noted below is a synthesis of ideas and themes established during the course of this book but informed by the two elements of "reconciling" in the SCPC tradition, namely forgiveness and discipline. However, the field of SCPC offers an array of lenses that address the human dynamics at work in matters relating to racial reconciliation, white privilege and racism since, in reconciling, it seeks to call back together the estranged. It is this unique perspective that can offer a bridge between the two sides in the ongoing debate inside Adventism on the closure or continuance of Regional Conferences–beyond the merely historical and theological perspectives advanced to date. As an Adventist, I take the Bible as my authoritative source from which my theological foundation is established. The inspirational writings of Ellen G. White (a white woman whom the church considers a prophet), has enabled me to comprehend the Bible better, and the SCPC field has helped to clarify the human situations.

The field of SCPC operates in the context of providing care within community and restoring to wholeness our common humanity. Through an array of spiritual practices, practical wisdom, therapeutic traditions, intercultural understanding, and a more expansive religious worldview, the field has attempted to contextualize the universal nature of the human condition. It has also become more self-reflective to include how the impact of social location and privilege can complicate care. Indeed, there has been a revaluing of difference, argues pastoral theologian Nancy Ramsay, so that issues of race, culture, gender, class, religion are now renegotiated. Postmodernity is embraced so that assessing justice, power differentials, marginalization, and oppression come into wider focus. In addition, love as a relational ethic is used to assess any justice considerations rather than simply being viewed as a

---

[24] This observation is made by South African Theologian John W. de Gruchy, who writes that the word 'reconciliation' "is so overloaded with ambiguity in some contexts and so emptied of significant meaning in others that we may well wonder whether it remains a useful term in universal discourse." John W. de Gruchy, *Reconciliation: Restoring Justice* (Minneapolis: Fortress Press, 2002), 25.

stand-alone command.[25] It is these significant contributions to the issue of racial reconciliation that the field of SCPC brings to this text.

It should be noted that an inherent challenge exists in achieving racial reconciliation at the macro level (the national church), compared to the micro level (members of the local church). Generally speaking, at the macro level there is a concern for church polity and policy, and to a lesser extent, interrelatedness, while at the micro level it is the reverse. I believe that this reality could make reconciliation more manageable for church administrators who must relate to each other in ways substantively different than local members (collegiality vs. camaraderie). Since the SDA Church is a hierarchical institution in which members generally have a positive regard for leaders, a top-down reconciliation process may be challenging but certainly possible. Hence, the primary target of this text are church leaders, though the voice of local church members should not be lost in this dialogue; notwithstanding the odds of a trickle-down effect are greater than a bottom-up, at least in my estimation. However, individual members will have an important role to play in actualizing racial reconciliation. Anecdotally, I have found in pastoring multiethnic churches both in Great Britain and the United States, that there appears to be a willingness on the part of these congregants to embrace cultural diversity if they are led in such a direction. Hence, I believe that there is a reciprocal process between leaders and congregants in any racial reconciliation effort in which one motivates and sustains the efforts of the other.

The arguments of this book will be outlined as follows. In chapter two, a literature review will explore the contributions of SCPC and related fields in addressing the subjects of racial reconciliation, white privilege, and racism. Three categories of literature on racial reconciliation have been identified. The first includes advocates of "reconciling" in the SCPC tradition, as well as the field's treatment of white identity and racism. Since there is little in the way of Adventist scholarship in the area of racial reconciliation, a rationale for why this is so, as well as a review of

---

[25] Nancy J. Ramsay, "Contemporary Pastoral Theology: A Wider Vision for the Practice of Love," *Pastoral Care and Counseling: Redefining the Paradigms* (ed. Nancy J. Ramsay; Nashville: Abingdon Press, 2004), 160, 161, 171.

racism in Adventist literature are explored. The second discusses the books authored by clergy practitioners arising from the evangelical racial reconciliation movement of the late 1980s through the 1990s. The third highlights the published works of those who are either engaged in or observers of the peace and justice movement, which seeks to establish common ground in divided societies. There is also a review of some selected literature addressing white privilege within the SCPC and other psychosocial disciplines. A historical overview of the SDA church and the world it emerged from is offered in chapter three. Attention is paid to the church's millennial movement roots with its belief that as society moves closer to becoming a Christian one, Christ will return to usher in the end of the world. However, internal inconsistencies slowed the Christianizing of America, argue sociologists Michael Emerson and Christian Smith, notably regarding the issue of slavery.[26] One factor that could have influenced the decision of the SDA Church to adopt a segregationist stance is the post-Civil War reunification process, and the role played by race and religion in that sectional union. The prophetic and influential role of Ellen G. White on the church's irresolute approach to work among blacks is discussed, as the church moved from a desegregated to a segregated stance, in order to alleviate white hostilities to the propagation of the nascent denomination's beliefs. How the church handled dissent by black clergymen such as James K. Humphrey and Lewis Sheafe is also considered. Also, probed is an unfortunate incident involving a black woman named Lucy Byard and the Washington Sanitarium, own and operated by the SDA Church. Her untimely death, attributed to a lack of immediate medical care because she was black, served as the catalyst for white church leaders to address the demands of blacks for equality and desegregation, by agreeing to establish Regional (Black) Conferences. The effectiveness of these new governance structures over the last sixty-five years, along with a discussion of attempts at racial reconciliation by the SDA Church, is also delineated. By way of comparison, Chapter 3 concludes by investigating how the issue of racial discrimination and black

---

[26] Michael O. Emerson and Christian Smith, *Divided by Faith: Evangelical Religion and the Problem of Race in America* (Oxford: Oxford University Press, 2000), 30f.

disenfranchisement by white Adventists in the United Kingdom in the 1970s was tackled, resulting in a reduction in the racial disparity of black Adventists.

In this book, opponents of Regional Conferences will be referred to as Idealists and proponents as Pragmatists. The rationale for these choices was to avoid more combative labels such as opponents and proponents. Despite the unanimous consent to approve the resolution establishing Regional Conferences on April 9, 1944,[27] the vigorous debate that preceded the vote in many ways has continued to the present. In presenting the arguments advanced by Idealists and Pragmatists, I will analyze both for their strengths and weaknesses, with the aid of literature from SCPC and other fields, as noted above.

Chapter 4 lays out the arguments advanced by Idealists — those who desire to see the dissolution of Regional Conferences. Idealists are of the opinion that Regional Conferences represent a visible sign of the church's racial legacy and current divisions. The debate gained currency when on May 25, 2006, William G. Johnsson who is white, and who served as editor of the flagship journal of the SDA Church, broached the issue as one of four substantive problems church administrators must consider.[28] Johnsson's "What will it take to bring us together?" question can best be framed as the "unity defense" for dissolving Regional Conferences, and it is the normative posture for most exponents of this view. However, little is often said about a process of reconciliation, the assimilation of black members and administrators into the general church structure, or the resultant effect of abolishing Regional Conferences on both black and white members.

---

[27] Delbert W. Baker, "Regional Conferences: 50 Years of Progress," *Adventist Review* (Nov. 2, 1995), 14.

[28] The four questions are: Will the church in North America be flexible enough to accommodate the changes that lie just ahead? What will be the role of our institutions — our hospitals, schools, publishing houses, etc.? When will Adventists in North America honestly face the challenge of the movies? And, what will it take to bring us together? William G. Johnsson, "Four Big Questions," *Adventist Review* (May 25, 2006): http://www.adventistreview.org/issue.php?issue=2006-1515&page=8 (accessed 8/17/10).

Chapter 5 outlines the strengths and weaknesses of the arguments advanced by Pragmatists, those who wish to see Regional Conferences maintained. Calvin Rock, who is black, best typifies Pragmatists since his doctoral dissertation offers cogent analysis and support for a structural framework that integrates a black minority within a once white majority denomination. Rock's defense of the structural accommodation in the form of Regional Conferences, is that given the reality of "white flight" and the need of blacks for "cultural solidarity," a greater harm will be done should these institutions be tampered with.[29] Pragmatists, who tend to coalesce around this cultural solidarity defense in its various formulations, may be challenged by a debate over the Church and cultural engagement as encapsulated by H. Richard Niebuhr's classic *Christ and Culture*. Given the hope that a transformative engagement of Christ and culture was anticipated by Niebuhr, Pragmatists could be challenged on the need for faith in the possibility of change to the social order, including increased intercultural and interethnic solidarity.

Scholars in various disciplines have sought to articulate an ethical stance when addressing the odious issue of racism and its concomitant white privilege. Chapter 6 attempts to establish both the rationale and the processes for racial reconciliation from an SCPC perspective. Of the theological significance of reconcile-iation, Scottish theologian James Denney declares that it "is the central and fundamental experience of the Christian religion; the doctrine of reconciliation is not so much one doctrine as the inspiration and focus of all."[30] The term "reconciliation" is principally a New Testament (NT) concept, which conveys the sense of exchanging places with the other, being in solidarity with and not against the other. The Apostle Paul is credited with developing the doctrine of reconciliation, though the idea is inherent whenever estrangement or hostility is to be surmounted and unity restored.

---

[29] Calvin B. Rock, *"Institutional Loyalty Versus Racial Freedom: The Dilemma of Black Seventh-day Adventist Leadership"* (Ph.D. diss., Vanderbilt University, 1984), 4.

[30] James Denney, *The Christian Doctrine of Reconciliation* (New York: George H. Doran, 1918), 6.

Pastoral theologians under consideration include Edward P. Wimberly who focuses on issues of oppression and empowerment; James Poling who challenges social inequities, framing them as "evil;" Carroll Watkins Ali, Lee H. Butler, and Homer U. Ashby, Jr, all emphasize a communal approach to overcoming racism and advocate for a survival and liberation strategy for blacks; and Archie Smith, Jr., who contends that black cultural heritage should be embraced as a resource to empowerment.[31] Other pastoral theologians, such as Sharon G. Thornton, have grounded their discourse on racism and its remedies in a suffering motif, whereas Donald Chinula focuses on caregiving among oppressed communities. Still others like Nancy J. Ramsay share practical considerations for combating racism.[32] Theologian Fumitaka Matsuoka also provides a theological perspective on racial reconciliation by exploring issues of alienation and hope in the midst of a culture of oppression, while systematic theologian Miroslav Volf grounds his reconciliation discourse in solidarity and self-donation of the cross of Christ.[33] This rich understanding of pastoral care

---

[31] Edward P. Wimberly, *American Churches and Communities* (Nashville: Abingdon Press, 2000); and Wimberly, *African American Pastoral Care* (Nashville: Abingdon Press, 2008); James Newton Poling, *Deliver Us from Evil: Resisting Racial and Gender Oppression* (Minneapolis: Fortress Press, 1996); Ali, 19; Homer Ashby, *Our Home Is Over Jordan: A Black Pastoral Theology* (St. Louis, MO: Chalice Press, 2003), 9f; and Archie Smith, *Navigating the Deep River: Spirituality in African American Families* (Cleveland: United Church Press, 1997), xvi-xvii; Lee H. Bulter Jr., *Liberating Our Dignity, Saving Our Souls* (St. Louis, MO: Chalice Press, 2006), 158.

[32] Nancy J. Ramsay, "Navigating Racial Difference as a White Pastoral Theologian," *Journal of Pastoral Theology* 12, no. 2 (2002): 13. Marsha Foster Boyd and Carolyn Stahl Bohler, "Womanist-Feminist Alliances: Meeting on the Bridge," in *Feminist and Womanist Pastoral Theology* (ed. Bonnie J. Miller-McLemore and Brita L. Gill-Austern; Nashville: Abingdon Press, 1999), 190

[33] Thornton views Christ's suffering on the cross as ascribing meaning to the masking and minimizing of the reality of pain. Sharon G. Thornton, *Broken Yet Beloved: A Pastoral Theology of the Cross* (St. Louis, MO: Chalice Press, 2002), 3. By solidarity, Volf refers to "struggling on the side of, rather than simply suffering together with, solidarity may not be severed from self-donation. All sufferers can find comfort in the solidarity

considerations and the practical applications outlined can contribute to a viable way forward for SDA Church leaders in grappling with the history of racism within the church.

There is a consensus within the reconciliation literature that no one methodological framework for achieving racial reconciliation exists for all situations.34   Within the Evangelical religious community, differing approaches towards racial healing have been advanced by clergy with a passion for the ministry of reconciliation. Since no other situation in recent memory is more emblematic of a racial reconciliation process than was South Africa's Truth and Reconciliation Commission (TRC),35 it will be evaluated for its

---

of the Crucified; but only those who struggle against evil by following the example of the Crucified will discover him at their side. To claim the comfort of the Crucified while rejecting his way is to advocate not only cheap grace but a deceitful ideology." Miroslav Volf, *Exclusion and Embrace: A Theological Exploration of Identity, Otherness, and Reconciliation* (Nashville: Abingdon Press, 1996), 24. Chinula speaks of the oppressed community searching for the "Beloved Community." Donald M. Chinula, *Building King's Beloved Community: Foundations for Pastoral Care and Counseling with the Oppressed* (Cleveland, OH: United Church Press, 1997), xiv. Matsuoka reflects on alienation during oppression. Fumitaka Matsuoka, *The Color of Faith: Building Community in a Multiracial Society (Cleveland, OH: United Church Press, 1998).*

34 This reality is affirmed by the following statement: "While common goals, hopes, and aspirations may be shared, in the end the method of finding healing, establishing justice and securing peace will and must differ." Miguel A. De La Torre, *Liberating Jonah: Forming an Ethics of Reconciliation* (Maryknoll, NY: Orbis Books, 2007), 87f.

35 Books proliferate on the subject of the TRC of South Africa include: Charles Villa-Vicencio and Wilhelm Verwoerd, ed., *Looking Back Reaching Forward: Reflections on the Truth and Reconciliation Commission of South Africa* (Cape Town: University of Cape Town Press, 2000); Lyn S. Graybill, *Truth and Reconciliation in South Africa: Miracle or Model?* (Boulder, CO: Lynne Rienner Publishers, 2002); Michael Battle, *Reconciliation: The Ubuntu Theology of Desmond Tutu* (Cleveland, OH: Pilgrim Press, 1997); Audrey R. Chapman and Hugo van der Merwe, eds., *Truth and Reconciliation in South Africa: Did the TRC Deliver?* (Philadelphia: University of Pennsylvania Press, 2008); Gregory Baum and Harold Wells, *The Reconciliation of Peoples: Challenges to the Churches* (Geneva: WCC Publication, 1997); and Martin Meredith, *Coming to Terms: South Africa's Search for Truth* (New York: Public Affairs, 1999).

central premise, namely restorative justice, which includes "truth, dialogue, and reparations to victims from the state."36 Other reconciliation approaches, including those arising out of the peace and justice movements, are considered to establish a framework for racial reconciliation within the Adventist context. Of particular interest is the work of Eric K. Yamamoto on the issue of Interracial Justice. I argue that Yamamoto offers a compelling four stage model of racial reconciliation (Recognition, Responsibility, Reconstruction, and Reparation) that, with some adaptation, can serve as a constructive approach to this complex but necessary work of racial healing in the SDA Church.37

Other areas of consideration include conflict management, integrated problem-solving, and decision making. How conflicts are diagnosed, and alternative possibilities developed, as well as the range of decisions made by those involved in reconciliation, both individually and collectively, are vital considerations that the SCPC tradition can elucidate. Of equal importance to reconciliation are the intrapsychic processes that contribute to stalemates, intransigence and self-interested motives. I will also demonstrate how a cognitive behavioral understanding for counteracting biases can help in addressing cognitive distortions and erroneous beliefs that may often serve to undermine reconciliation.

The final chapter is a summary conclusion, which seeks to adapt Yamamoto's Interracial Justice model to the Adventist context. Some thoughts will be shared on the reasons within Adventism for the complicity of silence on both sides of the debate regarding racial reconciliation. An appeal will be made for a ministry of reconciliation to be placed at the heart of Adventist practice, and with it, racial reconciliation. Only in so doing can the church accurately reflect the sentiments of its "Statement on Racism" — that

---

36 Hugo Van der Merwe, "Reconciliation and Justice in South Africa," *Reconciliation, Justice and Coexistence: Theory and Practice* (ed. Mohammed Abu-Nimer; Lanham, MD: Lexington Books, 2001), 190.

37As an internationally recognized law professor at the University of Hawaii, Yamamoto was co-counsel to Fred Korematsu in the successful reopening of the infamous WWII Japanese American internment case Korematsu v. U.S. (contributing to congressional reparations) in 1984. Eric K. Yamamoto, *Interracial Justice: Conflict and Reconciliation in Post-Civil Rights America* (New York: New York University Press, 1999).

the "Seventh-day Adventists want to be faithful to the reconciling ministry assigned to the Christian church. As a worldwide community of faith, the Seventh-day Adventist Church wishes to witness to and exhibit in her own ranks the unity and love that transcend racial differences and overcome past alienation between races."[38] This statement implicitly attests to the desire of church leaders to do what is necessary to achieve this noble standard. I believe that any signal emanating from leaders at the North American Division of SDAs to engage in overcoming past alienation, can and must, be met by all black leaders of Regional Conferences as well as the other conference and union administrators in a national, racial reconciliation process. Such a process could also be championed by the Adventist academic community, who can provide both a theoretical framework, as well as practical considerations to ensure success. It is hoped that this book can be a helpful addition to any such deliberations.

The chapter also affirms the perspective that what matters most is not the continuance or closure of Regional Conferences, but rather an ongoing process of racial reconciliation, with the goal of achieving forgiveness and equity. Or, as de la Torre frames it, "to establish justice and peace," since there "can be no reconciliation as long as power structures that continue to benefit the few at the expense of the many remain in place."[39] Since the debate within Adventism in the U. S. revolves around Regional Conferences, it would be logical to take a stand on their future, but such a stance is beyond the scope of this book. Consequently, further research remains necessary regarding the future of Regional Conferences, should the form of racial healing advocated in this book be actualized.

For the purpose of this book the designation of "black(s)" will be used for individuals of African descent, "persons of color" for individuals considered in the U.S. to be ethnic minorities, and "white(s)" for individuals of European descent. Establishing a

---

[38] "A Statement on racism," can be viewed on Appendix A. Seventh-day Adventist Church: Official Statements (June 27, 1985): http://www.adventist.org/beliefs/statements/main-stat18.html (accessed 12/12/10).

[39] De La Torre, 90.

definition for racial reconciliation has been difficult since there are few working definitions. For the purpose of this research, racial reconciliation is a dimension of the ongoing divine mandate to overcome alienation between ethnic groups through identification and in solidarity with each other, which can result in peacemaking and restored relationships. The word reconciliation is preferred to other related words and phrases, like "conflict resolution," "conflict mediation," "peacebuilding," "peaceful coexistence," "reconstruction," and "restorative justice movement," given its theological significance and the fact that it is an acceptable term for religious and nonreligious entities engaged in peacemaking.[40]

The racial reconciliation model of lawyer Eric K. Yamamoto, which he calls "Interracial justice," is defined as "hard acknowledgment of the historical and contemporary ways in which racial groups harm one another, along with affirmative efforts to redress justice grievance and rearticulate and restructure present-day relations."[41] "White flight," which is discussed in this book, refers to whites abandoning their communities as a minority group exceeds a particular threshold–deemed to be about 25 percent. Both racism and white privilege have been defined earlier in this document. The word evangelical is used in the context of Protestant churches that emphasize conversion and being "born again," being missionary minded, viewing the Bible as the ultimate authority, and stressing the centrality of Christ sacrificial death on the cross as redemptive. The term spiritual or spirituality is being used in preference to the term religious since I intend to convey the "personal quest for understanding answers to ultimate questions about life, about meaning, and about relationship to the sacred or transcendent, which may (or may not) lead to or arise from the development of religious rituals and the formation of community."[42] The Regional (Black) Conferences, like state Conferences, are third in a four-tier Adventist hierarchy beginning with the General

---

[40] The restorative justice movement differs from the others mentioned since its focus is on repairing the harm caused or revealed by criminal behavior.

[41] Yamamoto, 9f.

[42] Harold G. Koenig, Michael E. McCullough, and David B. Larson, *Handbook of Religion and Health* (Oxford: University Press, 2001), 18.

Conference (the world church) and its extended territories abroad, World Divisions (13 geographical territories composed of a collection of missions, conferences, or states into Unions). This is followed by Unions (a collection of missions and conferences), Conferences (a collection of churches), and Churches (a gathering of members).

The target audience of this book are primarily SDA leaders, and the message conveyed is that work of racial reconciliation is necessary, urgent and difficult, but not impossible. There are two secondary audiences: First, SDA members – whose exposure to this disputation and the underlying issues that hinder the quest for a way forward – may be motivated to urge church leaders to find a solution and end the debate. Second, the academic community in general and the Adventist academic community in particularly who could give voice to the issues highlighted and become motivated to seek alliances with church leaders, ensuring that racial reconciliation is given the attention it deserves.

The obvious limitation of this text is that, while it seeks to bring the need for racial reconciliation into the collective consciousness of all concerned, consciousness-raising is insufficient, redressing is imperative. While I offer a theoretical framework grounded in the historical nature of the problem of racial inequity and its concomitant symptoms, finding the agency to actualize its recommendations rests in the hands of church leaders, who may ultimately operate on the basis of self-interest. Beyond the scope of this book is the prospect of the SDA church revisioning its entire social justice ethos, extending it beyond its humanitarian aid program ADRA (Adventist Development and Relief Agency), its Religious Liberty department, and its extensive education and healthcare activities around the world.

Also outside the scope of this book, though not beyond the subject matter, is the issue of gender equality in Adventism and, specifically, women's ordination and the hierarchical glass ceiling that withholding ordination enforces.[43] While the role of forgiveness

---

[43] At the November 2010, NAD Year End Meeting the delegates voted to request a waiver from the GC to allow women with a "commissioned minister's" credential [a local jurisdiction license in lieu of ordination] to be eligible to stand as candidates for president of church

is relevant to this book, it is only reviewed in the context of the literature on racial reconciliation. Given the importance of church leaders, any future study of this topic should include personal interviews with church leaders to gain their insights into the past and present state of race relations in the SDA church. I would be the first to admit that it is impossible to prevent my own social location as a black clergyperson and behavioral health worker to not be influenced by the affective elements of this book, but effort was made to observe and contain any bias, or at least make it conscious, so that it could be processed in an explicit manner.

Surprisingly, while the issue of race relations in the SDA church has garnered some attention from Adventist scholars (mainly historians and ethicists), largely, it remains the great "unsaid." Adventists have generally addressed racial reconciliation in either journal articles, a section of a chapter, or a chapter of a book, from a historical and theological perspective, but not from an SCPC perspective using an interdisciplinary approach. It is hoped that this study will provide insight for "reconciling," a foundational pillar of the pastoral care tradition that Clebsch and Jaekle viewed as most promising. At the outset of this research, I learned more in the direction of the Idealists stance based upon my experience of Adventists in Britain. There, we dealt with much the same issues of racial injustice towards blacks, but instead of separate structures, we achieved a more inclusive resolution. Midway through my research, I learned more in the Pragmatists' direction as I explored the entrenched nature of white privilege. By the end of the study, I had become too realistic for the Idealists and too optimistic for the Pragmatists. Idealists appear willing to minimize racism and the virulence of white privilege while Pragmatists emphasize the need for cultural solidarity over community, but neither have a passion for racial reconciliation. Standing in the midst of this confluence is both limiting yet liberating.

---

institutions, including conferences and unions. These are presently the exclusive domain of males, since the SDA church does not permit women's ordination.

Review of Relevant Literature

Reconciling and Racism in the SCPC Field

This literature review, though not exhaustive, explores the contributions by the SCPC field, Seventh-day Adventism, clergy practitioners involved in the racial reconciliation movement, the peace and justice movements, and the social science literature in the area of reconciliation and racism. It will be shown that some of these groups have been more prolific and proactive while others have been reserved and reactive in dealing with racism and efforts directed at healing such human affliction.

In chronicling the extant literature on the meaning, mandates, and methods specifically of racial reconciliation within the SCPC tradition, it was striking to discover few publications that extensively address the subject, and where racial reconciliation was addressed, it was part of a wider argument.[1] This discovery was

---

[1] As noted earlier, the following individuals in particular were chief exponents of "reconciling": Anton T. Boisen, Wayne E. Oates, and Charles V. Gerkin. Furthermore, the following references say little if at all, about racial reconciliation, but mention is made of either racism or reconciliation in general: William A. Clebsch and Charles R. Jaekle, *Pastoral Care in Historical Perspective: An Essay with Exhibits* (Englewood Cliffs, NJ: Prentice-Hall, 1964), 17-28, 81; William Robert Miller, "Dynamics of Reconciliation," *Pastoral Psychology* 18.8 (1967): 29; Wayne Oates, *Pastoral Counseling in Social Problems: Extremism, Race, Sex, Divorce* (Philadelphia: Westminster Press, 1966), 12; Leroy Aden and J. Harold Ellens, eds., *Turning Points in Pastoral Care: The Legacy of Anton Boisen and Seward Hiltner* (Grand Rapids, MI: Baker Book House, 1990); Anton T. Boisen, *The Exploration of the Inner World: A Study of Mental Disorder and Religious Experience* (New York: Harper & Bros, 1936); Walter C. Jackson, III, "The Oates Agenda for Pastoral Care," *Spiritual Dimensions of Pastoral Care: Witness to the Ministry of Wayne E. Oates* (ed. Gerald L. Borchert and Andrew D. Lester; Philadelphia: Westminster Press, 1985); Wayne E. Oates, *The Christian Pastor*, 3rd ed. (Philadelphia: Westminster Press, 1982); Charles V. Gerkin, *Widening the Horizons: Pastoral Responses to a Fragmented Society* (Philadelphia: Westminster Press, 1986);

particularly alarming since, as has been noted previously, "reconciling" is one of the core functions within the pastoral care tradition. Evidence of this glaring omission is best illustrated in the SCPC's own *Dictionary of Pastoral Care and Counseling* (DPCC) which has no entry for "racial reconciliation" and only makes passing reference to "reconciling" — largely repeating the definition advanced by Clebsch and Jaekle. It should be noted that an expanded version of the DPCC published in 2004 includes seven essays which seek to address some of the shortcomings of the earlier edition, including offering insights into contextual and cultural changes and new paradigms.[2] By way of comparison, the dictionary has entries for the other six established pastoral care functions, measured in columns on a twin-column page as follows: for *healing* there are seven columns of information; for *sustaining,* two and a half columns; for *guiding,* three columns; for *prophesying,* six columns; and for *liberation,* three columns, whereas there is only one-third of a column for *reconciling.*[3] Why this disparity for a pastoral function that has the most promise and is central to an understanding of the work of Christ — "reconciling the world to himself" (2 Cor. 5:19)?

One possible answer to the question of the underdeveloped pastoral function of reconciling may be traced to the historical context in which the field of pastoral care and counseling (PCC) emerged, incorporating psychological theories that served to elucidate the human condition in a way that theological understanding could not. This paradigm shift led to a more individual-centered approach to pastoral care when previously it

---

and Charles V. Gerkin, *Prophetic Pastoral Practice: A Christian Vision of Life Together* (Nashville: Abingdon Press, 1991).

[2] Rodney J. Hunter, gen. ed., Nancy J. Ramsay, expanded edition ed., *Dictionary of Pastoral Care and Counseling* (Nashville: Abingdon Press, 2005.

[3] See the following entries in Hunter and Ramsay, *Dictionary of Pastoral Care and Counseling*: Larry Kent Graham, "Healing," 497-501; Leroy Aden, "Comfort/Sustaining," 193-95; Kenneth R. Mitchell, "Guidance, Pastoral," 486-87; Harvey Seifert, "Prophetic/Pastoral Tension in Ministry," 963-66; Romney M. Moseley, "Liberation Theology and Pastoral Care," 645-46.

was more community-centered.[4] For a field emerging in the mid-1900s focused on spiritual care and arising out of an American society steeped in racial disparity, segregation, and discrimination, discussion of restoring fractured relationships and ending estrangement between blacks and whites would seem to be fertile territory. Is it possible that the published scholars in the field at the time — all white and almost all male — lacked perspective, since their cohort represented the forces of oppression directed at blacks? In exploring the failure to embrace this ministry of reconciliation, William R. Miller laments that "Life is a constellation of largely lost opportunities for reconciliation, in which our brother asks us for bread and we give him a stone."[5] Miller's rationale for the PCC field's early reluctance to engage in reconciling is one of inconsistency, where reconciling with a stranger is preferred to someone familiar since this limits the level of confrontation. He further observes that "what passes for reconciliation is only obeisance to some benign formula, and doesn't really involve us in any genuine give-and-take with the other."[6]

The work of pastoral theologian Nancy J. Ramsay in seeking to redefine the field, making it more contemporary and inclusive, must be commended. In her book, *Pastoral Diagnosis*, she urges that pastoral caregivers learn to critically evaluate their theological, philosophical, ethical, and cultural assumptions in dispensing diagnosis and treatment.[7] Ramsay's personal reflections on navigating racial difference as a white professor are instructive. She writes of the need to engage with white racial identity and the

---

[4] Joretta L. Marshall, "Methods in Pastoral Theology, Care and Counseling," *Pastoral Care and Counseling: Redefining the Paradigms* (ed. Nancy J. Ramsay; Nashville: Abingdon Press, 2004), 144. The author rightly acknowledges four categories of individuals underrepresented (white women, ethnically and culturally diverse persons, international scholars, and homosexuals) in the PCC field, and that women as well as blacks now use a theology of liberation to restore a "communal contextual paradigm" to the discipline.

[5] William Robert Miller, "Dynamics of Reconciliation," *Pastoral Psychology* 18.8 (1967): 29.

[6] Miller, "Dynamics."

[7] Nancy J. Ramsay, *Pastoral Diagnosis: A Resource for Ministries of Care and Counseling* (Minneapolis: Fortress Press, 1998), 9-25.

awareness of how unwittingly whites generate racism and then avoid complicity. Of whites, Ramsay argues, "Our priority needs to lie in deconstructing the internalization of privilege that reproduce racism."[8] Others, she writes, are disadvantaged due to their non-white heritage, hence the need for whites to develop critical self-awareness in order to resist the inherent injustices of privilege. Developing a community of colleagues as conversational partners to engage in the deconstruction of racist's elements of white identity is just one way to overcome racism.[9] Ramsay offers six practical steps that have helped her in her journey in combating racism: 1) cultivate relations with other whites who can hold her accountable to confronting racism; 2) find racial diverse conversational partners to gain differing perspective; 3) learn from experience to confront guarded aspects of her identity; 4) increase awareness of her ethnic history and identities; 5) read and consult more extensively on a range of sociopolitical, historical and ecclesiastical issues; and 6) expand imagination with the help of other white antiracist models.[10] These self-reflective steps could be particularly useful to the Adventist academic community if they chose to engage in racial reconciliation.

Finally, Ramsay makes an invaluable contribution in helping to redefine the paradigm for the pastoral care field. One important acknowledgment is the shift toward relational justice. With justice as a central theme of the field, liberation is expanded beyond freedom from psychological and spiritual oppression to include freedom from literal bondage and the redistribution of resources, power, and privilege. Also added is a communal-contextual paradigm, which gave rise to issues of gender, race, and sexual orientation, as well as an intercultural paradigm, which recognized the importance of cultural pluralism, a corrective for the dominant Eurocentric culturalism.[11] This more inclusive trajectory in pastoral

---

[8] Ramsay, *Pastoral Diagnosis*, 13.

[9] Ramsay, *Pastoral Diagnosis*, 14-15.

[10] Ramsay, *Pastoral Diagnosis*, 24.

[11] Nancy J. Ramsay, "A Time of Ferment and Redefinition," *Pastor Care and Counseling: Redefining the Paradigms*, 9-22. The intercultural paradigm is more comprehensively addressed by Emmanuel Y. Lartey,

care has empowered the marginalized to voice their concerns and seek redress.

From a historical perspective, Clebsch and Jaekle assessed reconciling to be the leading pastoral function during the evolution of the early Christian Church, preceded by Roman persecution and the readmission into the Church of lapsed members who had recanted their faith under the fear of death but who now sought forgiveness during more peaceful times.[12] Pastoral theologian Sharon Thornton is in agreement with Clebsch and Jaekle on the evolution of reconciling in the pastoral care tradition. She further states that, as Christianity extended its reach around the time of the Constantinian era, reconciliation became synonymous with adhering to Church standards and practices so that harmony existed between the lives of parishioners and the teachings of the church.

Later, reconciliation became closely aligned with believers seeking redress for injustices as common grievances were given consideration. Thornton affirms that "rituals of exorcism, healing, and reconciliation were combined to redress the brokenness in the community and point its members to a new and more just way of living."[13]   Reconciliation also gained prominence during the Renaissance and Reformation periods, but it was less the mode of seeking divine forgiveness and more an act of discipline, as some Protestants were brought back into the fold during the Counter-Reformation.[14] This history of reconciling is, for Thornton, evidence that reconciliation should not be regarded as a pastoral function but as a practice. By practice, she means the "things that Christian people do together over time in response to and in light of God's active presence for the life of the world."[15] This reframing of the pastoral function has appeal since all believers fulfill priestly functions as they participate with Christ in the plan of salvation through the process of reconciliation. You could say that healing,

---

Pastoral Theology in an Intercultural World (Cleveland, OH: Pilgrim Press, 2006), 121-149.

[12] The authors noted that not all clergy were amenable to extending reconciliation to lapsed believers. Clebsch and Jaekle, 17f.

[13] Thornton, 140.

[14] Clebsch and Jaekle, 28.

[15] Thornton, 128.

guiding, sustaining, reconciling, prophesying and liberation are the tools, the interventions available to believers as they engage in the service of mediating a lost world to a loving God.

Clebsch and Jaekle viewed reconciling as the "most opportune pastoral function today,"[16] writing as they were during the 1960s, in the midst of the American Civil Rights Movement. Yet the silence on the number one issue of the day—racial reconciliation—by them and many of the thought leaders in the SCPC field is disconcerting. Clebsch and Jaekle did express optimism that the embrace of reconciling by the SCPC field "could precipitate the ministry of the cure of souls into a new realization of its therapeutic power for our time."[17]

Anton T. Boisen (1876-1965), lauded as the father of Clinical Pastoral Education (CPE), was the first to position the SCPC field in the direction of social action and ultimately to reconsider the potency of the ministry of reconciliation. Boisen's clinical method was an outgrowth of his theological perspective, namely his study of human experience. He internalized the tenets of the Social Gospel Movement in his first book, in which he articulates a theology of community. Boisen theorized that mental illness was not solely individual but communal and that it points in the direction of reconciliation and social change in the prophetic tradition.[18] While Boisen acknowledged that religious adherence would invariably fall short of its ideal, he nevertheless felt that pastoral care should strive to realize its highest potential through the medium of reconciliation and the prophetic ministry.

---

[16] Clebsch and Jaekle, 69.

[17] Clebsch and Jaekle, 82.

[18] Boisen contends that mental disorders can best be understood in their social context as the caregiver considers "what kind of society he wants to create and perpetuate and be identified with. Personal salvation can be found only in reconciliation with this deeper social self and in commitment to the task of transforming the personal and social life.... Religion is thus inherently social as well as personal. It is rooted in a loyalty that is looked upon as so important that for it the individual is ready to live and, if necessary, to die." Anton T. Boisen, *The Exploration of the Inner World: A Study of Mental Disorder and Religious Experience* (New York: Harper & Brothers, 1936), 290.

Heavily influenced by Boisen, pastoral theologian, Wayne Oates (1917-1999), who remained sensitive to the problems of the South, advanced a theory of the social context of the pastor and his/her prophetic task. Oates conceptualized a more expansive definition for the pastoral counselor, one in which the pastor should not be seen as just a private counselor but "as a public figure, a person with corporate and community responsibilities."[19] Oates asserts that the pastor has a vital prophetic role in contemporary society, and he listed five principles of prophetic pastoral care. For example, he describes the principle of *"face-to-faceness"* in the reconciling of feuding sides, since resolving social conflicts and perspective-taking can only occur when the antagonists are together in the room. Another principle he enunciates is that of *clarification*, an indispensable part of problem-solving; and a further principle is *anticipation*, in which perceptiveness on possible outcomes are explored.[20] In setting forth these principles, Oates was attempting to propel the SCPC field in the direction of social consciousness vis-à-vis the ongoing antagonisms and racial hostilities that prevailed in his beloved South, prompting a discourse that could lead to restored relationships.

An additional formative figure in the SCPC field advancing the cause of reconciliation was Charles V. Gerkin (1922-2004), a student of Boisen, who claimed him as a "spiritual ancestor." Gerkin expanded on Boisen's "living human document" concept, making him instrumental in an expansion of the field into areas of social conflict. Gerkin was concerned with a theology based on praxis (a

---

[19] Wayne E. Oates, *Pastoral Counseling* (Philadelphia: Westminster Press, 1974), 143.

[20] Of the second principle he writes, "The objective of prophetic pastoral care is to produce a face-to-face, first hand relationship and to reduce indirect, secondhand attempts to manipulate and mange people from afar." The other principles are "balance between visibility and invisibility in pastoral practice" and "two-way communication." Wayne E. Oates, *Pastoral Counseling in Social Problems: Extremism, Race, Sex, Divorce* (Philadelphia: Westminster Press, 1966), 13-18.

social consciousness in the practice of ministry). He expressed the concern that the field of pastoral care was in need of some reenvisioning in order to better address social issues, including racism and the risk of nuclear holocaust. As he observes, many outside the field wondered whether pastoral care was adequately equipped to speak prophetically on social issues. A further concern of Gerkin was the perception that the field of pastoral care had been deluged with the same psychological theories that had delivered to the U.S. culture a self-absorbed preoccupation. He attempted to redress the balance and return the field of pastoral care to its roots.[21]

Finding inspiration from Old Testament scholar Walter Brueggemann's model for prophetic ministry, Gerkin advances a 6-part paradigm through which imaginative prophetic ministry can be enacted.[22] Elsewhere, Gerkin condenses these steps, casting them under the rubric of "a metaphor of care" with four themes: listening, responding, advocating, and hearing. Pastoral care in the prophetic tradition is, for Gerkin, more than responding to the needs of others and the wider culture. It must be advocacy-centered.[23] Advocacy for the marginalized, the underprivileged, and the victims of racism, sexism, ageism, etc., is part of the imaginative prophetic, pastoral approach. Thanks to the pioneering efforts of Boisen, Oates, and Gerkin, the field of pastoral care would chart a new course, from a minimalist approach of engaging with society, to a reorientation around meeting the challenges that face contemporary society. Their leadership facilitated a reorientation of the field, challenging it to champion issues of social justice and other relevant community issues.

---

[21] As he wrote, "my search is for a fresh vision of what the discipline of pastoral care involves, while at the same time preserving the gains of the past forty years, including the appropriation of psychological ways of thinking about human need and problems." Charles V. Gerkin, *Widening the Horizons: Pastoral Responses to a Fragmented Society* (Philadelphia: Westminster Press, 1986), 12.

[22] See Gerkin's six-part paradigm on page 116. Charles V. Gerkin, *Prophetic Pastoral Practice: A Christian Vision of Life Together* (Nashville: Abingdon Press, 1991), 74-84.

[23] Charles V. Gerkin, "On the Art of Caring," *Journal of Pastoral Care* 45.4 (1991): 399-408.

In a cluster of books within the SCPC field that addresses racism,[24] pastoral theologians like Edward P. Wimberly have for decades addressed "minority issues," particularly counseling blacks concerned with oppression and empowerment, reclaiming dignity, liberty, and wholeness, shame, and self-worth. Wimberly believes the role that the SCPC field can play in the lives of blacks is self-help empowerment, restoring nurturing relationships to meet their emotional needs, and reintegrating them into nurturing communities.[25] While his approach of self-help, mentoring and community support is salutary in addressing alienation and other lingering effects of racism, it ignores racial reconciliation, without which the fractious nature of the relationship between blacks and whites persists. More recently, Wimberly has adopted a narrative approach in summoning human agency among blacks, toward gaining insights, exploring new resources, acting appropriately, and bringing healing and reconciliation in relationships.[26] Wimberly's approach tends to be focused on helping the black community navigate through the symptoms of a racialized society rather than address more systemic issues plaguing the society.

Like Wimberly, black pastoral theologians Homer Ashby, Jr. and Archie Smith, Jr. share the same desire to empower blacks to survive despite injustices, while remaining strong and hopeful. Both appropriate the metaphor of the river to convey this perspective. For Ashby, the black church like "Deep River" in the spiritual is a

---

[24] Homer U. Ashby, Jr., *Our Home Is Over Jordan: A Black Pastoral Theology* (St. Louis, MO: Chalice Press, 2003); Donald M. Chinula, *Building King's Beloved Community: Foundations for Pastoral Care and Counseling with the Oppressed* (Cleveland, OH: United Church Press, 1997); James Newton Poling, *Deliver Us from Evil: Resisting Racial and Gender Oppression* (Minneapolis: Fortress Press, 1996); Archie Smith, Jr., *Navigating The Deep River: Spirituality in African American Families* (Cleveland, OH: United Church Press, 1997); Carroll A. Watkins Ali, *Survival and Liberation: Pastoral Theology in African American Context* (St. Louis, MO: Chalice Press, 1999); and Edward P. Wimberly, *Relational Refugees: Alienation and Reincorporation in African American Churches and Communities* (Nashville: Abingdon Press, 2000).

[25] Wimberly, *Relational Refugees*, 20-25.

[26] Edward P. Wimberly, *African American Pastoral Care*, rev. ed. (Nashville: Abingdon Press, 2008).

bulwark that enables blacks to survive white racism. It has amassed unique resources to effect deliverance, and it is an active participant with God in diverse ministries to achieve God's mission. This mission includes material successes as well as a rediscovery of a "black spiritual heritage." Ashby finally takes on the issue of reparations for blacks as part of this mission but doubts its viability since the U.S. will not even acknowledge it owes a debt.[27] Smith, on the other hand, emphasizes black spirituality and history as illustrative of a flowing river that can enable blacks to navigate the continued struggles of life in the United States. Since, like a river, life is a constant flow of change and transformation, a therapeutic approach to care for blacks, utilizing "principles of development of depth of meaning, reflexivity, and sense of agency," will help counter despair and nihilism.[28] These two pastoral theologians perhaps deliberately avoid subjecting the narrative of blacks to the oppressive conversation of white society but in doing so may leave vacant the racial reconciliation territory and its power to afford interethnic healing.

Womanist pastoral theologian, Carroll Watkins Ali's unique contribution to this discussion, is an expansion of the traditional pastoral functions to include liberation. Her argument for doing so is the individualistic and Eurocentric nature of SCPC and the ongoing need of blacks to constantly adjust to a culture of oppression while resisting the effects of oppression. Not intent on simply introducing the field to liberation, Ali asserts the view that reconciling is in need of revisioning with respect to ministry among blacks, but also as a ministry practice for healing strained relations between blacks and whites in the U.S. She remains, however, dubious of such a prospect given the increased strain in race relations. Ali's opinion is that blacks are in need of reconciliation with black communities and recovering lost historically rooted strategies for coping as an offset for nihilistic threats present in contemporary society.[29]

---

[27] Ashby, Jr., 135-37, 143-49.

[28] Both economic resources and internal consciousness resources will help to recover pride and self-worth in blacks. Archie Smith, 143, 153.

[29] Ali, 9. She goes on to specify the nature of this interpersonal reconciliation, by stating that, "it is vital to the survival and liberation of

Voicing concern about issues of social justice, particularly racism and gender discrimination, is practical and pastoral theologian James Newton Poling. Poling returns to the roots of the SCPC field by locating these social ills in a theological frame and denouncing them as an evil from which individuals and society must be delivered. He challenges SCPC to hold individuals and society responsible for abuses of power in personal, social and religious forms (his definition of evil), and he views white supremacy and male dominance as chief culprits. Poling's approach is built on a communal solidarity, which can then be used to challenge the privileged position of whites and males to "engage in a process of decentering power arrangements...in order to live within a world of relationality and mutuality with other persons and groups."[30]

A considered look at oppression by pastoral theologians is found in the book, *Injustice and the Care of Souls*, with the authors giving voice to some of the marginalized in society by insisting that justice and compassion are concomitant with the field of pastoral care.[31] Two specific chapters are relevant to this study since they come closest to the issues addressed in this text. In discussing antiracist pastoral care and the love-power dynamic, Sheryl A. Kujawa-Holbrook suggests that failure in true racial healing can be attributed in part to the dominant culture's disregard for the power differential that the marginalized experience. Antiracist care also reckons with white privilege and explores the effects of racism on a faith community and how to address it. Vital to antiracist pastoral care, argues Holbrook, is storytelling that conveys a perspective from various social locations. Next is the challenging of the melting pot theory which subsumes cultural difference into one identity, often that of the dominant culture, in favor of a mosaic in which

---

African Americans that we reconcile relations within the Black community that, ultimately, reunite the upper and lower classes of African Americans with each other and reduce and/or eliminate fratricide among male youth in particular." Ali, 140f.

[30] James Newton Poling, *Deliver Us from Evil: Resisting Racial and Gender Oppression* (Minneapolis: Fortress Press, 1996), xiii, 83, 172.

[31] Sheryl A. Kujawa-Holbrook and Karen B. Montagno, eds., *Injustice and the Care of Souls: Taking Oppression Seriously in Pastoral Care* (Minneapolis: Fortress Press, 2009).

difference is valued and viewed as enriching the community. Developing cultural competence is her third antiracist pastoral care recommendation since it strives to recognize and respond to cultural difference.[32]

The other significant essay is by Brita L. Gill-Austern who grapples with the interplay of difference and unity, and how failing to achieve this creative balance between the two leads to exclusion, oppression, and suffering. Austern's remedy for this exclusion is practical solidarity, which "means we do not simply feel compassion and empathy for others, but commit ourselves to be in the struggle for justice with them."[33] Recognition of our common humanity, need for wholeness, and healing from a troubled world, are key practices of practical solidarity. Austern advances to three movements with associated practices that could achieve practical solidarity. First, one must know one's home together with its in-built assumptions, particularly on issues of privilege and power; this should prompt self-examination and contrition. Second, one must take a pilgrimage away from home to encounter others and to deconstruct barriers erected to keep them out, leading to productive otherness engagement. Third, one must return home from the pilgrimage to integrate the new experiences with the old, arriving at a greater partnership with others.[34]

In *Liberating Our Dignity, Saving Our Souls*, pastoral psychologist Lee H. Butler Jr., unravels the constituent parts of African American cultural identity formation and settles on race, gender, and spirituality, with the aid of black and pastoral theology and black psychology and psychoanalytic theory.[35] From Butler's perspective, these eclectic sources have enabled him to construct more accurately the features of African American identity, which he calls the "Theory of African American Communal Identity

---

[32] Holbrook, "Love and Power: Antiracist Pastoral Care," *Injustice and the Care of Souls*, 19-27.

[33] Brita L. Gill-Austern, "Engaging Diversity and Difference: From Practices of Exclusion to Practices of Practical Solidarity," *Injustice and the Care of Souls*, 35.

[34] Austern, 36-44.

[35] Lee Butler, 1-9.

Formation."[36] His theory builds on identity development in the psychodynamic and psychosocial traditions with the addition of African American spirituality and their sense of community. Its two stages include a foundational and a constructive period in which childhood experiences provides the "blueprint for interpreting and constructing adult life."[37] Butler contends that his theory can assist in nurturing the soul and the complexities of life in which liberation is an ongoing challenge.[38] Perhaps it is a lot to ask of a theoretical framework, but its aim of a restored dignity and a saved soul is admirable. Nevertheless, Butler's theory illustrates how the instinctive drive for a God-centered humanity restores African American dignity, enabling them to be part of a resistance culture in pursuit of community.

In conceptualizing a more inclusive theological anthropology, pastoral theologian Emma J. Justes reveals how apparent differences cause division in areas of gender, race, class, sexual orientation and culture when such differences should lead to a more expansive worldview. Difference as adversarial, dualistic, and shameful limits the reality of our common humanity created in the image of God.[39] For Justes, overcoming these divisions requires a transformation prefaced on liberation from the oppression of hierarchical divisions and results in "our restoration to the oneness of our created nature and our redeemed nature in Christ."[40] From a classroom experience, Justes relates a teachable moment in which one group of her students found a creative way to maximize their participation given the time constraints.

Four lessons are highlighted: 1) an honest acknowledgement that being divided is easier than working together; 2) creative alternatives are preferred to 'either/or' propositions, which is achieved through mutuality and community over individuality and

---

[36] Lee Butler, 158.

[37] Lee Butler.

[38] Lee Butler, 172.

[39] Emma J. Justes, "We Belong Together: Toward an Inclusive Anthropology," *The Treasure of Earthen Vessels: Exploration in Theological Anthropology* (ed. Brian H. Childs and David W. Waanders; Louisville, KY: Westminster John Knox Press, 1994), 137-139.

[40] Justes, 145.

independence; 3) the struggle for creating synthesis requires analysis, and 4) shared outcomes require greater intimacy.[41] Her approach to a more satisfactory theological anthropology is meritorious for racial reconciliation since it requires the removal of historical distortions and the restoration of the oneness of humanity.

Finally, from the SCPC field come the observations by pastoral theologians Marsha Foster Boyd and Carolyn Stahl Bohler who, in dialogue, offer three pertinent insights in addressing race relations.[42] First, are the womanist and feminist values that inform their teaching, namely acknowledging the interdependence of human beings rather than the self-sufficiency embedded in the Christian tradition; thinking interdisciplinarily, honoring subjectivity, understanding power, and teaching inductively. Second, are the recurring dynamics between blacks and whites, including whites passively accepting the institutionalization of white power; despite multi-layers of truth telling, trust can emerge; whites should increase their knowledge on matters of race; whites should seek to heal their racism; and whites need to be alert to the sins of omission in racism. Third, they explore attempts by institutions to address diversity. Rigid boundaries for access to minorities in institutions remain despite affirmative action efforts, and many blacks in these institutions prefer to work in black institutions. Many institutions are electing to hire only the exceptional blacks, fearing that too many will lead to too much change. The authors conclude that a retrenchment on matters of race is occurring in institutions as gains made by blacks are reversed.[43]

Two things emerge from their assessment consistent with research in this book. First, they place a significant burden on whites to address their oft ignored racism and the privilege it provides them, and second, it offers limited hope that things will change since whites may be reluctant to engage at a level and frequency necessary for change to occur.

---

[41] Justes, 146-47.
[42] Boyd and Bohler, 190.
[43] Boyd and Bohler, 191-207.

Reconciliation and Racism in Adventist Literature

Given the pronouncements of one of Adventist's earliest pioneers, Ellen G. White, on the matter of race relations between blacks and whites and the historical challenges posed to the denomination by racial discrimination and disparity, it is surprising that the SDA Church has not had a more prominent stance on issues of reconciliation and racism in its published material.[44] Or, perhaps this should not be surprising, given the evidence documented by Adventist scholars Malcolm Bull and Keith Lockhart showing that the SDA Church, while concerned with the downtrodden, was nevertheless convinced, on the whole, that indirect approaches to racial discrimination and disparity were preferred to social protest.[45] Indeed, in the 1960s, Adventist leaders regarded the Civil Rights Movement as inappropriate interference in politics; they regarded its marches, for example, as coercive. Consequently, Adventist publications ignored issues of racial injustice until the late 1960s.[46] But it would not be until 1985 that the SDA Church issued its first official statement on the issue of race,[47] belatedly following in the footsteps of its messenger, Ellen G. White.

---

[44] Delbert W. Baker, *Make Us One: Celebrating Spiritual Unity in the Midst of Cultural Diversity* (Boise, ID: Pacific Press Publishing Association, 1995; Ronald D. Graybill, "Historical Contexts of Ellen G. White's Statements Concerning Race Relations" (Ph.D. diss., Andrews University, 1968); Ronald D. Graybill, *E. G. White and Church Race Relations* (Washington, DC: Review and Herald Publishing Association, 1970); Ronald D. Graybill, *Mission to Black America: The True Story of Edison White and the Riverboat Morning Star* (Mountain View, CA: Pacific Press Publishing Association, 1971); Frank W. Hale, Jr., *Out of The Trash Came Truth: The 45th Anniversary of the 1962 Challenge of the People, and for the People Against Racism in the Seventh-day Adventist Church* (Columbus, OH: F.W. Hale, 2007); Samuel Koranteng-Pipim, *Must We Be Silent: Issues Dividing Our Church* (Ann Arbor, MI: Berean Books, 2001); Sakae Kubo, *The God of Relationships: How the Gospel Helps to Reach across Barriers Such as Race, Culture and Gender* (Hagerstown, MD: Review and Herald Publishing Association, 1993); Alven Makapela, *The Problem with Africanity in the Seventh-day Adventist Church* (Lewiston, NY: E. Mellen Press, 1996); Caleb Rosado, *Broken Walls* (Boise ID: Pacific Press Publishing Association, 1990).

[45] Bull and Lockhart, [1989], 203.

[46] The author argues that Adventists viewed "the civil rights movement not as a great moral crusade but as a troubling instance of

As for the writings of White, her statements on racism need to be evaluated through the prism of a cultural crusader prior to 1899 and as a pragmatic practitioner after that date. White vehemently opposed the segregationist policy enacted by the SDA Church in 1889. She denounced the policy as unwarranted since it could perpetuate prejudicial attitudes. Yet, by 1899, following attacks on the workers and crew of the boat (The Morning Star) her son was using to evangelize blacks along the Mississippi River and the wave of anti-Reconstruction efforts, particularly in the South, she reversed herself to mitigate white prejudices.[48] Bull and Lockhart have provided an excellent analysis of Adventists' race relations stance. Their central thesis that the SDA Church's self-understanding of being a refuge from a hostile nation, all the while mirroring institutions and customs of the United States, reflects ambivalence in addressing social ills.[49]

Ronald D. Graybill was the first white Adventist scholar to wade into the apparent minefield of Ellen White's statements on race relations and to offer a coherent explanation for the shifts in her position regarding the issue of segregated congregations in the SDA Church. His dissertation and subsequent two books, cover the period in which Ellen White wrote on the subject of race relations in the SDA Church. The intent of his research was to clarify whether White's writings, with some suggestive racial overtones, were based on the prevailing and now-discredited scientific view of race, with its essential belief in the inferiority of blacks. One conclusion Graybill makes is that White's statements regarding segregation were made on the basis that Adventists working in the South, where racial hostilities were most acute, should be protected from acts of

---

improper involvement by religious leaders in politics. Part of the Adventist objection to the movement had to do with the coercion involved in boycotts and marches." Douglas Morgan, *Adventism and the Republic: The Public Involvement of a major Apocalyptic Movement* (Knoxville: University of Tennessee Press, 2001), 158-61, 159.

[47] Missing from this statement is any acknowledgment of culpability and expressions of remorse. Bull and Lockhart, [1989], 203; "A Statement on Racism."

[48] Ellen G. White, *The Southern Work* (Washington, DC: Review and Herald Publishing Association, 1966), 15, 83-84.

[49] Bull and Lockhart, [2007], xiii.

violence directed against them. Without this historical context, her segregation statements could be misunderstood, and charges of racism could be hurled. Graybill also affirmed that Ellen White believed "in the essential equality of the Negro and the Caucasian."[50]

Racial hostilities were also at the heart of White's statement regarding separate educational and religious services. Dealing with perhaps the most contentious issue–namely the rationale for the pre- and post-1908 statements of White in which she appears to contradict her previous denunciation of racial segregation and discrimination, Graybill argued that increased racial tensions led to "White's conviction that extreme caution must be exercised in order to prevent the closing of the Negro work entirely in the South."[51] He also confirmed that, despite these racial hostilities, White never outlined a prescription of segregation for all time and in all places; rather it was a "temporary [geographic] expedient."[52] It should be noted that Graybill's research was at the time lauded by church leaders since it appeared to extricate the SDA Church from a potential embarrassment that Ellen White's conflicting statements indicated a possible "black problem." Indeed, the most influential black leader at that time and beyond, E. E. Cleveland, wrote an endorsing forward to Graybill's first book. The endorsement served as a type of black imprimatur, which some regard as having dispelled any doubts that may have existed concerning White's race relations writings.[53]

Seeking to clarify the apparently contradicting statements of Ellen White, Graybill argues in his first book that, while his interpretative framework is neither exhaustive nor complete, it

---

[50] Ronald D. Graybill, *E. G. White and Church Race Relations* (Washington, DC: Review and Herald Publishing Association, 1970), 101-02.

[51] Ronald D. Graybill, 1970, 102.

[52] Ronald D. Graybill, 1970, 102.

[53] Cleveland writes, "Ronald Graybill has placed certain statements by Ellen G. White on race relations, which have been misunderstood, in their correct historical setting, and conclusively demonstrated their true meaning in terms of the situation that called them forth. In so doing he has performed a most valuable service for the church, by removing the cause of misinterpretation–ignorance of historical context." Ronald D. Graybill, 1970, 6.

enhances current understanding of these contradictions. In establishing his interpretive framework, he focuses on the waning years of Reconstruction and Southern white hostilities towards blacks and those whites who sought to help them. He also contrasts these racial hostilities towards blacks with Booker T. Washington's more naïve presentations on the achievements of some blacks, which was countered by the sociologist W.E.B. DuBois. Graybill reflects on the period 1895 to 1910 with its retrenchment of black freedoms including the right to hold public office and segregation being the accepted societal norm.[54] He notes that it was in this atmosphere that Ellen White writes of the church's outreach in the South veering towards an untimely end. Graybill concludes the book by affirming that Ellen White viewed blacks as equal to whites and that any differences were "the result of environmental influences."[55]

In his published dissertation, black Adventist theologian Alven Makapela seeks answers to the oft-asked question of church duplicity: Does the SDA church theologically uphold inclusion while actually practicing cultural exclusion of Africans? Makapela contends that the SDA Church was "unintentionally" the heir of white prejudice against people of African descent, so that despite an "Adventist perspective," misconceptions about African people have been unquestioningly appropriated through the lens of a secular worldview. Framing the church's problem with Africanity as sinful, Makapela questions why the SDA Church does not speak heartfelt truth to its white members.[56]

Black Adventist Systematic theologian Samuel Koranteng-Pipim aptly offers a conservative apologetic on hot-button issues confronting the Adventist Church, including racism. He asserts that while cherishing racial attitudes and practicing segregationist policies, most Adventists are convinced that racism is not a problem afflicting the church. Koranteng-Pipim describes racism as an ideology of supremacy that denies the fundamental tenets of Christianity and argues that most Christians, if not all, respond to it

---

[54] Ronald D. Graybill, 1970, 28-34; 82-87; 110-11.

[55] Ronald D. Graybill, 1970, 112.

[56] The author defines "Africanity" as "the totality of values, ways of being and acting which for many generations have developed out of the long African traditional experience and reality." Makapela, 2, 255.

only when it is politically expedient to do so. He sees reflected in the current Regional Conference structure ongoing racial division that is, among other things, a lingering embarrassment to the church. Challenging apparent myths regarding the necessity of maintaining these conferences, Koranteng-Pipim forcefully argues for the dismantling of "racially separate conferences" while improving race relations and instituting nondiscriminatory policies.[57]

In his edited book, *Make Us One*, black administer Delbert Baker proffers that without diversity, the SDA Church will not succeed, but that there was a time limit on the Church to take the historic opportunity to exhibit the gospel's power to unite as compared to culture's power to divide. Left unanswered is the question posed by one of the authors as to whether the church's engagement in a unique experiment for a Protestant church, namely a worldwide united fellowship, would succeed. Since the church's motivation for a positive outcome is more rooted in its theological self-understanding as the Remnant church than in a social consciousness or civic mindedness, the verdict is hard to cipher. Throughout the book, inclusiveness is emphasized, diversity is to be celebrated, and ethnic understanding and sensitivity are encouraged. However, while steps to solving cultural conflicts are explored, these steps are presented in a vacuum, as though the church has not had or continues to not have any interethnic conflicts to resolve. Thus, the "vexed question" remains.[58]

Hispanic Adventist sociologist Caleb Rosado names reciprocal learning as vital in developing cultural sensitivity. Using a socio-historical lens, Rosado views one of Christianity's principal task, the counteracting of societal stereotypes and prejudicial attitudes towards ethnic minorities. He observes that in the United States, homogeneous values dominate a heterogeneous society. Also identified is the danger of uniformity misconstrued as unity, which leads, paradoxically, to equally destructive ethnocentrism. For Rosado, ethnocentrism impedes interethnic relations structurally and socially, with those in the ascendancy holding sway over those

---

[57] Koranteng-Pipim, 305, 312, 341, 354, 400.
[58] Baker, *Make Us One*, 1995, 10, 24f, 216f,

in the diminutive position.[59] Sadly, Rosado similarly ignores specific references to ethnic tensions between blacks and whites that have been a feature of Adventism in several countries.

Finally, Calvin Rock's investigation into the dilemma facing black Adventists is framed as "institutional loyalty" over against "racial freedom." He charts the socio-political narrative of discrimination and demands as the SDA Church was coerced to confront the ugliness of individual and institutional racism. Rock assesses the ambivalent position of blacks within a majority white denomination by confirming that blacks can be both loyal and free as they have continued to pursue their struggle for equality and selfhood. Whether under church-sanctioned segregation or integration, where their political power was denied, the nature of black freedom, argues Rock, has been constant, while strategies of white church leaders have fluctuated to suit the times. Black protest has also had to survive "theological, socio-religious, and socio-political constraints that inhere in their denomination's beliefs and practices."[60] Since these beliefs and practices were advanced by white theologians, Rock is convinced that a black Adventist theology is a prerequisite to reinterpret freedom and faith. Viewing both liberation and reconciliation as insufficient principles upon which a black Adventist theology can be established, Rock opts for "restoration" as a means of individual renewal and social rectitude.[61]

Clergy Practitioners in the Racial Reconciliation Movement

Clergy practitioners who have been at the forefront of the evangelical racial reconciliation movement of the late 1980s through 1990s have documented their efforts.[62] An extensive review of this

---

[59] Rosado, 18, 31. He asserts that "While it is true that certain basic principles of Christian action and ways of doing things transcend culture, the gospel allows for much more latitude than the church is often willing to allow." 117.

[60] Rock, 1984, 64, 96.

[61] Rock, 1984, 162-64, 214-16. Of restoration, he writes, "As a conceptual framework for black theology, restoration gives ultimate meaning to one's understanding of the character and will of God as well as the nature and destiny of the human being," 213.

[62] Michael Battle, *Reconciliation: The Ubuntu Theology of Desmond Tutu* (Cleveland: Pilgrim Press, 1997); Tony Campolo and Michael Battle,

literature has been undertaken by Emerson and Smith who trace the history, theology, and practice of racial reconciliation by evangelicals. This theology they argue, was conceived by pioneers of the modern evangelical reconciliation movement as a four-part process: blacks and whites are to foster increased interpersonal relationships; structural inequality is to be recognized and resisted by all; whites, the architects, and beneficiaries of privilege, are to repent of personal, historical and social sins; and blacks are to be willing to forgive whites when asked to do so.[63] Social scientist Nancy Wadsworth has also studied this racial reconciliation movement and has concluded that the movement lacked

---

The Church Enslaved: A Spirituality of Racial Reconciliation (Minneapolis: Fortress Press, 2005); Laurene Beth Bowers, *Becoming a Multicultural Church* (Cleveland: Pilgrim Press, 2006); Brad Christerson, Korie L. Edwards, and Michael O. Emerson, *Against All Odds: The Struggle for Racial Integration in Religious Organizations* (New York: New York University Press, 2005); Susan E. Davies and Sister Paul Teresa Hennessee, eds., *Ending Racism in the Church* (Cleveland: Pilgrim Press, 1998); Curtiss Paul De Young, Michael O. Emerson, George Yancey, and Karen Chai Kim, *United By Faith: The Multiracial Congregation as an Answer to the Problem of Race* (Oxford: Oxford University Press, 2003); John W. de Gruchy, *Reconciliation: Restoring Justice* (Minneapolis: Fortress Press, 2002); Mark Deymaz, *Building a Healthy Multi-Ethnic Church* (San Francisco: John Wiley & Sons, 2007); Michael O. Emerson, *People of the Dream: Multiracial Congregations in the United States* (Princeton: Princeton University Press, 2006); Samuel George Hines and Curtiss Paul DeYoung, *Beyond Rhetoric: Reconciliation as a Way of Life* (Valley Forge, PA: Judson Press, 2000); Dennis L. Okholm, ed., *The Gospel In Black and White: Theological Resources for Racial Reconciliation* (Downers Grove, IL: InterVarsity Press, 1997); Norman Anthony Peart, *Separate No More: Understanding and Developing Racial Reconciliation in Your Church* (Grand Rapids, MI: Baker Books, 2000); Spencer Perkins and Chris Rice, *More Than Equals: Racial Healing for the Sake of the Gospel* (Downers Grove, IL: InterVarsity Press, 1993); George A. Yancey, *Beyond Black and White: Reflections on Racial Reconciliation* (Grand Rapids, MI: Bakers Books, 1996); and George A. Yancey, *Beyond Racial Gridlock: Embracing Mutual Responsibility* (Downers Grove, IL: InterVarsity Press, 2006). Since the research of Emerson and Smith on racial reconciliation within the evangelical community is thorough, repeating this history was deemed unnecessary, Emerson and Smith, 51-68.

[63] Emerson and Smith, 54-55.

sustainability due in part to the "different cultural tool kits employed by white and non-white evangelicals."[64] Wadsworth detects that ethnic minorities have a preference for more relationship-oriented models of reconciliation in contrast to the more politically oriented model preferred by whites, a perspective shared by Emerson and Smith.[65] These different perceptual realities leave many whites able to ignore white privilege, structural injustices, and their own involvement in sustaining these norms, whereas Christians of color tend to challenge and seek structural transformation to end racial disparities.

In light of the fact that Emerson and Smith, as well as Wadsworth, have conducted an excellent review of the publications arising from the racial reconciliation movement, my review will be limited to a few authors writing on multiracial religious communities and reconciliation reflections. Since co-authoring the groundbreaking *Divided by Faith*, Michael O. Emerson has coauthored several books with a multicultural congregational theme. Beginning with *United by Faith*, Emerson and his colleagues make a case for multicultural congregations being one of the answers to the problem of racial discrimination in the United States. They confirm that changing demographics show that the United States is soon moving towards having no overall majority ethnic group, yet 90 percent of worshippers attend "racially homogeneous congregations."[66] Since both demographics and improved race relations point in the directions of racially mixed congregations, the authors assert that where possible multiracial Christian congregations should be normative, and the book offers their rationale. They define a racially homogeneous congregation as "one

---

[64] Nancy Wadsworth, "Religious Bridging: Evangelical Racial Reconciliation as Race Project," lecture, American Political Science Association Conference, Chicago, 2007, http://www.allacademic.com//meta/p_mla_apa_research_citation/2/1/0/8/6/pages210866/p210866-1.php (accessed 8/17/10).

[65] Emerson and Smith, 6f. They further note that despite the fact that white evangelicals have "the subcultural tools to call for radical changes in race relations, they most consistently call for changes in persons that leave the dominant social structures, institutions, and culture intact," 21.

[66] DeYoung, Emerson, Yancey, and Kim, 4.

in which no one racial group is 80 percent or more of the congregation; just 7.5 percent of the over 300,000 religious congregations in the United States are racially mixed."[67] Given the immense racial barriers, valiant and insightful leadership of clergy and laity alike are prerequisites.

In *Against All Odds*, Emerson and his coauthors offer insights into how religious organizations and race relations operate in the U.S. Using an ethnographic methodology, they chart the experience of six religious volunteer organizations as they sought to become more racially and ethnically diverse. They appropriate the racial formation position of Michael Omi and Howard Winant in summarizing what they had learned from these six case studies.[68] Within these organizations, they observed tensions over competing racial projects by the different groups seeking influence. Often the victorious racial projects were detrimental to the organization's race relations efforts, leading to organizationally sanctioned racial divisions. White flight was deemed a considerable factor in the decline of whites where they were not the majority in these organizations, while diversity in the worship experiences was beneficial. Also, provided individuals had a supportive homogenous group; they reported a more enriched interracial experience. Their more hopeful finding was that where leaders modified their racial understandings and practices, over time, racial inequities were minimized.[69]

Finally, in *Beyond Black and White*, sociologist George A. Yancey challenges individuals and churches that have avoided racial reconciliation to move beyond the pretension of harmony to true unity in Christ. Yancey is in no doubt about where the burden lies in championing the cause of reconciliation: "the moral presence of the

---

[67] DeYoung, Emerson, Yancey, and Kim, 2.

[68] Omi and Winant "define racial formation as the sociohistorical process by which racial categories are created, inhabited, transformed, and destroyed." The theory has a two-step process, "historically situated projects in which human bodies and social structures are represented and organized," which is linked "to the evolution of hegemony, the way in which society is organized and ruled." Michael Omi and Howard Winant, *Racial Formation in the United States: From the 1960s to the 1990s*, 2nd ed. (New York: Routledge, 1994), 55f.

[69] Christerson, Edwards and Emerson, 2, 78f, 103f, 124, 182-85

church is essential in the battle against racism if racial peace is ever going to be possible in our time."[70] By taking the perspective of black and white Christians, Yancey probes the problem of racism in order to devise appropriate responses to it. Much of the book is spent countering misconceptions and strongly held beliefs of blacks and whites, including blacks charging whites of being racists; whites ignoring modern racism [stating racial discrimination is passé, yet minorities continue to seek advantages, which are now unfair]; and discomfort with interracial marriages and the offspring of such unions. Having an expanded vision that encompasses all ethnic groups is what it will take to move beyond black and white, a feat made possible only by repentance from the sin of racism, argues Yancey.[71]

In a more recent work, Yancey offers a critique of four secular approaches to addressing racism that has been embraced by Christians: Colorblindness, Anglo-Conformity, Multiculturalism, and White Responsibility. Not surprisingly, Yancey finds that these four models of addressing racism ultimately come up short because of the lack of a spiritual perspective. His favored paradigm is the mutual responsibility model, which is not dissimilar to his earlier thinking; in this model, both whites and blacks acknowledge areas of challenges which need to be repented of, making blacks and whites fewer adversaries and more collaborators. While the mutual responsibility model has much to commend it, it nevertheless minimizes the place of white privilege and institutional racism, since both adversely impact disparity, making shared responsibility anything but mutual.[72] Furthermore, blacks in the United States

---

[70] Yancey, *Beyond Black and White*, 1996, 7.

[71] Yancey, *Beyond Black and White*, 1996, 22f, 27f, 97f; 101f; 123f; 126f; 150-55.

[72] Yancey defines these four secular approaches as follows: The first is Colorblindness, which contents that racial reconciliation will evolve by focusing on racial advances and ignoring past discrimination; yet ignoring racial realities only serves those that benefit from racial discrimination and disparity. Next, Anglo-Conformity argues for the upward mobility of ethnic minorities as they assume white American values, but it ignores the fact that racism is at the heart of minorities' failure to succeed. Multiculturalism attempts to combat racial alienation and low self-esteem inflicted on ethnic minorities by the dominant culture through the emphasis

have had to contend with disproportionate discrimination and prejudices, so to hold them equally responsible for such behaviors inflicted upon them would appear to be unreasonable at best.

Reconciliation in the Peace and Justice Movements

In a world riven by perpetual violent conflicts, reconciliation, be it sacred or secular, continues to demand the attention of peacemakers, arbitrators, conciliators, envoys, ambassadors, governmental and nongovernmental officials, as well as those in the academy. Consequently, centers for global peace initiatives now populate many of the leading academic institutions the world over, and along with them have come volumes dedicated to the art of reconciliation, conflict resolution, and peacemaking. A sample of the most quoted volumes has been used in this review to indicate the direction the Peace and Justice movements have taken in pursuing peacemaking utilizing reconciliation strategies. That these movements have embraced reconciliation as a medium for conflict resolution should be instructive to the religious community where the issue of race relations remains unsettled.[73] As some of these

---

of the value of minority cultures. Multiculturalism is philosophically on par with cultural pluralism, since it allows for distinctive cultures to coexist without assimilation to the majority culture. Yet multiculturalism can lead to fractured or balkanized societies lacking in universal and social norms. Finally, White Responsibility centers racial conflict solely with the majority culture from which minorities must be liberated and empowered. The concept of white privilege is used by advocates of this model to demonstrate the subtle ways in which majority groups' benefit from their racial status. Yet, minorities cannot be completely absolved of all responsibility for racial conflict and disparity, since this leads only to defensiveness and anger among white majorities. Yancey, *Beyond Racial Gridlock*, 2006, 138-39.

[73] A sample of the most quoted volumes are as follows: Mohammed Abu-Nimer, ed., *Reconciliation, Justice and Coexistence: Theory and Practice* (Lanham, MD: Lexington Books, 2001); R. Scott Appleby, *The Ambivalence of the Sacred: Religion, Violence, and Reconciliation* (Lanham, MD: Rowman & Littlefield Publishers, 2000); Yaacov Bar-Siman-Tov, ed., *From Conflict Resolution to Reconciliation* (New York: Oxford University Press, 2004); Amy Benson Brown and Karen M. Poremski, eds., *Roads to Reconciliation: Conflict and Dialogue in the Twenty-First Century* (Armonk, NY: M. E. Sharpe, 2005); Herbert H. Blumberg, A. Paul Hare and Anna Costin, *Peace Psychology: A*

volumes do not specifically address racial reconciliation within religious communities, this literature review is confined to writings that come closest to addressing this issue and context and can demonstrate the evolution in how reconciliation is conceived. One compelling book on the subject of racial reconciliation was authored by Asian American law professor Eric K. Yamamoto, one of the first to address interethnic and interracial hostilities. Given demographic shifts in the United States, which are leading toward a nation of minorities, Yamamoto argues that reconciliation will remain an imperative as, otherwise, intergroup conflict and suspicion will continue to militate against lasting alliances. The key to resolving these conflicts, for Yamamoto, is interracial justice, defined as the awareness of the ways, past and present, ethnic groups have injured each other and how proactive steps towards addressing these grievances may lead to more positive relations.

To achieve interracial justice, Yamamoto argues for "race praxis" — a practical process of engagement, change and reflection — with four connecting dimensions. First is recognition, an empathetic realization of the anger and hope of the wounded; acknowledging the debilitating constraint one group imposes on another. Second,

---

Comprehensive Introduction (Cambridge: Cambridge University Press, 2006); Erin Daly and Jeremy Sarkin, *Reconciliation in Divided Societies: Finding Common Ground* (Philadelphia: University of Pennsylvania Press, 2007); John B. Hatch, *Race and Reconciliation: Redressing Wounds of Injury* (Lanham, MD: Lexington Books, 2008); Brian Hutchinson, *G. E. Moore's Ethical Theory: Resistance and Reconciliation* (Cambridge: Cambridge University Press, 2001); Ho-Won Jeong, *Peacebuilding in Postconflict Societies: Strategy and Process* (Boulder, CO: Lynne Rienner Publishers, 2005); John Paul Lederach, *Building Peace: Sustainable Reconciliation in Divided Societies* (Washington, DC: U. S. Institute of Peace Press, 1997); Robert L. Rothstein, ed., *After the Peace: Resistance and Reconciliation* (Boulder, CO: Lynne Rienner Publishers, 1999); Nicholas Tavuchis, *Mea Culpa: A Sociology of Apology and Reconciliation* (Stanford: Stanford University Press, 1991); Ronald W. Walters, *The Price of Racial Reconciliation* (Ann Arbor: University of Michigan Press, 2008); Andreas Wimmer, Richard J. Goldstone, Donald L. Horowitz, Ulrike Joras, and Conrad Schetter, eds., *Facing Ethnic Conflicts: Toward a New Realism* (Lanham, MD: Rowman & Littlefield, 2004); Everett L. Worthington, Jr., *Forgiveness and Reconciliation: Theory and Application* (New York: Routledge, 2006); Yamamoto, *Interracial Justice*, 1999.

Yamamoto acknowledges that ethnic groups are both aggressors and aggrieved in relationship to other groups and must take responsibility for both roles. Reconstruction is the third dimension, an active and mutual process of finding psychosocial healing through forgiveness and apologies. Finally, reparation is designed to deconstruct and decenter material and structural power differentials, removing disparity. Yamamoto utilizes a multidisciplinary approach using postcolonial, peace, ethnic and feminist studies, and indigenous healing practices as well as liberation theology as the theoretical underpinning of his dimensions of interracial justice.[74]

In *The Ambivalence of the Sacred*, historian R. Scott Appleby engages religion in peacebuilding more directly than does Yamamoto. His goal is to discover the role of religion and religious actors in violent conflicts, and how some of these actors justify their violent and nonviolent actions as a sacred duty. Appleby argues that, despite the plethora of religiously inspired violence the world over, religious peacebuilding is attempting to reshape these zones of conflict. Internal pluralism — the diverse beliefs and practices of a religious organization — is a key concept for Appleby, as it demonstrates the adaptable nature of religion. If exercised appropriately, this pluralism will seek to engage in an international dialogue on rights and responsibilities, promoting theologies of mission that foster respect for individual and religious liberty and prioritizing ecumenical and interreligious dialogue as a means of mitigating conflict.[75]

A collection of conference essays promoting peace and justice, *Reconciliation, Justice, and Coexistence*, offers useful theoretical frameworks for achieving reconciliation and peacebuilding. The book gives an excellent overview of the theory and practice of the peace and justice movement. Of particular relevance to this book are the twelve approaches to reconciliation outlined by Johan Galtung. Galtung, who perceives reconciliation to be a process that prepares the way for justice and peace, assesses the value of twelve reconciliation approaches but concludes that it is the synthesis of

---

[74] Yamamoto, 7f, 9f, 174f, 153-71.
[75] Appleby, 7, 19f, 28f, 212-13; 245f.

these approaches that lead to the best outcome.[76] Of the twelve reconciliation approaches, only five of the most relevant approaches are briefly assessed because of their individual focus on issues addressed in this book including reparations, forgiveness, truth-telling, conflict management, and emotional healing.

The Reparation/Restitution Approach addresses how the harm and resultant trauma caused by the aggressor is alleviated to some extent by repair and replacement, and the restoring of the status quo. This approach is more comprehensive than simply compensating the aggrieved since it could amount to nothing more than a payoff for a guilty conscience. The inherent obstacle to this approach is the unwillingness of both parties to agree on the restitution process or amount or, simply stated, "What is fair?" Further, it matters how influential the aggrieved are relative to the aggressors since aggressors tend to balk at being disadvantaged, as evidenced by the lack of progress on reparations for descendants of former slaves in the U.S. Next, the Apology/Forgiveness Approach envisages the expression and acceptance of a sincere apology for injurious behavior. This approach could be viewed as superficial since apologies are ultimately just words. Additionally, this approach is attitude and not behavior oriented, leaving the aggrieved with the burden of having to live with the symptoms of the injury long after the aggressor has been exonerated.[77]

The Historical/Truth Commission Approach seeks to explore in detail what actually occurred by vocalizing the facts. Yet, even this truth-telling can amount to little more than a descriptive without the needed prescriptive to ensure the necessary consequences for perpetrators. Also, this form of reconciliation could come at the expense of more substantive issues of structural and institutional

---

[76] The twelve approaches are: The Exculpatory Nature-Structure, Reparation-Restitution, Apology-Forgiveness, Theological-Penitence, Juridical-Punishment, Codependent Origination-Karma, Historical-Truth Commission, Theatrical-Reliving, Joint Sorrow-Healing, Joint Reconstruction, Joint Conflict Resolution, and ho 'o ponopono. Galtung recommends the *"ho 'o ponopono"* approach since it is more holistic, and it embodies the other eleven. Johan Galtung, "After Violence, Reconstruction, Reconciliation, and Resolution," *Reconciliation, Justice, and Coexistence,* 5-20.

[77] Johan Galtung, "After Violence, Reconstruction, Reconciliation, and Resolution," *Reconciliation, Justice, and Coexistence,* 6-8.

reforms. In the Joint Conflict Resolution Approach, leaders serve as representatives of the conflicting groups in bringing about resolution despite the fact that they may have been instrumental in initiating the conflict. However, its inherent strength may also its weakness, given the top-down nature of this approach in which those at the bottom are often excluded from any direct negotiations. A way to mitigate this passive involvement of the masses is to encourage individuals to discuss what went wrong and what might have averted the conflict. Finally, the Hawaiian *Ho`oponopono* Approach of facts and responsibility sharing, joining reconciliation and closure, is achieved as a moderator brings the two conflicting group together. The story of the conflict is written down on a piece of paper, provided both sides agree on its content, and later the paper is burnt ceremonially to symbolize closure. Prior to the burning, the most fortunate compensate the least fortunate for any expenses incurred.[78]

These five approaches to reconciliation collectively embody Yamamoto's Interracial Justice model in that they address how the actions of the aggressors have impacted the aggrieved and who should take responsibility for both intrapsychic and interpersonal consequences. The creation of an agreed upon metanarrative that expresses the essence of the conflict, while honoring painful trauma experiences, is in evidence. There is also the appropriate expression of an apology and forgiveness process, which leads to a just compensation process culminating in a ritual communal healing. Finally, the issue of reparations is addressed not simply as a means of compensation but as a restoration and renewal of tangible elements of the relationship.

Tackling the contrast between conflict resolution and reconciliation, peace studies professor Yaacov Bar-Siman-Tov and his colleagues assert that while conflict resolution may end a dispute, it does not prevent a renewed outbreak of conflict or harmonize fractured relationships between the protagonists. However, reconciliation goes beyond conflict resolution in that it addresses cognitive and emotional hindrances to normalized relations, and it seeks to restore and establish positive relations.[79]

---

[78] Johan Galtung, "After Violence, Reconstruction, Reconciliation, and Resolution," *Reconciliation, Justice, and Coexistence*, 12, 17-18.

[79] Bar-Siman-Tov, 4

The outcome of the reconciliation process should, therefore, include "mutual recognition and acceptance, invested interests and goals in developing peaceful relations, mutual trust, and positive attitudes, as well as sensitivity and consideration for the other party's needs and interests."[80] The authors see an important role for transformational leadership and forgiveness in the reconciliation process. The first lifts all involved in the reconciliation process to a higher level of motivation and the second provides a moral underpinning that most religious traditions have in common. Another perspective is advanced by Daly and Sarkin who argue for a reconciliation process that is not backward-looking but is a positive reframing of a society's goal to move forward. As these conflict-ridden societies such as South Africa, Lebanon, Iraq, Liberia and the former Yugoslavia emerge from interethnic hostilities, they are turning more demonstratively to reconciliation as a means of re-establishing social order. With this in mind, the authors aim for two basic goals: to revamp the prevailing conceptions of reconciliation, such as personal healing, interpersonal relations, community rebuilding, national stability and international peace; and to reconfigure a more relevant reconciliation process for these nations in transition.[81]

The contributions by the field of psychology to conflict resolution and peace studies, now called Peace Psychology, are also vital and can be traced to the father of American psychology, William James, whom Morton Deutsch calls "the first peace psychologist."[82] As a specialized branch of psychology, peace

---

[80] Bar-Siman-Tov, 15.

[81] As a consequence of these two assertions, Daly and Sarkin advocate for political and economic structural reforms along with personal healing, to ensure sustainable peace. Their conceptual justification for this new structural approach is a paradigm shift from an individual focus to a society focus, with nation-building and the establishment of a new social order — a redefinition of reconciliation. Hence, a national manifestation of reconciliation would be a joint commitment to a common purpose, with all ethnic groups sharing in this common vision. Daly and Sarkin, xii-xiv, 187, 199.

[82] Daniel J. Christie, Richard V. Wagner, and Deborah Du Nann Winter, eds., *Peace, Conflict, and Violence: Peace Psychology for the 21st Century* (Upper Saddle River, NJ: Prentice Hall, 2001), ix-x. An additional reference

psychology gained prominence during the nuclear arms race between the United States and the former U.S.S.R. as all branches of psychology explored theories and interventions to prevent a nuclear holocaust. The significance of peace psychology was established by the publication in 1986 of *Psychology and the Prevention of Nuclear War* and by the American Psychological Association establishing it as a new division. In the first-of-its-kind textbook entitled *Peace, Conflict, and Violence: Peace Psychology for the 21st Century*, the authors, mindful of the historic context of the discipline and given the global nature of conflict, ensured that concepts, theories, and practices were relevant for the multiplicity of violent and nonviolent global conflicts. They also located four key areas that peace psychology explores: violence, social inequalities, peacemaking and the pursuit of social justice.[83] Furthermore, they observed that the contemporary trends in peace psychology research are in peacekeeping, nuclear proliferation and disarmament, international terrorism, genocide, militarism, nationalism, environmentalism, and human rights violations.

Peace psychology adopts a multidisciplinary approach in its effort to bridge interethnic divides: philosophical, ethical, and religious thought; constructive themes from the world of art, music, and drama; and behavioral, social, and political science research. In the post-Cold War era, the field attempts to highlight the insidious nature of structural violence, largely induced by social, political, and economic resource disparity.[84] From this perspective, then, peacebuilding moves in the direction of social justice and parity in political and economic structures. Given the eclectic nature of the discipline, establishing specific foundational principles and assumptions is difficult since theories and practices proliferate. This diversity of thought allows for multiethnic and multicultural input and exchange, facilitating the movement towards "cultures of

---

is Herbert H. Blumberg, A. Paul Hare and Anna Costin, *Peace Psychology: A Comprehensive Introduction* (Cambridge: Cambridge University Press, 2006), 2.

[83] Christie, Wagner, and Winter, "Introduction to Peace Psychology," *Peace, Conflict, and Violence*, 7-11.

[84] Christie, Wagner, and Winter, "Introduction to Peace Psychology," 7.

peace."[85] Yet, this very fluid and ever-expanding discipline is challenged by the numerous complex issues involved in achieving significant change and the lack of expertise of peace psychologists in handling the multifaceted and multidisciplinary work of peace and social justice.[86] Hence, these challenges compound developing tensions that are influencing peace psychology.[87] Nevertheless, peace psychology will continue to play a pivotal role in assessing causes of social injustices, overcoming disparity in its myriad forms and providing a framework of interethnic peaceful coexistence.

One final review is merited since Everett L. Worthington, Jr. has distinguished himself as a research psychologist investigating psychosocial domains like marriage and family, forgiveness, stress, and coping, and now forgiveness and reconciliation. In *Forgiveness and Reconciliation*, Worthington, in his customary manner, builds on his theory of forgiveness to create a clinical theory of promoting forgiveness. Applicable to individuals and groups, Worthington's evidence-based approach is a method of reconciliation. For Worthington, forgiveness is a means of dealing with the injustice gap (an unresolved transgression). These transgressions are stressful and can best be handled by a transformation of one's personality. He reformulated his model of forgiveness on what he calls a biopsychosocial stress and coping theory of forgiveness, and with it,

---

[85] The United Nations designated 2000 as the International Year for the Culture of Peace, a concept with seven interdependent elements: social justice, human rights, nonviolence, inclusiveness, civil society, peace education, and sustainability. This multifaceted set of issues requires a multidisciplinary approach, which peace psychology seeks to fulfill. Daniel J. Christie, "Peacebuilding: Approaches to Social Justice," *Peace, Conflict, and Violence*, 277, 351f.

[86] Michael Wessells, Milton Schwebel, and Anne Anderson, "Psychologists Making A Difference in the Public Arena: Building Cultures of Peace," *Peace, Conflict, and Violence,* 352.

[87] These tensions include: "activism vs. analysis, universalism vs. relativism, proaction vs. reaction, and peaceful means vs. peaceful ends." Deborah Du Nann Winter, Daniel J. Christie, Richard V. Wagner, and Laura B. Boston, "Conclusion: Peace Psychology for the Twenty-First Century," *Peace, Conflict, and Violence*, 366.

he shows the role of affect in emotional forgiveness.[88] Along with forgiveness, he articulates a fourfold intervention process of decision, discussion, detoxification, and devotion to achieve reconciliation. Since this is a psychotherapeutic approach, Worthington provides clinical vignettes to illustrate how the forgiveness and reconciliation process works with individuals. However, he resorts to familiar interpersonal conflict resolution strategies to foster healing in intergroup conflicts, while admitting that there is insufficient data to support such usage. Worthington also acknowledges that neither forgiveness nor reconciliation is a panacea to societal peace,[89] but it at least places one on the right path.

Whiteness and White Privilege in Psychosocial Literature

In Critical Race Theory—the study of the relationship between race and power and the role of racism within society—disparity of resources is sustained by white hegemony.[90] Though often used interchangeably, the distinction between whiteness and white privilege is important. While white privilege addresses issues of unearned advantage favorable to people who have white skin over nonwhites; whiteness is considered a default standard and signifier of other ethnic groups, conferring dominance on whites in society.[91] Famed black sociologist and activist W.E.B. Du Bois was the first to reference white privilege when he observed that low-wage white workers "were compensated in part by a sort of public and psychological wage. They were given public deference and

---

[88] Worthington, 10, 170f, 198f. In addition, Worthington establishes a five-step process to achieve forgiveness, which he characterizes as "REACH": Recall the hurt, Empathize with the person who hurt you, Give an altruistic gift of forgiveness, Commit to the emotional forgiveness, and Hold on to forgiveness. Worthington, 262-266.

[89] Worthington, 266-68f.

[90] Roy L. Brooks, *Racial Justice in the Age of Obama* (Princeton: Princeton University Press, 2009), 90.

[91] Derald Wing Sue, "The Invisible Whiteness of Being," *Addressing Racism: Facilitating Cultural Competence in Mental Health and Educational Settings*, ed. Madonna G. Constantine and Derald Wing Sue (Hoboken, NJ: John Wiley & Sons, 2006), 15-17.

titles of courtesy because they were white."[92] Blacks continued to voice Du Bois' prescient insight, but it was only as white scholars began to engage the subject that whiteness and its privileges gained currency. Peggy McIntosh, an academic and antiracism activist, is credited with the modern reintroduction of this phenomenon, including originating the nomenclature of white privilege. In her classic article "Unpacking the Invisible Knapsack," she addresses the privileges of being white, a fact reinforced by the hidden nature of these in-built advantages that whites are raised not to see.[93]

There is now a substantial body of work focused on white privilege,[94] but this literature review will confine itself to Paula S. Rothenberg's edited *White Privilege: Essential Readings on the Other Side of Racism*, a collection of the classic readings on white privilege by central figures from different disciplines. The essays and articles are arranged into four sections: the invisibility of whiteness; historical perspectives on whiteness; the power of privilege, and how white privilege can be resisted. Rothenberg calls attention to white privilege by juxtaposing the moral outrage and guilt that most whites express regarding racism and most whites' silence or refusal of responsibility for the privileges that they as beneficiaries receive from racism. She also voices the consensus view that whiteness goes unnamed and unexplored because it has been uncritically normalized by society. Once exposed to privilege, argues Rothenberg, whites will be challenged by issues of fairness and justice, as well as self-interest and whether to remain silent or speak out against the system of privilege.[95]

---

[92] W. E. B. Du Bois, *Black Reconstruction in America: An Essay toward a History of the Part Which Black Folk Played in the Attempt to Reconstruct Democracy in America, 1860-1880* (New York: Russell and Russell, 1966), 700.

[93] Peggy McIntosh, "White Privilege: Unpacking the Invisible Knapsack," *White Privilege: Essential Readings on the Other Side of Racism* (ed. Paula S. Rothenberg, 3rd Ed: New York: Worth Publishers, 2008), 123-132.

[94] Melanie Bush, *Breaking the Code of Good Intentions: Everyday Forms of Whiteness* (Lanham, MD: Rowman and Littlefield, 2004); Laurie M. Cassidy and Alex M. Mikulich, eds., *Interrupting White Privilege: Catholic Theologians Break the Silence* (Maryknoll, NY: Orbis Books, 2007); Madonna G. Constantine and Derald Wing Sue, *Addressing Racism: Facilitating Cultural Competence in Mental Health and Educational Settings* (Hoboken, NJ: John Wiley & Sons, 2006); George J. Sefa Dei, Leeno Luke Karumanchery,

The three essays selected to respond to the invisibility of white privilege approach the issue from different angles. Richard Dyer observes that since race is not a distinction that whites use to understand themselves, they are able to function assuming themselves to be the norm and, as such, assume also that they can speak on behalf of all human beings. Consequently, white people need to appreciate their particularity and to see themselves as white. Harlon Dalton takes Dyer's point a step further by stating that many whites adopt a rugged individualistic motif which tends to minimize

---

Nisha Karumanchery-Luik, *Playing the Race Card: Exposing White Power and Privilege* (New York: Peter Lang, 2004); Joe R. Feagin and Eileen O'Brien, *White Men on Race: Power, Privilege, and the Shaping of Cultural Consciousness* (Boston: Beacon Press, 2003); Paula Harris and Doug Schaupp, *Being White: Finding our Place in a Multiethnic World* (Downers Grove, IL: InterVarsity Press, 2004); Matthew Frye Jacobson, *Whiteness of a Different Color: European Immigrants and the Alchemy of Race* (Cambridge: Harvard University Press, 1998); Robert Jensen, *The Heart of Whiteness: Confronting Race, Racism, and White Privilege* (San Francisco: City Lights, 2005); Kendall, *Understanding White Privilege*; Michael S. Kimmel and Abby L. Ferber, eds., *Privilege: A Reader* (Boulder, CO: Westview Press, 2003); George Lipsitz, *The Possessive Investment in Whiteness: How White People Profit from Identity Politics*, rev. ed. (Philadelphia: Temple University Press, 2006); Carole L. Lund and Scipio A. J. Colin, III., eds., *White Privilege and Racism: Perceptions and Actions* (San Francisco: Jossey-Bass, 2010); Terrance MacMullan, *Habits of Whiteness: A Pragmatist Reconstruction* (Bloomington: Indiana University Press, 2009); David R. Roediger, *The Wages of Whiteness: Race and the Making of the American Working Class*, rev. ed. (London: Verso, 1999); Paula S. Rothenberg, ed., *White Privilege: Essential Readings on the Other Side of Racism*, 3rd ed. (New York: Worth Publishers, 2008); Shannon Sullivan, *Revealing Whiteness: The Unconscious Habits of Racial Privilege* (Bloomington: Indiana University Press, 2006); Derald Wing Sue, *Overcoming our Racism: the Journey to Liberation* (Hoboken: Jossey-Bass, 2003); Beverly Daniel Tatum, *"Why Are All the Black Kids Sitting Together in the Cafeteria?" And Other Conversations about Race* (New York: BasicBooks, 1997); Thandeka, *Learning to be White: Money, Race, and God in America* (New York: Continuum, 1999); Stephanie M. Wildman, *Privilege Revealed: How Invisible Preference Undermines America* (New York: New York University, 1996); Linda F. Williams, *The Constraint of Race: Legacies of White Skin Privilege* (University Park: Pennsylvania State University Press, 2003); and Tim Wise, *White Like Me: Reflections on Race from a Privileged Son*, rev. ed. (Brooklyn, NY: Soft Skull Press, 2008).
[95] Rothenberg, "Introduction," *White Privilege*, 1-5.

notions of community, so collective concern is often viewed negatively as "groupthink" (minimizing conflict to reach a group census). Moreover, since whites tend to avoid speaking about their own racial identity, they are blindsided by the degree to which blacks are willing to explore their racial identity. Additionally, whites are baffled when blacks prioritize issues of racial identity and interact with them on the basis of their past encounters with other whites. Finally, Bell Hooks has observed that while whites may be oblivious to their whiteness, blacks have been scrutinizing the phenomenon since slavery, regarding it with suspicion, fear, and hatred, and yet seeking to imitate it. This gazing on whiteness by blacks is an affront to whites, who wish to maintain their invisibility while exerting control over the "dark other" as they keep themselves invisible.[96]

The authors of *How White People Became White* note that Eastern European immigrants to the United States initially had little racial awareness–given the social construction of race–but soon discovered its potency since they were ranked above blacks but below whites because of their varied languages and cultures. Therefore, the quest of these new immigrants was to become both American and white in the process of Americanization. Jews were also subjected to this Americanization process since they were often viewed by whites as an inferior race. The country at the time had a virulent strain of anti-Semitism, but by achieving middle-class status through education and increased wealth, Jews became part of the expanding view of whiteness. The people in the category of Hispanic, grouping together ethnicities from Latin America, were deemed to be white but separate from U.S. whites. Many Latinos had experienced racial classification as a legacy of the Spanish conquistadors before their arrival in the U.S. and some of their forebears' experience of discrimination, particularly in the Southeastern part of the country, is legendary. Their path to Americanization and assimilation, as with other ethnic groups, included the acceptance of white evaluations of the inferior nature of blacks as compared to whites, and having their ethnic identities subsumed into a white racial identity. Consequently, the authors

---

[96] Richard Dyer, "The Matter of Whiteness," *White Privilege*, 9-23.

contend that many Hispanics are beneficiaries of whiteness today while others remain excluded.[97]

George Lipsitz views whiteness as an organizing principle through which social and cultural transactions are conducted, hence his term "a possessive investment in whiteness," by which he means that throughout U.S. history the federal government has ensured that the gap between resources available to whites and other ethnicities widens. He references the New Deal Era, the Federal Housing Act of 1934, and the post-World War II era trade union rights as largely benefitting whites because of the discriminatory manner in which the rules were implemented. Whether in policy and procedures related to housing, urban development and renewal, income, education, healthcare, criminal justice, or the environment, disparity abounds. This disparity is compounded through attacks on civil rights activism by those mainly on the right of the political spectrum, under the misguided notion that such activism is anachronistic. In her essay entitled "The Constraint of Race," Linda Faye Williams identifies the race problem as a "white skin problem" and argues that unless this system of advantage is acknowledged and addressed; solutions to this age-old problem will remain elusive. Williams also suggests that income redistribution and changes in social policies can impact racial disparity. Charles W. Mills views the problem of whiteness as a global white supremacy, which expresses itself in racially hierarchical civic structures run by Europeans. This global dominance makes it difficult for the nonwhite world to break through with a concerted voice. Closing the gap between the ideals of liberal democracies and the reality of white supremacy is, for him, the color line battle.[98]

In order to make the system of unearned privilege more visible, Stephanie M. Wildman and Adrienne D. Davis identify the use of language as vital in the elimination of "isms." Isms, they argue, tend to individualize rather than globalize: they focus on larger categories rather than on specifics, and they are shorthand for undesirable. Thus, any discussion of race, sex, sexual orientation, or

---

[97] Philip C. Wander, Judith N. Martin, and Thomas K. Nakayama, "The Roots of Racial Classification," *White Privilege*, 29-63.

[98] George Lipsitz, "The Possessive Investment in Whiteness," *White Privilege*, 67-104.

class needs to address the power that fuels them. Their remedy is for whites to make privilege visible and to take ownership of their own racism.[99] In his discussion of privilege as paradox, Allan G. Johnson emphasizes the obvious point that privilege is defined in relationship with another group or category. Hence, one need not be white, male, or heterosexual to benefit from privilege since privilege comes from identification with a particular category–it's not who you are but who you are with![100]

Peggy McIntosh's seminal essay is useful for its practicality with its list of common occurrences that are taken for granted by most whites but which are illustrative of the privilege they exercise. Privilege, says McIntosh, is unearned entitlement that confers dominance. Challenging this system of privilege begins with breaking the silence and denial of its existence, including the notion of equality, when inbuilt benefits have already favored the privileged.[101] The power of privilege leads Robert Jensen to conclude that privilege is the affirmative action of whites in the United States; consequently, this awareness of privilege is the first step towards privilege recovery.[102] In the same vein, Tim Wise asserts that acknowledging privilege is not enough. He offers some practical considerations that include alliances with the underprivileged, protesting racial insensitivity, denouncing racial tracking in the classroom, curtailing white flight, and decrying the privileging of the elite. These suggestions all invite the holders of privilege to step outside of their comfort zone in an effort to mitigate privilege.[103] Leonard Pitts echoes a familiar refrain, namely, that blacks generally obsess over racism while whites generally do not—the key is somewhere in the middle.[104]

Finally, in resisting the power of privilege, Beverly Tatum urges that blacks and whites overcome their fear of discomfort,

---

[99] Stephanie M. Wildman with Adrienne D. Davis, "Making Systems of Privilege Visible," *White Privilege*, 114f.

[100] Wildman and Davis, 109-120.

[101] Peggy McIntosh, "White Privilege: Unpacking the Invisible Knapsack," *White Privilege*, 123-127.

[102] Robert Jensen, "White Privilege Shapes the U.S." *White Privilege*, 129-131.

[103] Tim Wise, "Membership Has Its Privileges: Thoughts on Acknowledging and Challenging Whiteness," *White Privilege*, 133-136.

[104] Leonard Pitts, "Crazy Sometimes," *White Privilege*, 137-141.

rejection and anger through constructive dialogue.[105]   Others admonish all to confront their own racism embedded from childhood, with a focus on the oneness of our collective humanity.[106] And Paul Kivel rehearses a pivotal suggestion made by Poling that whites establish alliances with blacks or "resistance communities."[107] However, resistance to being resistant itself needs to be tackled, and for this Kivel offers a twelve step guideline on how this hurdle can be overcome. First, one must assume that racism is ever-present, which is not a stretch, given the historic nature of legalized racial discrimination in the United States. Second, observing who are at the center of attention and power will provide insight into the holders of privilege. Third, awareness of how racism is denied, minimized or justified reveals the level of discomfort that the privileged have in addressing it. Four, be aware of the historical context of whiteness and racism since it has evolved over time due to exposure and challenge. Five, an appreciation for the nexus between racism, economic issues, sexism and other forms of injustice is useful since it reveals a common trend of marginalization. Six, knowledge of the previous steps lead to the inevitable "so what?" and the need to take stand against injustice. Seven, it is important to be strategic in order to target the major issues like the source of power. Eight, since the fight against racism and inequality, has been prolonged, not confusing a battle with the war is important. The fight is never over simply because some rights and freedoms are won. Nine, while name-calling and personal abusive behaviors are tempting, they have diminishing returns. Ten, supporting leaders of color in their fight for equality should be done consistently but not uncritically. Eleven, this is a community fight and not one for lone rangers since it is exacting. Finally, discussing these issues with the young as the next generation of adults could serve to mitigate the effects of

---

[105] Beverly Tatum, "Breaking the Silence," *White Privilege*, 147-151.

[106] Joe Feagin and Hernan Vera, "Confronting One's Own Racism," *White Privilege*, 153-157.

[107] Paul Kivel, "How White People Can Serve as Allies to People of Color in the Struggle to End Racism," *White Privilege*, 159.

racism.[108]   Kivel's twelve steps should find a home in any reconciliation process.

Summary

        This review of the literature on racial reconciliation from the SCPC field, Adventism, clergy practitioners, the peace and justice movement, and the psychology and social psychology fields, reflects an evolution in thinking regarding how interethnic reconciliation can effectively be accomplished in conflicted societies. All agree that the purpose of reconciliation is to achieve a more harmonious relationship between estranged parties, though there are variations in its definition.   Although there is no consensus on how reconciliation is to be accomplished–with interventions ranging from the intrapsychic to the interpersonal to the intergroup–there is some commonality on the elements of a process. These generally agreed-upon elements include identification of the cause and nature of the conflict, how the offended and offenders are affected by the conflict, the role of forgiveness (regret, contrition, apology) in resolving the conflict, and the nature of the post-conflict relationship. The SCPC field, Adventism, and clergy practitioners should be encouraged by the spiritual-ethical dimensions of reconciliation that are the basis for peacemaking within both the peace and justice movement and the social science fields. The fact that these latter fields have actively included guiding principles and interventional strategies from the realm of the spiritual and ethical in the reconciliation process should encourage SCPC, Adventism, and clergy practitioners to renew and sustain their participation this arena since they have much to contribute.

---

[108] Rothenberg Paul Kivel, "How White People Can Serve as Allies to People of Color in the Struggle to End Racism," *White Privilege*, 166-167.

A Historical Overview of the SDA Church in the United States and in Great Britain Relative to its Mission to Black Expansion and Protest

> The Color line has been drawn so incisively by the church itself that its proclamation of the gospel of the brotherhood of Jew and Greek, of bond and free, of white and black has sometimes the sad sound of irony, and sometimes there is in it the bitter cry of repentance.[1]

The historical developments discussed in this chapter are chosen to show how the birth of a religious movement at a time of extreme societal fluctuations — including racial tensions — was able to thrive despite growing pains. Some of the beliefs and practices of the SDA Church were informed both by millennial influences of its founders, and the racialized society from which it emerged. The role of one founder, in particular, Ellen G. White, is explored with reference to the church's mission to blacks. Since the racial attitudes of Adventists mirrored to some extent those of society in general, it is perhaps understandable that the church would pursue a policy of segregation. This policy, as well as discriminatory behaviors, resulted in the birth of Regional Conferences, which have facilitated (though not exclusively) the growth of Adventism among blacks in the United States. Also addressed is the expansion of Adventism in the U.K. and the role that blacks from the Caribbean played in this expansion. Their fight with racism both in the country and in their church will reveal some parallels between the church's approach to racism in the United States and the United Kingdom.

The Formation of the SDA Church

Organized in May 1863, in the midst of the American Civil War with approximately 3,500 members, largely in the northern United States, the SDA Church was an offspring of the apocalyptic Millerite movement of the early 1840s. The church was one of

---

[1] H. Richard Niebuhr, *The Social Sources of Denominationalism* (New York: Meridian Books, 1957), 263.

several fragments that survived the Great Disappointment of October 22, 1844.[2] It presently has a worldwide membership of over 18.5 million persons, with perhaps a similar number of casual adherents and unbaptized children in its ranks. Its annual growth rate is approximately 6 percent, and around 1.3 million members live in the United States. It is thought that by 2050 there could be as many as 100 million adherents worldwide.[3] The role of teenager Ellen G. Harmon[4] in the establishment of the SDA Church was significant for many reasons, including as a voice of protest at how church leaders were addressing the issue of race relations. Harmon's family, who had accepted the Millerite message, was expelled from the Methodist church. Ellen was only a teenager in 1844 when the church believes she began receiving visions from God. Ellen's visions, accepted by the nascent movement as revelations from God, were first used to encourage the dispirited Millerites. Later, these visions would be used to confirm new doctrinal beliefs of the fledgling movement, and with co-founders James White (her husband) and Joseph Bates, these believers grew from 100 in 1849 to 3,500 at the time of the church's incorporation.[5]

The church's distinctive beliefs are the seventh day Sabbath, the imminent return of Christ and the final judgment, as well as the importance of health reform. Like other members of the Millerite movement, the SDA church had until 1870 appropriated a 'shut door' policy–the belief that 'probation' had closed on humanity. According to this belief, salvation was no longer on offer since Christ had returned spiritually. Consequently, any outreach by members was conducted among former members of the Millerite movement. This policy was soon jettisoned, as outsiders joined the denomination, and with an emphasis on missionary outreach, the

---

[2] Baptist preacher William Miller had calculated with the aid of scripture – prophecies in the book of Daniel and the Revelation – that Christ was to return to the earth to inaugurate the kingdom of God. According to Miller's calculations, the day for this return was October 22, 1844. Naturally, the date came and went without the expected *Parousia*, leaving many Millerites disappointed and dejected.

[3] Bull and Lockhart, [2007], xiii.

[4] Ellen G. Harmon became Ellen G. White by marriage to James White.

[5] Bull and Lockhart, [2007], 7.

membership tripled to 16,000 by late 1880. By 1901, when the church underwent reorganization, it had 1,500 workers and a membership of 75,767.[6] Following the advice of Ellen White, the SDA Church branched out into education and healthcare so that today it boasts the largest private educational and medical institutions of any religious entity except for Roman Catholicism. It currently operates: 7,442 educational institutions; 24 food companies; 168 hospitals and sanitariums; 433 clinics and dispensaries; 130 nursing homes; and retirement centers; 33 orphanages and children's homes; and 10 airplanes and medical launches; 10 media centers; 62 publishing houses and branches, which produce publications in 362 languages; 125 Adventist Development and Relief Agencies; and its annual worldwide income is $2.7 trillion, which is processed through its headquarters in Silver Springs, Maryland.[7]

The Religious and Sociopolitical Context in Which the SDA Church Emerged
Millennialism Influences

The SDA church emerged during a milieu of change and social upheaval in U.S. history that, for Adventist scholar and administrator Norman Miles, was "probably the most crucial period with regard to race relations."[8] It was also a time of religious fervor

---

⁶ Six major changes were included in the reorganization: (1) organization of union conferences; (2) the transfer of ownership and management of all institutions to the organizations where they were located; (3) creation of departments – such as Sabbath School, education, and publishing—in the General Conference; (4) strengthening of committees by placing on them representatives of the different areas; (5) placing of responsibility for the details of church work on those located where the work was done; (6) creation of a representative General Conference Committee. Nancy J. Vyhmeister, "Who Are Seventh-day Adventists?" *Handbook of Seventh-day Adventist Theology* (ed. Raoul Dederen; Hagerstown, MD: Review and Herald Publishing Association, 2000), 11.

⁷ "Seventh-day Adventist World Church Statistics," Seventh-day Adventist Church http://www.adventist.org/world_church/facts_and_figures /index.html.en (accessed 2/19/10).

⁸ Norman K. Miles, "Tensions between the Races," *The World of Ellen G. White* (ed. Gary Land; Washington, DC: Review and Herald Publishing Association, 1987), 47.

triggering the Second and Third Great Awakening,[9] and encapsulated in what historian Ernest Sandeen called "millennial expectations… woven in into the fabric of early nineteenth-century life both in Europe and America."[10] Taking the second of these movements first, millennialism advanced the belief that Jesus Christ's return to the earth was imminent, at which point a thousand-year reign would ensue. It should be noted that millennialism encompassed more than a belief in a new divine order; rather it was an extensive philosophical approach to human history, a form of eschatology used to denote how this earth will end.

It was this millennial expectancy, closely aligned with a civilization in flux, that fueled evangelical fervor to save sinners and reform social institutions. Indeed, millennialism was the motivating force for the Social Gospel movement, epitomized in the writings of Walter Rauschenbusch. Rauschenbusch advocated that those longing for the coming of Christ's kingdom were to work for improvements in the social and employment conditions of workers in a burgeoning industrialized world. Rauschenbusch's view of Christ's kingdom was more here and now than hereafter, due to the transformative nature of the gospel.[11] Unfortunately, Rauschenbusch and other Social Gospel thinkers excluded from their

---

[9] Following revivals in the "burned over district" of upstate New York and in Kentucky, the Second Great Awakening, which took place from 1800 to 1840 was strongest in the western states. The third Great Awakening occurred from 1880 to 1910 and was characterized by new denominations' very active missionary work and the Social Gospel approach to social issues. "Great Awakening," *Britannica Online Encyclopedia* http://www.britannica.com/EBchecked/topic/242887/Great-Awakening (accessed 9/20/10).

[10] Ernest R. Sandeen, *The Origin of Fundamentalism: Toward a Historical Interpretation* (Philadelphia: Fortress Press, 1968), 7.

[11] According to Harlan Beckley, Rauschenbusch favored "an evolutionary view of the kingdom that mobilizes the available natural and social resources towards a social order of love and equality. Hence, Rauschenbusch understood the kingdom as building upon natural human instincts, especially the desire for fellowship, and upon existing social forces." Harlan Beckley, *Passion for Justice: Retrieving the Legacies of Walter Rauschenbusch, John A. Ryan, and Reinhold Niebuhr* (Louisville, KY: Westminster/John Knox Press, 1992), 56.

discourse on social justice the fight for racial equality and the church's role in this fight. This neglect of the greatest social ill of their time, surmises ethicist Preston Williams, was due largely to the fact that "racism was so endemic to American life that it was a ruling idea of all Americans and every age."[12] Williams further theorizes that not only were Social Gospel thinkers silent on the question of racial disparity, they "helped to create a method of analysis that makes more difficult, even today, a solution to the racial problem."[13] From Williams' perspective, the methodology of Social Gospel thinkers was to champion all causes except that of blacks, since doing so would also be an indictment of these white social reformers.

By the 1830's, there were essentially two rival millennial perspectives, postmillennialism and premillennialism, each differing on issues of the chronological sequence of end-time events, in the manner of the expected kingdom of God, and on the nature of control that Christ exercised over this kingdom. Postmillennialists believed that the events of the End would conclude the millennium with a grand resurrection and Judgment Day coinciding with the visible return of Christ at the end of the thousand years. Conversely, premillennialists held that there would be two resurrections, judgments, and Advents either side of the thousand years.[14] One millennial scholar further observes that premillennialists adopted an extremely negative view of humankind, considering human beings and society in general as putrid, and that "this state of things can be overcome only by the direct, cataclysmic intervention of God."[15] This belief would appear to rule out tampering with the social order but working within it to achieve the evangelical goal of converting individuals to 'the faith.'

---

[12] Preston N. Williams, "The Social Gospel and Race Relations: A Case Study of a Social Movement," *Toward a Discipline of Social Ethics: Essays in Honor of Walter George Muelder* (ed. Paul Deats, Jr.; (Boston: Boston University Press, 1972), 235.

[13] Williams, 233.

[14] Underwood, 4.

[15] Kenneth G. C. Newport, *Apocalypse and Millennium: Studies in Biblical Eisegesis* (Cambridge: Cambridge University Press, 2000), 12f.

Premillennialists were divided into two camps, historicist and futurist, with the former being more pronounced during the first half of the nineteenth century and the latter gaining ascendancy in the last half of the nineteenth century and remaining the most common evangelical interpretative framework today. Historicists had a "comprehensive outline of history in the apocalyptic prophecies; the futurist school expected most of these prophecies to be fulfilled in the future–during a brief period just before the Second Coming of Christ," writes Adventist historian Douglas Morgan.[16] Adventists have continued in the tradition of William Miller by adhering to a historicist premillennialism, and it is through this lens that the church's position on social change can best be analyzed. As Morgan observes, Adventists have been shy at any effort "to transform society as the primary vehicle of redemption," including avoiding conservative religious causes in favor of religious liberty.[17] This hesitancy towards social advocacy within Adventism has been labeled "self-interest" by Adventist theologian Sakae Kubo, who chronicles the church's shift in concern for the welfare of others. Kubo states that Adventist justification for the establishment of schools and hospitals was on the basis of "soul-winning purposes, not altruistic ones."[18] Despite the fact that the church's rationale for social engagement has modulated over the years from ulterior to more altruistic motives, Kubo insists that the church disabuse itself of the notion that assisting others be done "only where it serves their self-interest."[19]

Race, Religion and Reunion Post U.S. Civil War

---

[16] Douglas Morgan, *Adventism and the American Republic: The Public Involvement of a Major Apocalyptic Movement* (Knoxville: University of Tennessee Press, 2001), 7.

[17] Morgan, 2001, 9.

[18] Sakae Kubo, foreword to *The Silent Church: Human Rights and Adventist Social Ethics,* by Zdravko Plantak (Basingstoke, Hampshire: Macillan, 1998), xii.

[19] Kubo, xii.

In turning to the sociopolitical environment of the nineteenth century from which Adventism emerged, the profound question posited by the social reformer Frederick Douglass is apropos: "If war among the whites brought peace and liberty to blacks, what will peace among the whites bring?"[20]   The history of this period provides an uncomfortable, even harrowing response to Douglass' question, which he hints at with the following statement, "The fathers of the Republic as I have said had their trial ninety-nine years ago. The colored citizens of this Republic are about to have their trial now." The Republic was finding its footing following its War of Independence, but by the end of the 19th century it had a thriving economy courtesy of slave labor, welcoming the "huddled masses [whites] yearning to breathe free."[21] In the middle of the century, the loss of over half a million men to a Civil War (1861-1865) had "stripped it of its innocence and its slaves."[22] Prior to the Civil War, four million blacks lived mainly in the Southern States as slaves, with ten percent residing in the North.[23]   But fighting a war to guarantee their freedom was relatively easy compared to the

---

[20] He sounds this ominous note: "The Signs of the times, are not all in our favor. There are even in the Republican Party, indications of a disposition to get rid of us. Men are seeking new allies, and smiling on faces upon which they never smiled before the war." He also questioned, "when this great white race has renewed its vow of patriotism and flowed back into its accustomed channels, the question for us is: in what position will this stupendous reconciliation leave the colored people? Fredrick Douglass, "The Color Question," a speech delivered on July 5th, 1875, the Fredrick Douglass Papers at the Library of Congress, http://memory .loc.gov/cgi-bin/ampage?collId=mfd&fileName=23/23001/23001page.db &recNum=0&itemLink=/ammem/doughtml/dougFolder5.html&link Text=7 (accessed 2/19/10).

[21] A line from Emma Lazarus' sonnet "The New Colossus," engraved on a plaque at the Statue of Liberty.

[22] Norman K. Miles, "Tensions between the Races," *The World of Ellen G. White*, 48.

[23] Jon Butler, Grant Wacker and Randall Balmer, *Religion in American Life: A Short History* (Oxford: Oxford University Press, 2003), 242.

enormous undertaking of bringing reconciliation and reconstruction to a divided nation. The process of reconciliation was complicated by a need to understand the competing ideas of North-South sectional healing and racial justice, argues the foremost historian of the period, David Blight, who writes:

> The sectional reunion after so horrible a civil war was a political triumph by the late nineteenth century, but it could not have been achieved without the resubjugation of many of those people whom the war had freed from centuries of bondage. This is the tragedy lingering on the margins and infesting the heart of American history from Appomattox to World War I. For many whites, especially veterans and their family members, healing from the war was simply not the same proposition as doing justice to the four million emancipated slaves and their descendants. On the other hand, a simple justice, a fair chance to exercise their basic rights, and secure access to land and livelihood were all blacks ever demanded of reconstruction and beyond.[24]

Given the entrenched belief that blacks were not considered fully human as established by the Three-Fifths compromise between Northern and Southern states during the Philadelphia Convention of 1787, whites had difficulty accepting the new social order of black equality, established by the Thirteenth, Fourteenth and Fifteenth Amendments.[25] It is important to specify that this white dissonance was not limited to Southern whites, as Emilie Towne confirms; by

---

[24] The author confirms that the way the Civil War is remembered remains a significant point of contention. "Those who remembered the war as the rebirth of the republic in the name of racial equality would continue to do battle with the growing number who would remember it as the nation's test of manhood and the South's struggle to sustain white supremacy." David W. Blight, *Race and Reunion: The Civil War in American Memory* (Cambridge: Harvard University Press, 2001), 97.

[25] The Thirteenth Amendment ended slavery in the United States in 1865; the Fourteenth Amendment allowed blacks to have the same rights as whites in 1868; and the Fifteenth Amendment allowed blacks to vote in 1870. "Civil War Amendments," http://library.thinkquest.org/J0112391/civil_war_amendments.htm (accessed 9/21/10).

1860, in almost every area of Northern life, racial segregation existed. Also significant, says Townes, is the fact that among the things credited for the embrace by the South of extreme racism was "the relaxation of significant opposition to racism by the liberal North… [and that] Eventually, the North and South differed little on their race policies."[26] It is largely for this reason, as Blight intones, that fifty years after the Civil War, with the North and the South principally reconciled, blacks and whites were even more divided.[27] Indeed the title of his book, *Race and Reunion*, encapsulates his central thesis that the sectional merger came at the expense of racial disparity and segregation of blacks.

The Reconstruction era of 1863 to 1877, was designed to restore self-government to the eleven seceding states and to provide equality for blacks. However, Blight argues, it's vital challenge was to "determine how a national blood feud could be reconciled at the same time a new nation emerged out of war and social revolution."[28] Caught in the middle of this feud were recently freed blacks, who would come under the most severe brutality and violence imaginable. Blacks in the South lived in constant fear of their lives, with the birth of the Ku Klux Klan during this period. Many ex-slaves viewed the Klan as a form of the old slave patrol, lynching indiscriminately, raping black women, burning houses, schools and churches, and engaging in vigilante sadism.[29] Probing for psychological answers to this level of human barbarity, Blight identifies the trauma of defeat by white Southerners, whose world was upended, and whose indignation was aroused by former slaves being assertive by bearing arms, organizing unions and engaging in the political process, including the judiciary. Though no reliable statistics are available prior to 1882 for the total number of blacks

---

26 Emilie Townes, *In a Blaze of Glory: Womanist Spirituality as Social Witness* (Nashville: Abingdon Press, 1995), 52.

27 Blight, 4.

28 Blight, 31.

29 Victims of these heinous crimes included teachers, students, white and black politicians, and freedmen and their families. Blight, 113.

and whites that were lynched, from the years 1882 to 1968 a total of 4,743 has been suggested, with a ratio of 3 blacks to 1 to one white.[30]

Southern violence during Reconstruction is captured by Wilbur Cash's classic *The Mind of the South*, a book whose supporters and detractors both agree continues to exert significant influence on the study of the South.[31] Cash frames the South as besieged by racism, rampant individualism, a penchant for brutality, and impervious to being disparaged. He writes that "Stripped of a decade of all control of its government...the South was left with scarcely any feasible way to mastery save only this one of the use of naked force... [with] the Negro who was the obviously appointed scapegoat... to give the black man the works was just as effectually to strike Yankeedom, to serve notice of the South's will...."[32] From Cash's perspective, white Southerners displaced their anger on freed blacks in an attempt to cope with their own sense of loss, for a way of life that was brutally seized from them by Northern whites. Significantly for blacks, this level of violence reinforced centuries of ancestral trauma of personal and communal remembering that left them experiencing and re-experiencing "conflicted emotions of guilt and rage, humiliation and vengeance, and profound distrust."[33] This distrust has played a significant role in the interaction between blacks and whites to the present day. Therefore, one need not look further than the manner in which freed blacks were treated by whites during Reconstruction and beyond to provide a credible answer to Douglas's question.

While Blight argues for a sectional healing at the expense of racial justice, in *Forging the White Republic*, historian Edward J. Blum

---

[30] "Lynchings by State and Race, 1882-1968," under "Famous American Trails," [Shipp], faculty project, University of Missouri, Kansas City, http://www.law.unkc.edu/faculty/projects/ftrials.shipp/lynch ingsstate.html (accessed 9/21/10).

[31] Charles W. Eagles, ed., *The Mind of the South: Fifty Years Later* (Jackson: University Press of Mississippi, 1992).

[32] W. J. Cash, *The Mind of the South* (Garden City, NY: Doubleday Anchor Books, 1954), 126-27.

[33] Blight, 177. Blight later concludes with the observation that "The Civil War had become the nation's inheritance of glory, Reconstruction the legacy of folly, and the race problem a matter of efficient schemes of segregation." Blight, 387.

contends that the Reconstruction reunion of whites was achieved not only by race but also by religion, specifically Northern white Christianity. In addition, religion justified and encouraged "social and spiritual separation of whites and blacks, and in propelling the United States into global imperialism."[34] The confluence of nationalism and religion was exemplified in the term "Manifest Destiny." The phrase was first coined in 1845 by John O'Sullivan to signify the belief that the United States, with its Anglo-Saxon colonists, had been divinely appointed to gain territorial advantage over the Northern Hemisphere. H. Richard Niebuhr observes that this attribution "was turned into the notion of a chosen nation especially favored."[35] The tenets of this favored nation status were, for Southern Whites, "a nation in which the rights, privileges, and liberties of white men, especially slaveholders, were vigorously protected."[36] By implicating religion in the North-South reunion post-Civil War, Blum challenges established scholarship on the role of Protestantism as a reactive force, instead arguing that in every facet of U.S. society, there was a prevailing religious influence. Blum's approach holds currency, given the spiritual significance of Manifest Destiny.[37]

According to Blum, Northern religionists were complicit in discarding the 1860s' civic nationalism in favor of an ethnic nationalism of whiteness, prevalent in the antebellum North; the upshot was the abandonment of racial justice and the demonization of blacks.[38] This demonization of blacks had been established much

---

[34] Edward J. Blum, *Forging the White Republic: Race, Religion and American Nationalism, 1865-1898* (Baton Rouge: Louisiana State University Press, 2007), 3f.

[35] H. Richard Niebuhr, *The Kingdom of God in America* (Hamden, CT: Shoe String Press, 1956), 179.

[36] Blum, 5.

[37] Blum, 9.

[38] Blum also sees a political calculus in the approach of white temperance organizers, whom he claims "demonized African Americans and immigrants as unworthy of national citizenship." In addition, "the legacy of racial prejudice in the North and the desires of northern white Protestants to reach out to southern whites in the 1870s, 1880s, and 1890s led them to repudiate their Civil War-era commitments to building an integrated nation of racial equality." Blum, 15-16.

earlier in the amalgam of pseudoscientific and religious defenses of racism and slavery. Such justifications are widely chronicled and include the polygenesis theory, which argues for the creation of pre-Adam humans who were non-white and inferior, from whom Cain took his wife (Gen. 4:16, 17). Associated with polygenesis is the belief that Cain was the offspring of a union between the Devil and Eve during her encounter with the serpent at the tree of knowledge of good and evil (Gen. 3:1f). Also, the belief that the flood was triggered by an illicit intercourse between "sons of God" and "daughters of men" (Gen. 6:4) was used to denounce intermarriage between the blacks and whites. But the most potent racist defense of slavery was the notorious curse of Canaan extrapolated from Gen. 9:20-27, the incident of Noah's drunkenness and nude exposure, which plants the seed for "the centrality of honor in the white Southern mind. In the process, it problematizes the view that old South racism was a projection of white sexual fears and fantasies," observes religious studies Professor Stephen R. Haynes.[39] Noah's son Ham, who gazes on his naked father, avoids his father's curse, but his son Canaan, along with his posterity, is cursed with being "a servant of servants." This life of servitude becomes the principal theological rationale for a God-ordained enslavement of blacks by proslavery supporters; with Ham's actions being viewed as a violation of family loyalty, resulting in blacks being "devoid of honor and thus fit for slavery."[40]

It follows that such racial thinking and assumption of black inferiority, which Niebuhr acknowledged was the acceptable and prevailing attitude in post-Civil War America, was "accepted by the

---

[39] Stephen R. Haynes, *Noah's Curse: The Biblical Justification for American Slavery* (Oxford: Oxford University Press, 2002), 15-17. Haynes also challenges this assertion by noting that "Beginning with nineteenth-century abolitionists, who regarded the South as a modern-day Sodom in which 'men could indulge their erotic impulses with impunity,' the proslavery argument has been perceived as a rationale for dominance and sexual transgression. But careful study of the way Genesis 9 was read in antebellum America indicates that proslavery intellectuals were at least as deeply concerned with honor and dishonor as with sex and power." Haynes, 66.

[40] Haynes, 66-67.

church without subterfuge of any sort."[41] It is fair to say, however, that some northern clergy advocated for a universal humanity, as they resisted scientific and religious justification for racial difference. Prompted by a desire to assist former slaves and reunite a divided country, missionaries journeyed south to Christianize, educate, and provide financial resources to establish black institutions that would lay the foundations for a black middle class. From 1862 to 1870 over eight thousand black and white northerners made the trek south as saviors to a degenerated territory in an attempt to restore the union and with it, the nation's Manifest Destiny, self-understanding. Needless to say, these overtures to blacks were viewed with disdain by Southern whites, who felt threatened by the message of social equality for blacks. Violence accompanied Southern white hostility, instilling fear in northern missionaries, leading to a kind of reenactment of the Civil War conflict between defenseless schoolteachers and students and marauding white vigilantes. Despite the overwhelming odds against their efforts, Northerners left an enduring legacy that none of the violence and intimidation of Southern whites could erase. Universities like Atlanta, Fisk, Clark, Howard, and Lincoln, along with over twenty-five thousand other schools and thirteen thousand teachers educated in these reconstruction schools, are fitting testimonials to the courage and accomplishment of the outreach. The educational stride of Southern blacks speaks volumes, as a result of these institutions. The literacy rate of blacks stood at ten percent in 1865, almost doubling in five years. Twenty years later, literacy among blacks had reached fifty-five percent, and by 1940 it was eighty-nine percent, evidence of significant motivation by blacks to put their days of servitude behind them.42

By the mid-1860s, northern largesse and interest in racial justice diminished in favor of sectional healing for the purpose of reclaiming the Manifest Destiny motif. Northern Protestant leaders began appropriating Christian principles of forgiveness and reconciliation in accelerating the drive for a unified nation. However, the price to be paid for this drive for sectional healing was a retreat from their commitment to civic nationalism, Blum argues.

---

[41] H. Richard Niebuhr, *The Social Sources of Denominationalism*, 236.
[42] Blum, 54, 60, 79, 81, 82-83.

Northern Protestants convinced themselves that with the 15th Amendment racial justice was complete and that Southern whites would safeguard the well-being of blacks. Northerners also returned to viewing blacks as second-class citizens and an essential ingredient to restoring the white republic. Leading this charge for sectional healing over racial justice were the larger denominations and the more renowned preachers, such as Henry Ward Beecher and Dwight L. Moody.[43]

In much of his sermons, Beecher implored northern Protestants to forgive southern whites so that sectional harmony could transpire. Church historian Clifford E. Clark observes that while Beecher supported black equality, he did not want it to come at the expense of southern whites, as the following quote suggests: "Much as I see the natural rights of suffrage given to the freemen, I think it would be attained at too great a price if it involved the right of the Federal Government to meddle with state affairs."[44] Beecher's laissez-faire stance led him to believe that it was senseless to legislate equality for blacks if southern whites were not in agreement. This degree of faith in southern whites exposed Beecher to criticism from the likes of Frederick Douglass, who admitted to not being able to fathom this change of heart. By 1876, Beecher's perspective was the majority view held by the major northern denominations, and the reconciliation fervor was followed-up with a gradual withdrawal of funding to black interests in the South. So, influential were the northern Protestant leaders that the chief arguments used to advance sectional reunion in the country were Christian narratives. The reaction of many of the black denominations, including the African Methodist Episcopal Zion Church, was that they were not interested in forging closer ties between themselves and northern white Methodism, who sought sectional reunion while practicing racial discrimination.[45]

By the time Dwight L. Moody entered the fray in the late 1870s through the 1880s, during the Third Great Awakening, he was able to sway the political debate around sectional healing by

---

[43] Blum, 89, 90, 119.

[44] Clifford E. Clark, Jr., *Henry Ward Beecher: Spokesman for a Middle-class America* (Chicago: University of Illinois Press, 1978), 171.

[45] Blum, 95, 108, 111.

ironically "disparaging involvement in politics by religionists and accepting racial segregation as normative, so as not to offend white Southerners."[46] One encounter that forced Moody to face the issue of racism occurred in April 1976 in Augusta, Georgia. While Moody was vacationing in Augusta, he held a desegregated revival. With blacks occupying the first rows, a partition was erected to separate blacks and whites, something Moody opposed. Southern whites challenged Moody not to change the prevailing social conventions, and from then on, he would hold only segregated revivals so as not to risk unpopularity. Moody's popularity was unrivaled in his day, with a "who's-who" of the country's nobility, including President Ulysses S. Grant and international banker J. P. Morgan, often attending his revivals.[47]

Importantly, while denominations maintained their North/ South divide, Moody was able to transcend these intersectional animosities with his reconciliation and reunion message, while railing against social activism. But, argues Blum, "In the context of the mid-1870s, however, this general abandonment of politics had a specific meaning. It invariably meant a rejection of radical Reconstruction and its emphasis on black civil rights and civic nationalism."[48] Moody's storytelling homiletics tended to romanticize the Civil War, placate white Southerners, and minimize the grave peril the country went through, with its future in the balance and blacks' role in that future decidedly in doubt. His penchant to maintain his popularity with Southern whites by continuing segregated revivals did not go without criticism, with one clergy calling him responsible for erecting a caste system over Christianity.[49] Criticism also came from Frederick Douglass, who despised segregated congregations: "Of all the forms of negro hate in this world, save me from that one which clothes itself with the name of the loving Jesus… The negro can go into the circus, the theatre,

---

[46] Blum, 119.

[47] James F. Findlay, Jr., *Dwight L. Moody: American Evangelist, 1837-1899* (Chicago: University of Chicago Press, 1969), 279-280. Findlay further notes that for Moody, "To remain a popular religious hero he had to conform to national secular standards on this social issue…." Findlay, 281

[48] Blum, 127, 129.

[49] Blum, 142.

and can be admitted to the lectures of Mr. Ingersoll, but cannot go into an evangelical Christian meeting."[50]

The extent to which Moody's revivals affected both the spiritual tenor of the country as well as the political discourse on reconciliation and reunion is chronicled by Blum. This towering revivalist was an effective conduit, bridging Northern whites' yearnings for ethnic nationalism, and Southern whites' desire to restore the antebellum social order. His effective Southern strategy of capitulation to Jim Crow laws, ignoring sociopolitical issues, embracing Southern religious icons like Presbyterian minister William Plumer, and creating a narrative of the South that was sanitized of any of the prevailing horrors committed against blacks, assured him of the status as the preeminent preacher of his time, acknowledged as such by both North and South. Moody and Beecher would come to be acknowledged as "apostles of forgiveness" and "apostles of reunion," for their biblical message had helped to shape the conversation and frame the issues for a country and its politicians,[51] who sought to restore the Manifest Destiny motif, a motif not possible while division reigned. Among the many black intellectuals defying this white merger at the expense of blacks, was eminent sociologist and civil rights activist W.E.B. Du Bois. Given the Manifest Destiny motif and in the face of white disinterest in solving the "Negro problem," Du Bois dared to posit the question: "Is the civilization of the United States Christian?" His response speaks for itself:

> The precepts of Jesus Christ cannot but mean that Christianity consists of an attitude of humility, of a desire for peace, of a disposition to treat our brothers as we would have our brothers treat us, of mercy and charity towards our fellow men, of willingness to suffer persecution for right ideals and in general of love not only

---

[50] "Oration of Frederick Douglass," *The American Missionary* 39.6 (June 1885): 164, http://digital.library.cornell.edu/cgi/t/text/ pageviewer-idx?c=amis;cc=amis;rgn=full%20text;idno=amis0039-6;didno=amis0039-6;view=image;seq=0177;node=amis0039-6%3A10 (accessed 9/21/10).

[51] Blum, 145. The author makes this ominous concluding remark, "As the United States barged into the twentieth century, the supremacy of whiteness, the supremacy of the United States, and the supremacy of Christ had again become viewed as one in the same." Blum, 249.

toward our friends but even toward our enemies. Judged by this, it is absurd to call the practical religion of this nation Christian… we are not merciful, we are unmerciful toward friend and foe… we do not want to be martyrs, we would much rather be thieves and liars so long as we can be rich; we do not seek continuously, and prayerfully to inculcate love and justice for our fellow men, but on the contrary the treatment of the poor, the unfortunate, and the black within our borders is almost a national crime.[52]

It is in this climate that a dispirited group of believers would emerge to establish the SDA Church. This group was strongly influenced by many elements of the society and its history: the United States was experiencing a national identity crisis, with its nightmare of a smoldering Manifest Destiny, a sectional divide that cost the lives of over 600,000 men; a way of life in the South had been prematurely overturned, leaving a shattered collective white psyche, yearning for its past; a people's servitude may have been over, but their longing for acceptance, parity, and selfhood remained in the distance; a racial ferment impacted every aspect of society; religious traditions had to find new ways of reinterpreting falsely constructed, Bible-based distortions about blacks; and, a religious awakening with a millennialistic framework had emerged that was more concerned with the hereafter than the here-and-now. Having reviewed the religious and sociopolitical contexts from which the SDA Church emanates, I will now turn to the church's outreach to blacks and the impact of Ellen G. White on that outreach.

The SDA Church's Mission to Blacks and the Role of Ellen G. White

It is a rather perplexing historical reality enunciated by H. Richard Niebuhr that, "The existence of the racial schism in America is one of the clearest facts in the whole mixed pattern of American denominationalism"[53] In this regard, the SDA Church has been typical of most denominations in the United States, particularly as it sought to expand outside the confines of its Northern territorial

---

[52] Booker T. Washington and W. E. B Du Bois, *The Negro in the South: His Economic Progress in Relation to His Moral and Religious Development* (Philadelphia: George W. Jacobs & Co., 1907), 185-86.

[53] H. Richard Niebuhr, *The Social Sources of Denominationalism*, 239.

roots, as an essentially all-white movement. The Millerite movement from which the SDA church emerged, did have black members in its ranks in the 1840s. After the Great Disappointment of October 22, 1844, in which hopes of Christ's return to the Earth did not materialize, some blacks joined forces with the group that would become the SDA Church, but the number of black Adventists remained minuscule in the 1880s.[54] The history of the work in the South, which began informally in 1871, in the Southern states of Kentucky, and later Missouri, Georgia, etc., and other states, has been ably chronicled by many Adventist historians and theologians.[55] Some Northern white Adventists did venture South at the end of Reconstruction to help in the uplift of blacks, including Joseph Clarke and his wife, both teachers, who traveled to Texas, but found that they lacked the ministerial expertise. Their request for help was answered in April 1877 by former Union officer R. M.

---

[54] Louis B. Reynolds, *We Have Tomorrow: The Story of American Seventh-day Adventists with an African Heritage* (Washington, DC: Review and Herald Publishing Association, 1984), 19f.

[55] "S.D.A. Accomplishments in Interracial Relations," *Adventist Archives* (1934): http://www.adventistarchives.org/docs/RCO/RCO-01B.pdf#view=fit (accessed 9/24/10). Resources used for this discussion of the history of SDA work in the South are the following: W.W. Fordham, *Righteous Rebel* (Washington, DC: Review and Herald Publishing Association, 1990); Alfonzo Greene, "[Black] Regional Conferences in the Seventh-day Adventists Church (SDA) Compared with United Methodist [Black] Central Jurisdiction/Annual Conferences With White SDA Conferences, From 1940-2001" (Ph.D. diss., Loyola University Chicago, 2009); Clifford R. Jones, *James K. Humphrey and the Sabbath-Day Adventists* (Jackson: University Press of Mississippi, 2006); Douglas Morgan, *Lewis C. Sheafe: Apostle to Black America* (Hagerstown, MD: Review and Herald Publishing Association, 2010); David K. Penno, "An Investigation of the Perceptions of Clergy and Laity Concerning Race-Based Organizational Segregation in the Southern Union Conference of Seventh-day Adventists" (Ph.D. diss., Andrews University, 2009); Rock, "Institutional Loyalty Versus Racial Freedom"; Reynolds, *We Have Tomorrow*; Bull and Lockhart, *Seeking A Sanctuary*; Richard W. Schwarz and Floyd Greenleaf, *Light Bearers: A History of the Seventh-day Adventist Church* (Nampa, ID: Pacific Press Publishing Association, 2001; Arthur W. Spalding, *Origin and History of Seventh-day Adventists* (4 vols.; Washington, DC: Review and Herald Publishing Association, 1962).

Kilgore, who labored under difficult circumstances in Texas for eight years. White Texans opposed his efforts, claiming that Kilgore was another Yankee who had come "to preach nigger equality," a charge he rebuffed.[56] Yet, in this rebuttal is epitomized the general approach of white Adventists to the "race problem," tacit submission to Southern customs in order to avoid alienating Southern whites by reaching out to blacks. Indeed, it was Kilgore, who by force of argument–based on his experience of working in the South–would be most influential in steering the church away from its integrated approach to a segregated approach to congregational worship.

In their interpretation of this period, in which Adventists sought southward expansion, Bull and Lockhart posit that blacks were not in their purview, and that church workers were surprised by the active segregation policies of the South. They then charge that "It was an appropriate beginning to Adventist dealings in race relations, for from that time to the present day, Adventist have never relinquished the idea that good relations between the races are best served by some kind of segregationist policy."[57] As previously stated, most aspects of Northern life were racially segregated by 1860, so whether or not these Adventists laboring in the South should have been surprised is questionable. The thorny issue of submitting to the prevailing mores of segregating black and white members in the South was contested at GC sessions in 1877, 1885, 1887, and 1889. Given his experience in Texas, Kilgore's position on segregation prevailed, for reasons of political expediency, namely the reluctance of white church leaders to hinder the potential growth of white converts.[58] This policy of segregation, which was already mirrored in society and served as a perpetual reminder to blacks that they were neither free nor equal, sowed the seed for what would later germinate into a push for black self-determination in the form of Regional Conferences.

By the end of the 19th century, a divide, largely along racial lines pitted those favoring racial equality including integrated worship services, with those who would rather preserve the status

---

56 Schwarz and Greenleaf, 226.

57 Bull and Lockhart, [2007], 279.

58 Schwarz and Greenleaf, 226.

quo, by preaching the gospel without incurring the animus of Southern whites. Parenthetically, the tensions between these two groups are mirrored in the current debate over Regional Conferences, only now, the roles are reversed. For it is the largely black leadership who are the Pragmatists intent on preserving the current system, while the largely white leadership, are now the Idealists, seeking a more integrated approach.

At a camp-meeting held in Nashville, Tennessee, on October 2, 1889, the first black protest of their treatment by white Adventists erupted. Articulating the apprehensions of black members was the first ordained black SDA minister, Charles M. Kinney, who is understood to be the "Father of Black Adventism." Kinney, who was to be ordained at the camp-meeting, decried efforts by white church leaders to segregate black members. Kinney threatened a boycott of his own ordination, and the leaders acquiesced.[59] Kinney then outlined to the workers at the camp-meeting what he acknowledged to be radical ideas to address in a constructive manner the "colored-line question." His twelve-point plan delineated the need for structural accommodation: "where the two races cannot meet together without limitation in the church, it is better to separate." While convinced that the gospel could overcome prejudicial attitudes, Kinney felt that the prevailing racial climate was an "obstacle" to the propagation of the gospel.[60] Thus the blueprint for Regional Conferences was established, a plan that was in sync with Kilgore's own position of segregated congregations. By July 11th, 1890, Kilgore presented his solution to the race question, which he identified as being the socially unacceptable association of black and white members in worship services. In a report to the GC committee, he outlined a position he had already articulated in an article in the *Review and Herald* the previous year.[61]

---

[59] Clifford R. Jones, 91.

[60] Charles M. Kinney, "Statement on the Concept of Regional Conferences," *Seventh-day Adventist Church, General Conference Archives* (Oct 2, 1889): http://blacksdahistory.org/files39717569.PDF (accessed 9/27/10). See Appendix B.

[61] GC Committee meeting (July 11, 1890): http://www.adventistarchives.org/docs/GCC/GCC1890/index.djvu; In his article, Kilgore acknowledges the difficulty Northern whites have in understanding the "color line question," and he emphatically states that

On March 21, 1891, Ellen G. White addressed the GC leadership on the "perplexing questions" of race. This speech was later published as a 16-page pamphlet and forms the first of several articles written by White between 1891 and 1897, which were compiled in the book *The Southern Work*.[62] White had clearly anticipated that her controversial message on race relations would not receive universal acclaim, as she acknowledged: "I know that which I now speak will bring me into conflict. This I do not covet, for the conflict has seemed to be continuous of late years; but I do not mean to live a coward or die a coward, leaving my work undone."[63] Here she refers to the obvious problem that the issue of race was becoming by denouncing the 1890 GC decision to acquiesce to white prejudice by permitting segregated churches, advanced by Kilgore. Her words are emphatic: "You have no license from God to exclude the colored people from your places of worship. Treat them as Christ's property, which they are, just as much as yourselves. They should hold membership in the church with the white brethren. Every effort should be made to wipe out the terrible wrong, which has been done to them."[64] Unlike her contemporaries Beecher and Moody, White was unambiguous about the ungodly nature of racism, which is perhaps why she remains revered by most black Adventists.

Despite such candor, there are early signs of Ellen White's ambivalence on the matter of race, for in the very next sentence she decries those in favor of miscegenation. "At the same time, we must not carry things to extremes and run into fanaticism on this question. Some would think it right to throw down every partition wall and intermarry with the colored people, but this is not the right thing to teach or to practice."[65] Though anti-miscegenation is beyond the scope of this study, it nevertheless offers insights into White's

---

"any effort made on the part of those from the North to break down the distinction between the races, thus ignoring popular prejudice, is simply fanatical and unwise." *Review and Herald* (October 29, 1889, 683): http://www.adventistarchives.org/docs/RH/RH18891029-V66-43__B/index.djvu (accessed 9/27/10).

[62] White, *The Southern Work*, 1966, 10.
[63] White, *The Southern Work*, 1966, 10.
[64] White, *The Southern Work*, 1966, 15.
[65] White, *The Southern Work*, 1966, 15

worldview that, despite her prophetic role, she remained a product of her racialized society.

In spite of this appeal to the GC "to send to this class [black] laborers who will work in Christ's name, who will not fail nor be discouraged,"[66] nearly three years would elapse before anyone would take up her challenge. James Edson White, the second child of Ellen and James White, is regarded by Adventists as the pioneer of the work among blacks, with his strategy of sailing along the Mississippi river in a steamboat, "The Morning Star," in 1895, preaching the gospel message. Following a spiritual renewal, Edson White had developed an interest in working for blacks in the south from Dr. J. E. Caldwell, who himself had been working for blacks in Knoxville, Tennessee. It was Caldwell who had informed Edson of his mother's 1891 GC appeal for vigorous action to be taken on behalf of the "colored people."

Alarmingly, as Schwarz and Greenleaf observe, as Edson made inquiries about the text of his mother's appeal, no one at the GC seemed to be cognizant of it. Were it not for the alertness of a painter at the church's printing press plant, who recalled seeing the "forgotten tract in an unused office," it may have been lost indefinitely.[67] Such indifference on the part of GC officials to such an important document, which espoused a mission to Southern blacks, reinforces the previous observation of Bull and Lockhart that early Adventists had scant regard for the spiritual welfare of blacks. Could the widely held belief that blacks were soul-less have anything to do with this indifference?[68] It is also possible that White's stinging rebuff to these leaders for their unchristian action in endorsing segregation, produced intransigence and disdain, rather than compassion and contrition?[69]

---

[66] White, *The Southern Work*, 1966, 15.

[67] Schwarz and Greenleaf, 229.

[68] This popularized notion that blacks did not have souls was eloquently challenged by W. E. B. Du Bois in his book, *The Souls of Black Folk* (New York: New American Library, 1969).

[69] Schwarz and Greenleaf, 229. Additionally, an authority on Ellen White's approach to race relations alludes to a similar conclusion — that the March 20, 1891 tract "had been promptly forgotten at the time." R. Ronald D. Graybill, *Mission to Black America*, 17.

Under the guidance of White, in 1896 church leaders at the GC purchased a 360-acre plantation in Huntsville, Alabama to develop an industrial training school for blacks. Called Oakwood Industrial School, which to some extent was modeled after Booker T. Washington's Tuskegee Institute, the school opened in the fall of 1896, with sixteen boarding students. The institution was managed by S. M. Jacob, an Iowa farmer, and by 1898 enrollment stood at fifty-five students. In 1904, its name was changed to Oakwood Manual Training School, and by 1917 it received both its charter to grant degrees, and a name change to Oakwood Junior College.

However, it was not until 1932 that Oakwood Junior College received its first black president, J. L. Morgan, following discontent among the students, a sharp decline in student enrollment, and charges of racial prejudice by many of the white staff and administrators. With Morgan's appointment came the decision to have an all-black faculty, and under his leadership, Oakwood established itself as the training center and hub for black Adventists. The school was granted senior college status in 1942 with 1,997 students; with this new status came a new president, Frank L. Peterson, who would usher in a decade of change. Undoubtedly, the most transformative ["golden age"] years of Oakwood College were the fourteen years (1971-1985) under the leadership of President Calvin B. Rock—mentioned earlier as a central character in the current debate about Regional Conferences. Student enrollment grew from 684 to 1,326; a feature of this growth was its international outreach.[70] As a graduate of Oakwood College in 1985, I was a part of this overseas outreach, attending the college as a citizen of the United Kingdom. The development of the college reached another landmark when on January 1, 2008; it was renamed Oakwood University. The university president is now Leslie N. Pollard, and student enrollment stands at 1,900, just 97 short of its 1942 total.

Evangelizing Southern blacks was not a priority for Adventists into the 1890s, particularly since they had already established overseas missions in Europe. Ellen White was scathing in her criticism of such neglect, as this quote indicates: "Sin rests upon us as a church because we have not made greater effort for the

---

[70] Mervyn A. Warren, *Oakwood! A Vision Splendid: 1896-1996* (Huntsville, AL: Oakwood, 1996), 129-42, 153f, 212-16.

salvation of souls among the colored people. It will always be a difficult matter to deal with the prejudices of the white people in the South and do missionary work for the colored race. But the way this matter has been treated by some, is an offense to God."[71] Social acceptability and self-preservation were not White's concerns prior to 1908, and her desegregation commitment was undiminished, as this 1895 passage indicates:

> Men have thought it necessary to plan in such a way as to meet the prejudice of white people, and the wall of separation in religious worship has been built up between the colored people and the white people. The white people have declared themselves willing that the colored people should be converted. They have no objection to this…yet they were not willing to sit by the side of their colored brethren and sing and pray and bear witness to the truth which they had in common.[72]

Yet, in a letter addressed to a Southern church worker on June 5, 1899, White was already beginning to indicate that a cautious approach in the South was needed, perhaps a precursor to her advocating a policy of segregation. She writes, "The field is one that needs to be worked with the greatest discretion. Any mingling of the white people with the colored people, as sleeping in their houses, or showing them friendship as would be shown by the whites to those of their own color, is exasperating to the white people of the South."[73] By 1899, all indications are that White's increasing ambivalence over segregated worship was now resolved since she urged that, "The breaking down of distinctions between the white and the colored races unfits the blacks to work for their own class, and exerts a wrong influence upon the whites."[74] White appears to

---

[71] White, *The Southern Work*, 1966, 15. In his Ph.D. dissertation, Roy E. Graham expresses doubt that the ambivalence of whites to evangelize blacks was due to "evil prejudice" but rather "a genuine desire to avoid making it more difficult to preach the SDA message to all races and classes." Such a response shows the lengths that some contemporary white historians have gone to defend the past practices of the church. Graham, 251.

[72] White, *The Southern Work*, 1966, 19-20.

[73] White, *The Southern Work*, 1966, 83.

[74] White, *The Southern Work*, 1966, 96.

have bowed to the inevitable policy of segregation on the basis of expediency, adopted by church leaders a decade earlier, an interpretation voiced by Bull and Lockhart, who conclude that White's aspirations for Adventists were those of an "unobtrusive people who avoided undue conflict."[75]

In a pamphlet called "Proclaiming the Truth Where There Is Race Antagonism," written on October 19, 1908, Mrs. White bows to the social pressure and moves into lock step with the prevailing norms. She intones with pathos, that

> I am burdened, heavily burdened, for the work among the colored people. The gospel is to be presented to the downtrodden Negro race. But great caution will have to be shown in the efforts put forth for the uplifting of this people. Among the white people in many places there exists a strong prejudice against the Negro race. We may desire to ignore this prejudice, but we cannot do it. If we were to act as if this prejudice did not exist we could not get the light before the white people. We must meet the situation as it is and deal with it wisely and intelligently.[76]

With the paradigm shift achieved, White built upon the themes of caution and wisdom, as well as indifference and neglect among church leaders, to finally countenance segregated worship services. Her pragmatism gave way to compromise, leading to the essential formulation of an Adventist race relations policy that held sway into the new century.[77] She formalized her position thus:

> Let as little as possible be said about the color line, and let the colored people work chiefly for those of their own race. In regard to white and colored people worshiping in the same building, this cannot be followed as a general custom with profit to either party — especially in the South. The best thing will be to provide the colored people who accept the truth, with places of worship of their own, in which

---

[75] Bull and Lockhart, 2007, 193.

[76] "Proclaiming The Truth Where There Is Race Antagonism," pamphlet written on October 19, 1908, and reproduced in *Testimony for the Church* (Mountain View, CA: Pacific Press Publishing Association, 1948), 9:204-05.

[77] Interestingly, the authors removed this assertion in their revised edition. Bull and Lockhart, [1989], 196.

they can carry on their services by themselves. This is particularly necessary in the South in order that the work for the white people may be carried on without serious hindrance. Let the colored believers be provided with neat, tasteful houses of worship. Let them be shown that this is done not to exclude them from worshiping with white people, because they are black, but in order that the progress of the truth may be advanced. Let them understand that this plan is to be followed until the Lord shows us a better way.[78]

In qualifying her segregation stance, White offers this caveat, "Where demanded by custom or where greater efficiency is to be gained, let the white believers and the colored believers assemble in separate places of worship."[79] This would clearly imply that she was in favor of integrated services as the norm and segregated services as the exception. However, White's segregation stance, with its caveat, was taken as license by church leaders — who had already arrived at such a position — to implement a generalized policy of segregation and discrimination. Despite her acquiescence, White saw her new position as a temporary measure that would be reversed in the future, when more harmonious relations existed between blacks and whites; at which point presumably, the Lord would reveal "a better way." It is duly noted that White informed readers that the expedient nature of her approbation should be clearly explained to blacks so that they would not be left with the wrong impression about the church's stance on race relations.

Assuming the need for expediency in the face of Southern white hostility towards blacks and those whites working on behalf of blacks, it is alarming that in the previous year, 1907, White was becoming more extreme in her language, embracing conventional racist ideology. Driven by millennial expectations, with their resistance to social change, White insists on black submission in the face of white supremacist attitudes and activities:

---

[78] White, "Proclaiming the Truth Where There Is Race Antagonism," in *Testimonies for the Church,* vol. 9, 206.

[79] White, "Proclaiming the Truth Where There Is Race Antagonism," 208.

The colored people should not urge that they be placed on an equality with white people. The relation of the two races has been a matter hard to deal with, and I fear that it will ever remain a most perplexing problem. So far as possible, everything that would stir up the race prejudice of white people should be avoided... I know that if we attempt to meet the ideas and preferences of some of the colored people, we shall find our way blocked completely. The work of proclaiming the truth for this time is not to be hindered by an effort to adjust the position of the Negro race. Should we attempt to do this we should find that barriers like mountains would be raised to hinder the work that God desires to have done... The time has not come for us to work as if there were no prejudice... All things may be lawful, but all things are not expedient.[80]

Understandably, Adventists have attempted to explain away White's about-face. Most notably, Roy Branson wrote a three part series in the April 1970 *Review and Herald*, with the title "Ellen G. White, Racist or Champion of Equality."[81] Branson concludes that White's reversal was impacted by: the crisis of the 1890s, in which there was a rollback of black freedoms achieved under Reconstruction; Southern white violence against her son, Edson White, and his team of workers along the Mississippi, who were ordered never to return; her process of aging, in which a "zealous

---

[80] White, "The Color Line," manuscript dated September 1907, and published in *Testimonies for the Church* 9.214.

[81] Roy Branson, "Ellen G. White, Racist or Champion of Equality," *Review and Herald* (April 9, 1970): http://www.adventist archives.org/docs/RH/RH19700409-V147-15__B/index.djvu (accessed 9/27/10); Branson, "Ellen G. White, Racist or Champion of Equality: Slavery and Prophecy," *Review* (April 16, 1970): http://www.adventist archives.org/docs/RH/RH19700416-V147-16__B/index.djvu (accessed 9/27/10); Branson, "Ellen G. White, Racist or Champion of Equality: Slavery and Prophecy: The Crisis of the Nineties," *Review* (April 23, 1970): http://www.adventistarchives.org/docs/RH/RH19700423-V147-17__B/ index.djvu (accessed 9/27/10); Delbert Baker, *Make Us One*, 1995, 83-103; Koranteng-Pipim, 353-383; Ronald D. Graybill, *E. G. White and Church Race Relations*, 1970.

reformer" at age 35 had become a cautious moderate at age 76.[82] Branson's rationale for White's actions is plausible enough, for indeed, Southern white hatred directed towards blacks following their Civil War defeat, led to unspeakable racial violence.

Additionally, White's maternal instincts would surely have been tested at the news of her oldest living son's near-death experience at the hands of vigilantes. However, White's prophetic voice, in which she challenged prevailing conventions within both civil society and the Adventist community, evolved into a pastoral voice of political expediency, exhibited by other contemporary religious leaders, including Beecher and Moody.[83] It is therefore not surprising for scholars such as Bull and Lockhart to conclude that White's comments illustrate that the denomination had not changed significantly from an "all white movement, with a mission to a white America, and blacks were not allowed to jeopardize the evangelistic objective of the denomination."[84]

The narrative of the Adventists' early mission to Southern blacks was ad hoc, and an afterthought, a fact reinforced by the insistence of church leaders, and latterly, White herself, that nothing should be allowed to impede the church's effort to evangelize Southern whites. Consequently, it would only be a matter of time before the simmering disquiet of blacks, with their experience of segregation and discrimination within the country and inside the church, would be vocalized. In the opening chapter of his book, *The Souls of Black Folks*, Du Bois pointedly asks the "unasked

---

[82] Branson, "Ellen G. White, Racist or Champion of Equality: The Crisis of the Nineties," Part 3, April 23, 1970, *Review and Herald* (Washington, DC: Review and Herald Publishing Assn., 1970).

[83] Adventist historian R. Clifford Jones arrives at a similar conclusion. He writes, "Notwithstanding her pointed statements condemning slavery and racism, Ellen White was a product of her times, whose social theories and practices conspired to produce in her a pragmatism that continues to confuse Blacks to this day, and that begs for explanation and understanding." R. Clifford Jones, 99.

[84] Two things should be noted. First, this statement had been redacted from the revised version of the authors' book. Second, during the year in question, 1906, there were only 562 black Adventists. Bull and Lockhart, 1989, 197.

question…How does it feel to be a problem?"[85] This characterization of blacks as a "problem" has been wedded to them since they were first brought to the American continent. And following the Civil War, which was supposed to usher in their freedom, the question only gained currency, and no more so than in the Christian faith.

Like all other denominations, the SDA Church has struggled in its effort to integrate former slaves and former slave owners into the same faith tradition. Within this psychodrama of finding location and placement, blacks have continuously sought one thing: belonging! In their quest for belonging and self-determination, they have concluded with Kinney that to cease being a problem to whites, their souls needed to find rest in their own organizational structures, where their lament to the God of their deliverance could be vented without the scrutiny or approbation of whites. As the history of Regional Conferences will reveal, the desire for spiritual liberation by blacks would coincide with white church leaders' wish to be free of their "Negro problem."

The History of Regional [Black] Conferences

Ellen G. White continued her advocacy of blacks to a reluctant church hierarchy, and by 1909, with a black membership of 900, the GC established the North American Negro Department, with a mandate to oversee the black work, but thoroughly under the control of white leaders.[86] Alas, it would take another nine years before the department was headed by a black, in the person of W.H. Green. Further, Rock observes that black protest during this period revolved around employment equality in the church and representation on church committees, with an emphasis on

---

[85] Du Bois, *The Souls of Black Folk*, 1969, 43.

[86] GC president A. G. Daniell, in his speech to the GC session in 1909, acknowledged failings in the church not advancing the black work further due to underfunding and shortage of human resources. Daniell's frank admission, of underfunding the black work is emblematic of the problem blacks faced in dealing with white church leaders. *Advent Review and Sabbath Herald* 86.23 (June 10, 1909, 13): http://www.adventistarchives.org/docs/RH/RH19090610-V86-23__B/index.djvu (accessed 9/27/10). The North American Negro Department later evolved into the Office of Human Relations. Schwartz and Greenleaf, 323.

integration, as blacks sought acceptance.[87] Given the manner in which the work among blacks evolved, with each advance towards equal justice encountering white resistance, the church was gradually moving towards an inevitable stalemate – making some form of structural accommodation necessary. Along the way, there would be some high-profile black clergy defections from the church, due to racial inequities. Writing in his autobiography, W.W. Fordham is pointed in his criticism of white church leaders of this period: "During the long years of struggle within the Seventh-day Adventist Church, there were those who would no longer swallow their crumbs—men such as Charles Manns and J.K. Humphrey – while others swallowed their crumbs from the table with much impatience, praying and hoping that the day would soon come when they would be accepted as equals at the 'table of brotherhood.'"[88]

The next significant event on the road to black self-determination in the midst of racial disparity occurred on April 29, 1929, at a GC committee meeting. A delegation of black clergy submitted a recommendation that the GC "consider the organization of Negro conferences... that will function in all of their departments exactly as the white conferences now function, and be united to the entire body in the usual organized way."[89] The black delegation requested that the proposal be given due consideration by a commission that would report its findings to the GC's Autumn Council. At the Autumn Council on September 26, 1929, the commission's recommendations were presented, but excluded was the central request from black leaders for their own conferences.[90]

---

[87] Rock, "Institutional Loyalty versus Racial Freedom," 1984, 28.

[88] W.W. Fordham, *Righteous Rebel* (Washington, D C: Review and Herald Publishing Association, 1990), 69. Due to the limitations of this study, exploring the rationale for these major black clergy deflections, and their impact in delaying an already delayed work, will not be pursued. However, excellent scholarship on two central figures, James K. Humphrey and Lewis C. Sheafe, are chronicled in the following texts: R. Clifford Jones, *James K. Humphrey and the Sabbath-day Adventists*, 2006; and Douglas Morgan, *Lewis C. Sheafe: Apostle to Black America*.

[89] "Three Hundred Twenty-Fifth Meeting, General Conference Committee Minutes," (April 29, 1929): 45-46.

[90] Interestingly, no mention is made of the main purpose for the commission's genesis; instead, blacks were given token administrative

One wonders if the dismissive nature of the commission's approach to the central request for black conferences did not have lasting effects, such as black defections.[91]

In 1944, when Gunnar Myrdal published his seminal work, *An American Dilemma*, he theorized that "the Negro problem is predominantly a white man's problem," which is too complex to resolve and too difficult to be ignored.[92] Trapped in a vortex of inertia, white SDA leaders drifted into a firestorm in 1944, at the church's Spring Council. As black SDAs began their educational advancement, making them more able to compete on equal terms with their white colleagues, a shift from "paternalism to competition" resulted, leading white leaders to become "more committed to denying blacks equal status in the church."[93] A tragic incident would form the catalyst for the "enough already" stance of blacks in 1943, when a black woman, Lucy Byard, entered the Washington Sanitarium in Takoma Park, Maryland for a non-lethal illness. Discharged without being treated because of her race, Byard was taken to the Freedmen's Hospital, where she died of pneumonia.[94]

The Byard incident galvanized black members, who formed the National Association for the Advancement of World-wide Work among Colored Seventh-day Adventists to lobby the GC for an end to these inhumane and discriminatory practices. Their lobbying efforts were salutary. The GC president J.L. McElhany commenced formal dialogue with the black clergy, although a possible solution

---

offices and added to various committees, under the supervision of white leaders. A financial recommendation included a 1:2 ratio distribution of funds, "based on a practically equal constituency of white and colored membership." "Three Hundred Eighty-Third Meeting, General Conference Committee Minutes," (September 26, 1929): 947-49.

[91] Fordham concludes that the response of white leaders to the entreaty of the black delegation was the trigger for J. K. Humphrey's defection. Fordham, 71.

[92] Gunnar Myrdal, *An American Dilemma: The Negro Problems and Modern Democracy* (New York: Harper and Bros, 1944), lii, xlv.

[93] The authors interestingly observe that "The competitive phase of race relations helps to explain why blacks often revert to a self-imposed segregation." Bull and Lockhart, [1989], 203.

[94] Schwarz and Greenleaf, 501.

of total integration, amenable to most blacks, was deemed impracticable for white leaders. With heightened racial tensions following the Byard incident, workers gathered in Chicago for the GC Spring Council premeetings, with high expectations mixed with ominous foreboding. There was a range of opinions among the blacks, with some in favor of the status quo, some for complete integration, and still others in support of black conferences that could best "resolve the tensions without compromising the essential unity of the body."[95]

By reversing the 1929 Autumn Council decision, to reject Regional Conferences, GC president James. J. McElhany insisted that Regional Conferences should be included among a range of possible options, though he was clear to state that church leaders did not come with "cut-and-dried answers." Seeking to afford black self-determination while maintaining church unity, McElhany was adamant that, "If I thought anybody was proposing a Conference organization that would drive a wedge between the races I would oppose it."[96] Legal scholar Derrick Bell originated the "interest convergence principle," commonly known as the "white self-interest principle." The principle states that "the degree of progress blacks have made away from slavery and towards equality has depended on whether allowing blacks more or less opportunity best served the interests and aims of white society."[97] It is difficult not to conclude from the history of the formation of Regional Conferences that Bell's principle was at work since white church leaders acquiesced to black demands for racial justice because it was in their own self-interest. So changed occurred, when racial justice, and the interest of a church

---

[95] Delbert W. Baker, "Regional Conferences: 50 Years of Progress," *Adventist Review* (Nov 2, 1995, 1371-1374): http://www.adventist archives.org/docs/RH/RH19951102-V172-49__C/index.djvu. (accessed 9/28/10).

[96] Minutes from the "Pre-Spring Council," April 8, 1944. With this vote to establish Regional Conferences, Bull and Lockhart hold that it "cemented the principle of separate development, which had been implicit from the moment blacks first turned up at Adventist gatherings." Bull and Lockhart, [1989], 198.

[97] Derrick J. Bell Jr., *Race, Racism and American Law*, 2nd ed. (Boston: Little Brown, 1980), 39.

hierarchy desperate to mitigate public embarrassment from the Byard incident, converged.

Finally, the white church hierarchy was now prepared to bow to the inevitability of black structural accommodation, given the racial inequities blacks continued to be victims of, both within and outside the church. As church historian George R. Knight acknowledges, the recommendation was not universally acclaimed, but it was a necessary "compromise in a situation in which complete racial equality was not going to be granted."[98] Once this long-awaited concession was made to allow Regional Conferences, and despite the vigorous debate, the following recommendation was approved at the April 10, 1944, pre-meeting and unanimously assented to at the Spring Council:

> WHEREAS, The present development of the work among the colored people in North America has resulted, under the signal blessing of God, in the establishment of some 233 churches with 17,000 members; and,
> WHEREAS, It appears that a different plan of organization for our colored membership would bring further great advance in soul-winning endeavors; therefore,
> We -recommend, 1. That in unions where the colored constituency is considered by the union conference committee to be sufficiently large, and where the financial income and territory warrant, colored conferences be organized.
> 2. That these colored conferences be administered by colored officers and committees.
> 3. That in the organization of these conferences the present conference boundaries within each union need not be recognized.
> 4. That colored conferences sustain the same relation to their respective union conferences as do the white conferences.
> 5. That the General Conference Committee appoint three members of a commission to join with other members to be appointed by each union conference committee concerned, for a study of report to the respective union committees,

---

[98] George R. Knight, *Organizing To Beat The Devil: The Development of Adventist Church Structure*, ed. Gerald Wheeler (Hagerstown, MD: Review and Herald Publishing Association, 2001), 150.

and that in cases additional appropriations, organization of colored conferences be deferred until after the 1944 Autumn Council, in order to ascertain whether or not this will be possible.

6. That the 1930 plan of colored organization for the Southern States be adopted for all territories in North America with sufficient members, but where the constituency is not sufficiently large to warrant the organizations of colored conferences.[99]

And so, following years of tumult for the church, and second-class status for blacks, Adventists overcame their inertia by attempting a solution to the almost irresolvable and unavoidable problem of race relations between blacks and whites.

This paradigm shift in Adventist organizational structure has its detractors, but none can contravene the phenomenal impact the nine Regional Conferences have made on the work among blacks in the United States. Beginning with seven Regional Conferences (Allegheny, Lake Region, and Northeastern in 1945; South Atlantic and South Central in 1946, and Central States and Southwest Region in 1947), after the historic decision of 1944, the black membership grew exponentially, from 17,000 to 23,000 in 1950, to 37,000 in 1960, to 70,000 in 1970, to 130,000 in 1980, to 193,000 in 1990, and to 280,000 in 2010.[100] As with membership expansion, so too, has the tithe base of the Regional Conferences experienced significant increases over the intervening period, from $511,000 in 1944 to $145 million in 2004. As compelling as these statistics are, the wealth of administrative experience that black leaders have acquired leading these conference structures, has also been noteworthy. This administrative experience

---

[99] Spring Meeting, Three Hundred Ninety-Sixth Meeting, General Conference Committee, Chicago, Illinois, *Adventist Archives* (April 10, 1994, 1315): http://www.adventistarchives.org/docs/GCC/ GCC1944-04-SM/index.djvu (accessed 9/28/10).

[100] Delbert Baker, *Make Us One*, 1995, with current figures accessed from the Office of Regional Conference Ministry, http://www. regionalministry.org (accessed 9/29/10). Two additional Regional Conferences were formed by the partitioning of existing conferences: Allegheny Conference dividing into Allegheny East and Allegheny West Conferences in 1967, and South Atlantic split into South Atlantic and Southeastern Conferences in 1981.

has translated into significant ascent by blacks in the church's hierarchical structure, increasing black representation on all levels of the SDA church, resulting in them shaping worldwide church policies. Despite this administrative advance, the ratio of black to white church administrators remains disproportionate compared to their white counterparts.

Yet for all of its successes, Regional Conferences are not replicated across the entire country. Indeed, Regional Conferences have been successfully resisted on the West coast, despite vigorous debate in the late 1970s and, more recently, in the early 2000s. It was unsurprising that some opposed Regional Conferences on the West Coast—specifically in the territory of the Pacific Union Conference (PUC)—since some blacks from the PUC had opposed the landmark decision of 1944. Earl A. Canson, Sr. and Major C. White, both long time administrators at PUC, where for two decades influential in persuading blacks to repel efforts from backers of Regional Conferences. Rock writes that Canson "quietly managed to defuse most black political unrest on the Pacific Coast, while, at the same time, championing the cause of integration."[101] Instead of Regional Conferences, on the Pacific Coast, there is a Region system – a subset of the local Conference formed on the basis of ethnicity, language, and geography – with semi-autonomy to conduct the affairs of their constituency (Black, Hispanic, Asian-Pacific, and White). It is probably true to say that Region Coordinators have some of the administrative responsibilities of the Regional Conference presidents, but lack the ultimate decision-making authority of these presidents. Also, compared to the growth in membership, financial strength, and administrative opportunities within the Regional Conferences, the Region system falls short of the mark, leading some

---

[101] In assessing Canson's stance, Rock praises him for his diplomatic skills, which he writes "are appealing to white leadership, and provide him enough victories to placate the majority of the blacks in his area." Rock, "Institutional Loyalty versus Racial Freedom," 1984, 108-109. In his dissertation, Alfonso Greene reports that prior to 1969, "not one union conference in North America included an African American administrator. Out of nine unions, just two unions employed blacks in departmental positions. Greene, 292.

blacks to reflect on what might have been, were there Regional Conferences on the Pacific Coast.

Despite the obvious progress of Regional Conferences, some blacks remained unconvinced that this structural accommodation was producing the integration and parity at the higher echelons of Adventism in the United States. During the 1960s, one prominent black leader, Warren Banfield, reportedly lamented the fact that "Blacks were practically invisible at the union, division, and General Conference levels."[102] This invisibility was a decided strategy of white leaders, observe Bull and Lockhart, who concluded that discrimination intensified as the "white majority became more committed to denying equal status in the church," once the relationship between blacks and whites moved from "paternalism to competition."[103] The level of frustration among black Adventists at the racism within the denomination, a denomination they regard as God's last-day Church possessing the authentic gospel message, can be summarized in the opening line of an article by black church leader and pioneering evangelist E. Earl Cleveland: "The ghetto is girding for survival." Cleveland's point is set in stark terms, given the historical context of the assassinations of John Kennedy, Jr., Robert Kennedy and Martin Luther King, Jr., and the fading prospect that whites in this country would accord blacks' their constitutionally-guaranteed privileges. According to Cleveland, for black Adventists to survive, they must again petition the church leaders to provide them with Regional [Black] Union Conferences[104] — the next level up from local Conferences.

With the Civil Rights Movement triggering social change in U. S. society in general, black Adventists sought changes to the church's discrimination policies. Discussion of establishing Regional Unions was a central agenda item at the quadrennial advisory meeting of the GC Regional Department in Miami, April 7-10, 1969, where a recommendation to the GC was voted. A commission, consisting of 71 blacks and 21 whites was approved by the GC, and at their first meeting on January 13, 1970, their deliberations

---

102 Schwarz and Greenleaf, 504.

103 Bull and Lockhart, [1989], 202.

104 E. Earl Cleveland, "Regional Union Conferences," *Spectrum* 2.2 (Spring, 1970): 41.

coalesced around two approaches: that the present structure is expanded and that Regional unions be initiated. The core argument for those seeking to maintain the current arrangement was that it reinforced racial divisions between blacks and whites, and for those in favor of the new structures, it increased black self-determination within the church hierarchy. The motion to establish Regional Unions was tabled until serious considerations could be given by the GC regarding alternative approaches.

The commission reconvened on April 16, 1970, and essentially adopted a sixteen-point proposal approved at the Spring Meeting of the GC days earlier. These practical proposals appear to be the first preemptive attempt at remedying the structural racial disparity and discrimination that has afflicted the SDA Church. Importantly, the proposal was accompanied by an additional funding stream established by the GC called the "Regional Capital Reversion Fund," for the purpose of capital improvements and church scholarships within the Regional Conferences.[105] Following the adoption of these proposals, the SDA Church elected its first black secretary of the NAD, Charles C. Bradford, who would later go on to become president of that administrative body. Additional administrative strides were made as other Union Conferences elected their first black secretaries and other office holders.[106]

---

[105] "Whereas, The present structure of Regional Conference organization has been blessed of God in soul-winning endeavor, and Whereas, It now seems in order to suggest that the organizational idea move up one step, Voted, That we recommend to the General Conference that a representative committee be appointed to study the advisability of the organization of a Regional Union or Regional Unions in the United States." In the article, at least ten arguments are advanced by both sides of the debate. Neal C. Wilson, "Recent Developments in the Field of Human Relations in North America," *Review and Herald* (June 4, 1970, 147): http://www.adventistarchives.org/docs/RH/RH19700604-V147-23__B. pdf#view=fit (accessed 11/4/10). The sixteen-point proposal was recorded in the minutes of the Spring Meeting of the GC and it can be found in Appendix C: http://www.adventistarchives.org/ docs/NAD/NAD1970-04/index.djvu (accessed 11/4/10).

[106] Once the proposal was adopted, the first black NAD administrator and departmental director in the United States was elected,

Significantly, the sixteen-point proposal would become a template for resolving the ethnic conflict in the United Kingdom SDA Church. Despite the relative effectiveness of the sixteen-point proposal, it was not the outcome that some black leaders had favored. There was less of a consensus among blacks regarding Regional Unions than there had been for Regional Conferences. Historian Joel Williamson's critique of the black-white relations in the South is instructive, as he observes a challenging paradox:

> It is that black people have to get out of white society in order to get into it, and they have to get into it in order to get out. They have to get into the society to get a minimum of those palpable things that people need in order simply to survive–material goods, education, government, a minimum of justice, law, and order. But yet because white people are prejudiced they have to get out, to withdraw to themselves in some degree, to maintain a sense of worth and self-esteem...having suffered the slings and arrows of white prejudice as they had, and having the surety of further hurts by the laws of inertia and momentum, some black leaders began to move to pull black people away from white people.[107]

Perhaps this paradox helps to explain why throughout much of the 1970's, the unabated push for Regional Unions proved unsuccessful, thwarting the hopes of blacks seeking further racial redress. The level of dissatisfaction experienced by some blacks is articulated by Rock, who observes that "It is a cause of great frustration for black leadership that the church, for the most part, has historically found it necessary to oppose whatever model of interaction they happen to advocate."[108]

The final push for Regional Unions came in 1978 when the *Review and Herald* published position papers from opposing sides of the debate. Rock, whose position in favor of Regional Unions can be

---

and by 1972 seven other blacks were elected as administrators and fourteen as departmental directors in union conferences. Greene, 293.

[107] Joel Williamson, *The Crucible of Race: Black/White Relations in the American South Since Emancipation* (New York: Oxford University Press, 1984), 505f.

[108] The author lists the twin approaches of blacks in their quest for parity. Rock, "Institutional Loyalty Versus Racial Freedom," 1984, 49.

summarized on the basis of the cultural difference between blacks and whites and a glass ceiling that black leaders have difficulty shattering, was opposed by psychologist Alan Anderson, who viewed Regional Unions as a simple solution to a complex problem.[109] The minutes of the October 12, 1978, Annual Council of the GC recount a day-long discussion of Regional Unions, with two black leaders, G.R. Earle and Rock, as chief advocates. Neal C. Wilson, president of the NAD — who was later elected to replace the GC president Robert H. Pierson (whose surprise resignation due to ill health took effect January 3rd, 1979) — set out the GC position, which ultimately prevailed.[110] Notwithstanding this final rejection, blacks have nonetheless seen marked improvements in ascending Adventist hierarchy, including Charles Bradford becoming the first black to lead the NAD in 1979 — a direct response to black protest it would appear — though his qualifications for the position were exceptional.

This review of the evolution of Regional Conferences has attempted to establish the struggle of blacks, in their fight for self-determination and equality with whites, some of whom were sympathetic, others incalcitrant, and still others indifferent. This struggle was part of a greater effort being pursued by blacks in the wider society. It was also a struggle that some justifiably abandoned, believing that white church leaders would never relent. Ellen White's "ambivalent legacy" on the matter of race relations has also been shown to have empowered white church leaders to transmute the racial separatism that she had sanctioned "as a temporary expedient into a basic operational principle while ignoring her strong affirmations of equality,"[111] as Morgan rightly

---

[109] "Should the Church Organize Black Unions in North America?" *Review and Herald* 155.36 (September 7, 1978): http://www. adventistarchives.org/docs/RH/RH19780907-V155-36__B/index.djvu (accessed 11/28/10).

[110] The minutes report the vote as follows, "To indicate, at this time, that it is not wise to request the approval of the General Conference for the organization of two regional unions." Annual Council, Minutes of Meeting — North American Division Committee on Administration (October 12, 1978, 2:00pm): http://www.adventistarchives.org/docs/NAD/NAD1978-10/index.djvu (accessed 11/27/10).

[111] Morgan, *Adventism and the Republic*, 2001, 158, 159.

argues. Black Adventists' protest for equality and self-determination has undoubtedly been successful, judging by the effectiveness and expansion of Regional Conferences. Ironically, however, it is this very protest, and what it has accomplished over the last sixty-five years, that has now placed the object of their protest — Regional Conferences — at the center of debate within Adventism.

Before concluding this chapter, a depiction of race relations in the SDA Church in the United Kingdom (my home country) follows, to explore the ways in which black and white British Adventists dealt with their own struggle with racial discrimination. This depiction will show parallels and contrasts between racial redress in the United States and in the United Kingdom.

Racism and Redress in the SDA Church in the United Kingdom

> It is hopeless for the Negro to expect complete emancipation from the menial social and economic position into which the white man has forced him, merely by trusting in the moral sense of the white race.[112]

Post-war immigration into the United Kingdom is deemed to have been inaugurated with the arrival from the Caribbean of 430 Jamaican men on June 21, 1948, in Tilbury, Essex, on the former trooper ship the SS Empire Windrush. It should be noted that there were blacks living in the United Kingdom prior to the arrival of the Anglo-Saxons, some of whom served as soldiers in the imperial Roman army. Caribbean blacks were also recruited by the British to serve in the armed forces in World War II. Many of the Caribbean Islands were part of the expansive British Empire, and the 1948 Nationality Act had ensured that the Islands' populations were British citizens. Their British passports, therefore, entitled them to visit or remain in the United Kingdom as residents. After the War, worsening economic conditions in the Caribbean, and the need for an expanded labor force to reconstruct a war-torn Europe seeking to rebound served as an incentive for immigration from the Caribbean. Consequently, ten years after the Windrush, there were some 125,000 West Indians living in the United Kingdom; by 1981 there were over 500,000, and by 2001, 565,876 individuals identified themselves as

---

[112] Reinhold Niebuhr, *Moral Man and Immoral Society: A Study in Ethics and Politics* (New York: Charles Scribner's Sons, 1932), 252.

Black Caribbean, amounting to 1 percent of the total British population. These newcomers to the United Kingdom faced rampant racial discrimination and prejudice, with two-thirds of all whites having a low opinion of blacks, viewing them as uncivilized, uneducated, oversexed, and inferior to whites. Of these two-thirds, 50 percent were extremely prejudiced, unwilling to have any contact or communication with blacks and opposing interracial marriages. Unsurprisingly, the racial disparities of the 1960s and 1970s led to race riots in the 1980s in the United Kingdom.[113]

Since religious institutions are but a reflection of their social context, the same racial discrimination, and prejudice that were a part of British society were on display within the SDA Church. Immigration to the UK from the Caribbean resulted in an instant infusion of SDA members, particularly from the Island of Jamaica. Indeed, of the number of Caribbean immigrants attending churches in the UK, 25 percent attended SDA Churches in the mid-1960s, so that by 1978, blacks exceeded 50 percent of the 13,000-membership total.[114] As of December 2009, the membership in the British Union Conference (BUC) stood at just over 30,500.[115] While statistics on the ethnic complexion of the BUC are unavailable, a loose approximation based on observation, suggests a ratio of 80 percent blacks to 20 percent whites. Perhaps for this reason, the history of the SDA Church in the United Kingdom has attracted the interest of historians, theologians, and church officials, each confirming to varying degrees the significant role played by Caribbean immigrants to the expansion of British Adventism.[116] The Adventist mission to

---

[113] Peter Fryer, *Staying Power: The History of Black People in Britain* (London: Pluto Press, 1984), 1, 373-75; Mike Phillips and Trevor Phillips, *Windrush: The Irresistible Rise of Multi-Racial Britain* (London: Harper-Collins Publishers, 1998), 2-6, 96.

[114] Robin Theobald, "The Politicization of a Religious Movement: British Adventism Under the Impact of West Indian Immigration," *British Journal of Sociology* 32. 2 (June 1981), 203.

[115] http://www.adventistinfo.org.uk/about/c_status.php (accessed 11/16/10).

[116] They include: D. S. Porter, *A Century of Adventism in the British Isles* (Grantham, England: Stanborough Press, 1974); Nigel Garth Barham, "The Progress of the Seventh-day Adventist Church in Great Britain, 1878-1974" (Ph.D. diss., University of Michigan, 1976); Roswith I. H. Gerloff, *A*

the United Kingdom had a humble beginning with an Englishman named William Ings, who distributed Adventist literature in the port city of Southampton while visiting relatives in 1878. Ings reported that the people he spoke with were receptive, and he hoped that the GC would send "one of our best ministers" to evangelize the British Isles.[117] The Church responded by sending workers, but the effort was painstakingly slow, with historians Harry Lenard and Nigel Barham both attributing the time-consuming effort not to the quality of the American missionaries, but to the fact that they were foreigners — a dislike prevalent among British Adventists today.[118] However, in a letter in the *Review and Herald*, one of these missionaries, John Loughborough, attributed the lack of success to the social class structure of the country.[119]

Twenty-five years after Adventists arrived in the United Kingdom, the BUC was officially organized in 1902, with a membership of 798, and by the arrival of the first Caribbean blacks on the Windrush in 1948, the predominately white membership

---

Plea for British Black Theologies: The Black Church Movement in Britain (Frankfurt am Main: Peter Lang, 1992); Robin Theobald, "The Politicization of a Religious Movement," 1984, 202-23; Robin Theobald, "The Seventh-day Adventist Movement: A Sociological Study with Particular Reference to Great Britain" (Ph.D. diss., University of London, 1979); D.N. Marshall, ed., *The Story of Seventh-day Adventists in the British Isles 1902-1992* (Grantham, England: Stanborough Press Ltd., 1992): http://www.adventist history.org.uk/documents/souvenirmessenger1902-1992.pdf (accessed 9/30/10); Herbert Griffiths, "The Impact of African Caribbean Settlers on the Seventh-day Adventist Church in Britain 1952-2001" (Ph.D. diss., University of Leeds, 2003).

[117] Ings recounts his experience in a letter that was recorded in the church's official organ. "Missionary Work in England," *Review and Herald* (July 11, 1878, 19): http://www.adventistarchives.org/docs/RH/RH18780711-V52-03__B/index.djvu (accessed 11/4/10).

[118] British nationalism was prevalent in the 19th century, given the territorial expansion of the British Empire. Barham, 60f; Marshall, 4.

[119] Loughborough acknowledges "that society here is divided into classes." "Southampton, England," *Review and Herald* (January 22, 1880): 60, http://www.adventistarchives.org/docs/RH/RH18800122-V55-04__B/index.djvu (accessed 11/4/10).

stood at 6,376.[120] Over the next twenty-five years, as its membership doubled, the BUC and its constituent entities,[121] would be transformed by immigration from the Caribbean. However, this transformation did not come without its consequences, largely to the national identity of the BUC, leaving the membership of this once all-white institution, apprehensive. In a journal article analyzing the impact of this immigration, Adventist historian Robin Theobald writes of "unease and bewilderment" among white Adventists who felt that their churches were being "taken over by an alien group."[122] As noted earlier, the British aversion to foreign influences appears evident in this instance. A prominent white church leader, Martin Anthony, recounts that by 1958 the membership of the BUC was 8,252, consisting of 90 percent "of native British stock."[123] By 1974 the membership of the BUC was 12,511,[124] and as Barham reports, virtually all the new congregations that were established and almost all baptisms after 1960 were of blacks. This displacement of white Adventists by blacks led to a clash of the two cultures, white flight, and consternation among the all-white hierarchy about a trend that was likely to spell the demise of white Adventism in the United Kingdom.[125]

---

[120] Annual Statistical report for 1902, http://www.adventist archives.org/docs/ASR/ASR1902_B/index.djvu (accessed 11/4/10).

[121] The BUC is currently comprised of two local conferences — the South England Conference and the North British Conference — and three smaller organizations called missions (the Scottish, Welsh and Irish Missions).

[122] Added to this sense of alienation was the growth of stereotypes: blacks were "too fundamentalist and too enthusiastic in their beliefs... too noisy and too demanding, unreliable, bad timekeepers, had too many children and, worst of all for pious Adventists, were not too rigorous in their observances of proper relations between the sexes." Theobald, 1981, 206.

[123] Marshall, ed., *A Century of Adventism in the British Isles* (Grantham, England: Stanborough Park, 2000, 12): http://www. adventisthistory.org.uk/documents/CenturyofAdventism.pdf (accessed 11/4/10).

[124] Annual Statistical report for 1974, http://www.adventist archives.org/docs/ASR/ASR1974B/index.djvu (accessed 11/4/10).

[125] Barham, 217.

This level of white anxiety within the BUC is best illustrated in the centennial edition of the church's newspaper, of October 1974. The publication contained a chapter on the impact of Caribbean immigration on the church, which was viewed by most blacks and some whites as contentious since it highlighted only the negative impact of this emergent group on the church. It referenced the BUC's humanitarian relief efforts following hurricane Charlie in August 1951, with this comparison: "It [hurricane Charlie] blew away more than houses and institutions in the West Indies. It blew away British Adventism as it existed for three-quarters of a century."[126] The remainder of the chapter reads more like a lament on the demise of white Adventism in the United Kingdom than it does a brief history of the most expansive period in the church's development.[127] Theobald considered this chapter one of the reasons for a backlash from black Adventists, who were of the opinion that "their white brethren did not want the blacks in 'their' churches."[128] In his dissertation, Herbert Griffiths contests the assumption that the stagnation of white Adventists was due to Caribbean immigrants, by observing that by 1960 the BUC, aware of this stagnation, had reaffirmed a resolution that ministers [by implication, white

---

[126] One Adventist historian appears to see few redeeming qualities in the increase in membership of the BUC. Dennis S. Porter, "1918-1945: The Church in the Age of the Doctors," *Messenger: Centennial Historical Special* (Grantham, England: Stanborough Park, 1974), 40.

[127] One can detect further despair as the author projects into the future catastrophic failure of Adventism, with the eventual death of the "white work" and the inability of the next generation blacks to withstand the rising tide of British secularism. Porter writes, "While the decline in white membership continues to the point where there will be no white Adventist church in Britain, or has it already been halted? How successful will the West Indians be in holding their second and third generation, and if they are unsuccessful and the white members are not replaced, what will become of the Church as a whole? *Messenger: Centennial Historical Special,* 44.

[128] The author observes that the chapter ignored the substantial financial contribution of the black membership, choosing to focus instead on an earlier practice of black members sending remittances, including tithes, back to their home families and churches in the Caribbean. Theobald, "The Politicization of a Religious Movement," 1984, 206, 208.

ministers] needed to emphasize evangelism and "undertake systematic house-to-house work and dynamic regular baptismal classes in the church."[129]

As British society struggled to adjust to the wave of Caribbean immigrants and the increasing tensions between blacks and whites, British Adventism was perhaps experiencing these tensions more acutely — as an already religious white minority was quickly becoming a minority within a minority. This evolving situation appears to have precipitated an existential crisis for white Adventism, which saw an increase in BUC membership — largely black membership — as a diminution of white presence and power. The reaction of white Adventists to this unfolding displacement, what one administrator called "a state of siege,"[130] included "white flight" — the phenomenon of "welcome, puzzlement, [and] departure,"[131] — and the centralizing of power in the hands of white church leaders at the expense of the now black majority.

While white reaction to the dramatic reversal in membership in the BUC was an understandable social phenomenon, it nevertheless was rather fatalistic, since it spoke of demise without any contingency planning to reverse such trends — and with no apparent follow-up of the 1960 resolution. Furthermore, it appears to reflect a group, not at ease with the central tenet of the gospel they proclaim — a gospel to the world irrespective of social, ethnic,

---

[129] Griffiths, 183. He also observes that church leaders were concerned that the clergy were engaged in work outside of the church, what they called in one document, "Sidelines," and as such the work of evangelism was being neglected. Indeed, one church leader's own analysis of the decline in white members bucks the prevailing view that it was Caribbean immigration at the center of the decline: "The writer [Martin L. Anthony] suspects that the influence of immigration on White attendance has been exaggerated, and that a considerable proportion of those who lapsed in church fellowship would have done so anyway, and used immigration as an excuse for their lapsation." Griffiths, 184-85.

[130] Anthony accurately chronicles the psychology of white Adventists during these unsettling times, by reflecting on the anxiety of "native British" regarding the "survival of 'the white work.'" Martin L. Anthony, "1945-1981: Decades of Change," in *A Century of Adventism in the British Isles*, 28.

[131] Gerloff, 279.

cultural or linguistic background. Black educator Frank Hale Jr. best captures this tension when he writes, "The crucial challenge to Adventism in race relations is posed by the contradiction between its rhetorical commitment to fellowship without racial barriers, on the one hand, and the racial inequities which are typical of most of its own life as a church, on the other."[132] In her assessment of the white leaders of the BUC, Gerloff speaks of a lack of attentiveness in establishing black leaders or collaborative power-sharing between blacks and whites. Rather, notes Gerloff, many white clergy viewed the influx of Caribbean members into the BUC as problematic.[133]

The fight for equitable representation and power-sharing within the BUC was joined by the newly minted London Laymen's Forum (LLF) in 1973, comprised of black Adventists who called attention to the racial disparity inflicted upon them by the white leadership, which dominated the BUC. According to one of the founding members of the LLF, black educator and administrator Orville Woolford, the forum, viewed as "troublemakers" by white leaders, promoted a four-pronged agenda: (1) arrange more evangelistic outreach efforts in the cities (funding for which white leaders had resisted, so as to minimize black growth); (2) establish Adventist schools and a youth center in London; (3) increase the small number of black clergy so that they can offer pastoral care to the largely black membership; (4) and desegregate the church's administrative structures.[134] This mobilization by black Adventists, coupled with the withholding of funds remitted to the South

---

[132] Frank Hale, Jr., "Commitment vs. Capitulation," *Spectrum* 2.2 (Spring 1970): 31.

[133] Gerloff, 278.

[134] Orville Woolford, "The 70s Struggle: A Black Perspective," in *A Century of Adventism in the British Isles*, 34. Barham acknowledges the dearth of black clergy — only five or six during this period — stating that this was due to the lack of qualified individuals, a situation facilitated by white leaders who did not encourage blacks to attend the local SDA College for ministerial training. Neither were there any black administrators within the BUC, especially given the fact that black Adventists contributed almost 50 percent of the funding for the BUC. Barham, 219.

England Conference (SEC) by some large churches in London, had the desired effect.[135]

By 1974 the leadership of the BUC prepared a memorandum soliciting financial resources and personnel from the GC to facilitate a more collaborative effort among blacks and whites, but the GC failed to respond. It is possible that an unresponsive GC was partially due to the lack of a fully integrative approach to the work in the BUC. Instead of complete integration, the white BUC leadership sanctioned a referendum of the BUC membership in 1976 on the establishment of a Regional Conference, modeled after those in the United States. But the GC leadership opposed the reorganization of the BUC to include Regional Conferences. The advice coming from the LLF to the black membership regarding the referendum was that they had sought integration, but that the Regional Conference structure was the preferred option of white leaders, so they were reluctantly endorsing an affirmative response to the referendum. Given this ambivalence, it was not surprising that the referendum was overwhelmingly rejected by the BUC membership by a five to one margin.[136]

As with the struggle for racial equality by black Adventists in the United States, British blacks experienced the same resistance to full integration by white Adventist leaders. In both instances the default stance of white leaders was segregation, when blacks sought integration, affirming the previously stated analysis of Bull and Lockhart that "good race relations between the races are best served by some kind of segregationist policy."[137] Since the white leadership of the BUC appeared to view the need for substantial change as unnecessary, following the results of the referendum, the LLF

---

[135] Theobald outlined the political ramification of these churches withholding tithe to the SEC including possible exclusion from the "sisterhood of churches." Officials concluded that to penalize the majority of faithful members for the actions of a few "militants who had infiltrated the respective church boards" would not be prudent. This assertion by officials appears to be more reactionary than grounded in fact, since members of the LLF were members of these large churches, so they hardly qualify as infiltrators. Theobald, "The Politicization of a Religious Movement," 212.

[136] Woolford, 34; Schwartz and Greenleaf, 511.

[137] Bull and Lockhart, [1989], 195.

continued to press for reform through their publication, the *Comment*, aware of the words of Martin Luther King, Jr., that "freedom is never voluntarily given by the oppressor; it must be demanded by the oppressed."[138] In this struggle for equality, LLF leaders had also established communications with black leaders in the Regional Conferences in the United States, gleaning strategic information to advance their cause. Interestingly, once the fight for parity was achieved, black leaders who were beneficiaries of the struggle failed to establish alliances with the black leaders in the United States who were partially responsible for their presence and elevation in the United Kingdom.[139]

The continued demands of black Adventists were finally met when a delegation from the GC, including the President, Robert Pierson, two vice-presidents and an under-treasurer, brokered a deal on March 8, 1978, famously called the "Pierson Package." Comprised of nine recommendations and modelled after the "Sixteen-points" proposal, the "Pierson Package" advocated for a significant increase in black ministerial leadership and clerical staff at all levels of the administrative structure of the BUC, reorganized membership of boards and committees to include blacks, improved

---

[138] Martin Luther King Jr., *Why We Can't Wait* (New York: New American Library, 1964), 79.

[139] The reason for an apparent distance of Caribbean leaders in the United Kingdom from black leaders in the United States is too complex to be addressed in this dissertation, but there is growing evidence of tensions between Caribbean blacks and African Americans. It has been noted that harmony between the two groups "is most often undermined by passive cultural characteristics such as stereotyping, speech, accent, and foods. Cultural differences tend to generate distorted stereotypical images that constrain meaningful dialogue and understanding." Rock, 1996, 97. Others observe that a re-education is needed to increase awareness among the African Diaspora of the negative stereotypes and myths that need to be dispelled. Jennifer V. Jackson and Mary E. Cothran, "Black Versus Black: The Relationship among African, African American, and African Caribbean Persons," *Journal of Black Studies* 33, no. 5 (May 2003): 576-604; Milton Vickerman, "The Responses of West Indians to African-Americans: Distancing and Identification," *Research in Race and Ethnic Relations* (ed. Rutledge M. Dennis; Greenwich, CT: JAI Press, 1994), 7; Molefi Kete Asante, *Afrocentricity* (Trenton, NJ: Africa World Press, 1991).

access to organizational facilities for blacks, and an increase in interethnic understanding.[140] Confronted by the black majority from below, the white leadership of the BUC acquiesced in the face of pressure from above at the GC. As Schwarz and Greenleaf astutely observe, "The British Union was left with little choice but to press for a meaningful integration."[141] The implication of Schwarz and Greenleaf's remarks underline the immense pressure that white leaders were subjected to, from blacks, GC officials, along with pushback, presumably, from their own white constituents.[142] Unquestionably, the political reality of the white leadership affirming the Pierson Package was tantamount to voting themselves out of office eventually–like turkeys voting for Thanksgiving–given the political strength of the black majority. It did not take long for this latent political force to become kinetic, ushering in a wave of black leadership, beginning in 1981 with Silburn M. Reid as the first black president of the SEC, the largest conference in the BUC, and ten years later Cecil R. Perry, president of the BUC. Presently, blacks hold the highest offices in all three major administrative organizations (BUC, SEC, and NBC), with little to suggest that this trend is reversible.

The transition from an all-white leadership structure in the BUC to one that was more representative did not come without casualties; including several white ministers exiting the United Kingdom and fewer whites pursuing the ministry as a profession. This diminution of whites in ministry in the United Kingdom may have contributed to a lack of impetus to halt the steady decline in the numbers of white Adventists. It should be noted, though, that the attrition rate of white Adventists was clearly on a downward trajectory at the time that black immigration to the United Kingdom was approaching its peak. It would appear that rather than develop

---

[140] The nine recommendations in the Pierson Package can be found in Appendix D. Marshall, 37.

[141] Schwartz and Greenleaf, 511.

[142] Some white members opposed the Pierson Package on two grounds: (1) the election to union and conference offices of men with no experience of work in Britain; (2) and the increased representation of Blacks on conference committees. These objections are rightly suggestive of a white superior attitude, notes Griffiths, 197-98.

strategies to halt the decline of white members, white leaders seemed to have coalesced around the notion of maintaining white rule; fearing what one British newspaper at the time reported as "the public image of [the SDA Church] being a West Indian organization."[143]

One observation pertinent to this book is the approach taken by a consultative committee as it advanced a racially reconciled outcome within the BUC. It was an approach that to some extent was mirrored in the resolution of racial discrimination in Adventism in the United States. The approach to racial reconciliation adopted by the SDA church in the United States and the United Kingdom can be analogized using two psychotherapy modalities: solution-focused brief psychotherapy (SFBT) and psychoanalytically-oriented psychotherapy. As its name suggests, SFBT is geared towards achieving the client's desired outcome rather than dwelling on causation and the past; in essence, it is present-and-future-oriented. It is also a time-sensitive therapy. On the other hand, psychoanalytic therapies tend to have a longer duration; given that an individual's challenges have developed over a period of years, addressing them will take just as long.[144] Psychoanalytic therapies operate on the premise that the client must gain insight into repressed impulses, childhood trauma, and unconscious conflicts that are impacting behavior. The SDA Church has advocated more of an SFBT approach to racial reconciliation, resolving with dispatch decades of racial discrimination and disparity, while ignoring causation. As this text will show, at the heart of reconciliation is the restoration of ruptured relationships, and this can hardly be achieved while unresolved issues from the past remain. This quick-fix approach to reconciliation is akin to removing only at the surface level a splinter, while a fragment remains deeply embedded, and the skin re-grows, leaving an area sensitive when touched.

Summary

---

143 "Black Adventists Demand Greater Share of Power," in June 1976, *The Observer*, quoted in Gerloff, 275.

144 Sol L. Garfield, *The Practice of Brief Psychotherapy* (New York: John Wiley & Sons, 1998), 1-28.

This historical overview of the SDA Church's mission to blacks in the United States reflects a church emerging at a time of tremendous upheaval in which racism was the political currency of the realm. Religious fervor prompted by the Great Awakening, and embodied in millennial expectations for a new divine order, revealed reluctance among Adventists to engage in social change. Adventists also accepted much of the country's social norms, including its view that segregation should be normative for whites in their dealings with blacks. Since most Civil War historians acknowledge that racial disparity and segregation was the price paid for sectional healing after the Civil War, some also recognized the role of Christianity in this project of national reconciliation. Not surprisingly then, when Adventists eventually established a presence among blacks, they assumed a segregationalist posture, so as not to discourage evangelistic efforts among Southern whites. As the prophetic voice of the church, Ellen White initially advocated integration, she later had a change of heart, while hoping for the day when relations between whites and blacks would be normalized.

Continued segregation, coupled with racial discrimination by white church leaders, precipitated a race relations crisis, which saw both black defections and demands. These demands eventually ushered into existence Regional Conferences, and with them came extraordinary growth in black membership, financial resources, and leadership. Despite these successes, the debate rages on about their very existence being a throwback to an era of racial discrimination and oppression – something the church would sooner forget. When the experience in the BUC is considered, which in many ways mirrored that of the United States Adventists, a pattern of white racial prejudice and discriminatory practices against blacks emerges. In both instances, racial reconciliation was accomplished on the basis of rectifying the consequences rather than the exploring the cause of the injustices. Also, both situations reflect the central message of black psychiatrist Frantz Fanon's *The Wretched of the Earth*, that the colonized must realize that colonists never concede anything without a struggle and that gains made through concession, are achieved by colonists who are no longer prepared to take "no" for an answer.[145]

Parenthetically, the "Sixteen-point" proposal did mark a fundamental shift in the church's engagement in legislating social change, to achieve improved race relations between blacks and whites. Despite this fact, the reconciliation approach of the SDA Church in both instances is comparable to one of the misunderstandings of reconciliation identified by theologian Robert J. Schreiter—reconciliation as a hasty peace. This form of reconciliation is often advocated by perpetrators who, upon realizing the consequences of their actions, seek to get beyond it — "let bygones be bygones," on the basis of forgiveness. This, however, only trivializes and ignores history. Also, in attempting a hasty peace, the causes of suffering are not examined and, left unexamined, suffering will probably continue.[146]

---

[145] Frantz Fanon, *The Wretched of the Earth* (tr. Richard Philcox; New York: Grove Press, 2004), 1-62.

[146] Schreiter explains that "To trivialize and ignore memory is to trivialize and ignore human identity, and to trivialize and ignore identity is to trivialize and ignore human dignity. That is why reconciliation as a hasty peace is actually the opposite of reconciliation. By forgetting the suffering, the victim is forgotten and the causes of suffering are never uncovered and confronted." Robert J. Schreiter, *Reconciliation: Mission and Ministry in a Changing Social Order* (Maryknoll, NY: Orbis Books, 1992), 19.

Arguments in Favor of the Dissolution of Regional Conferences in the SDA Church in the United States

> Those who benefit from social injustice are naturally less capable of understanding its real character than those who suffer from it. They will attribute ethical qualities to social life, if only the slightest gesture of philanthropy hides social injustice.[1]

As U.S. society has become increasingly intolerant of the overt racism and discriminatory attitudes and actions that were normal occurrences just a generation ago, vestiges of this inauspicious era have come under increasing scrutiny.[2] While the motivation for such scrutiny can be questioned, society in general benefits from the equalizing, liberalizing and democratizing of social structures and institutions that have excluded individuals on the basis of ethnicity, gender, sexual orientation, education, religion, social status, wealth, or any other category.

Interestingly, such epic societal changes are often not preceded by periods of national reflection on how and why such injustices were permitted in the first place so that they can be avoided in the future. The Women's suffrage movement, for example, fought to give (at the time white) women the right to vote and to seek elective office. It achieved success in 1920 with the Nineteenth Amendment. Similarly, the Civil Rights Movement achieved a string of victories beginning with the Civil Rights Act of

---

[1] Reinhold Niebuhr, *Moral Man and Immoral Society: A Study in Ethics and Politics* (Louisville: Westminster John Knox Press, 2001), 80.

[2] Addressing the shift in racial attitudes in the United States and the motivation for such shifts, Schuman et al revise Myrdal's belief that the American Dilemma was "in the heart of the American," by noting that "what he surely meant was that it was located in the values and norms of our society, and that most Americans are capable of feeling pressure from these values and norms—if not out of personal guilt, then from social shaming when they are blatantly violated." Howard Schuman, Charlotte Steeh, Lawrence Bobo, and Maria Krysan, *Racial Attitudes in America: Trends and Interpretations* (Cambridge, MA: Harvard University Press, 1997), 315.

1964. However, both movements were missing thoughtful reflection about how the situations arose. Within the current debate over Regional Conferences, the same also appears to be true—agitation to remedy the once acceptable, but now embarrassing social norm, and then moving on to the next cause. Left unprocessed and unresolved are the underlying causes, triggers, and damages from these discriminatory actions. This chapter will reflect on central themes presented by Idealists as they seek to advance their position for changes to the present administrative structure, where the largely black constituents find their spiritual home within Regional Conferences. The Idealists' position has been distilled to three arguments: The Love-Unity Ethic, Segregation, and the Age of Obama.

Arguments of Church Leaders, Administrators, and Theologians

When former GC president Jan Paulsen implored young SDA professionals to be agents of change in both the church and the community during a discussion on September 29, 2009, he was questioned about the continued existence of Regional Conferences. His response is instructive of his thinking on the subject: "We are one family...If we don't act like one, shame on us."[3] Paulsen does not first offer thoughtful reflections on the historical grievances and racial discrimination that precipitated his predecessor's grudging offer of Regional Conferences to blacks, rather than their preferred option of full integration of the SDA church. Instead, he makes a pitch for family unity via shame. On the one hand, he implies black complicity in the problem, creating division by the mere existence of a structural accommodation that was mutually agreed upon in 1944. On the other hand, current church leaders may also be implicated, since few appear to be attempting possible solutions to this apparent family discord. As previously quoted, Paulsen urged the young adults at this forum to challenge church leaders with the assertion that the rationale for Regional Conferences is no longer socially

---

[3] "Let's Talk Encore: D.C. young professionals talk change with Adventist Church President." *Adventist News Network* (September 29, 2009): http://news.adventist.org/2009/09/lets-talk-encore-dc.html (accessed 8/25/10).

acceptable.[4] It is, however, laudable that Paulsen appeals to the organic and evolving nature of the SDA Church and the dynamic world which it thrives in, by urging that the church make its core values relevant and reliable.

Perhaps typical of most religious organizations with an official organ, the SDA Church in the United States took notice when the editor of the *Adventist Review* summoned the community's collective attention with his May 25th, 2006 editorial, "Four Big Questions." Utilizing editorial prerogative, and speaking in prophetic tones, William G. Johnsson called attention to the issue of race relations in the SDA Church with his final question. Reminiscent of Rodney King's famed question to the crowd — "Can we all get along?" — as he attempted to quell the riot that broke out in 1992, following the acquittal of police officers caught on camera assaulting him, Johnsson's question implies estrangement and the need for reunion: "What will it take to bring us together?"[5] In letters to the editor, many offered critiques and compliments regarding the arguments used by Johnsson to frame his response to the question, including a lengthy rebuttal by Calvin Rock.[6]

Johnsson's argument for more togetherness can be distilled into two headings, the first being an honest evaluation of the historical, sociological and political consequence of racism in the United States, and then a challenge to church leaders about the next steps forward. In the first, Johnsson provides a personal testimonial on his battle with racial attitudes, labeling himself as a "racist." To his credit, Johnsson resists the temptation to situate his discussion of racism in a vacuum. Instead, he positions himself squarely as a perpetrator. However, his admission is proceeded by deniability on the race question in this country, by confessing that he did not fully understand the nuances of black and white relationships since he is an Australian. This confession is typical of many nationalized or native whites in the United States, who may or may not be oblivious

---

[4] "Let's Talk Encore: D.C. Young Professionals talk Change with Adventist Church President."

[5] Johnsson, "Four Big Questions."

[6] "Readers Respond to Four Big Questions," *Adventist Review* http://www.adventistreview.org/issue/php?=660%action=print (accessed 8/6/10).

117

to the white privilege they enjoy, irrespective of their experience with racism. Johnsson does acknowledge some elements of white privilege, including not being susceptible to racial profiling while driving his car and not having others disparage him racially in private, while publicly commending him. Neither does Johnsson gloss over the SDA Church's past discriminatory actions towards blacks, nor does he clearly identify institutional racism as embedded in the culture of the church.[7]

Second, Johnsson challenges church leaders on the danger of inertia and the need for charting a new direction. He acknowledges the commendable successes of Regional Conferences in general and black Adventists in particular for ensuring doctrinal purity, a fervor for evangelism, and an expansion of black members and church leaders, as well as joint black and white initiatives to increase community engagement. But he also challenges some whites in leadership, who view the separation of the races as both satisfactory and perhaps even necessary. Johnsson finally questions the feasibility of the currently divided church structures, thoughtfully couching it in the context of generational woundedness, which requires attitudinal and emotional healing. Such healing will not take place without a "striving toward the ideal" and arriving at a place of "visible unity."[8] Though Johnsson avoids the language of reconciliation, this appears to be the direction of his commentary. One wonders why he does not speak of reconciliation, this fundamental pastoral function, and Christian practice. Nevertheless, Johnsson must be credited with at least voicing the need for some form of preliminary reconciling work before any talk of deconstructing Regional Conferences is embarked upon, unlike the next individual under consideration.

Since the writing of his book, *The Eleventh Commandment*, Dwight Nelson has been prominent in calling for the end of Regional Conferences. He declares Regional Conferences to be separate but equal administrative structures that were necessitated by the country's racial past but were now anomalous and anachronistic. Imploring a business model comparison, Nelson argues that if separate-but-equal organizations are so successful, why do Fortune

---

[7] Johnsson, "Four Big Questions."
[8] Johnsson, "Four Big Questions."

500 companies not adopt them? Then Nelson makes the dubious claim that other denominations in the country are abandoning their racial divisions and are uniting in "ecclesiastical solidarity."[9] While it is true that most Christian denominations have jettisoned their racial past, like the Southern Baptist Convention, which issued an apology in 1995 for upholding slavery, yet the divide remains between it and the National Baptist Convention (its black counterpart). Similarly, the United Methodists called for racial reconciliation at their May 2000 General Conference, yet they, too, are separated from the African Methodist Episcopal, the African Methodist Episcopal Zion, and the Methodist Episcopal Churches. This is evidence against ecclesiastical solidarity in two of the largest Protestant denominations in the United States.

Nelson then declares the Cross of Christ to be antithetical to the push by whites to segregate themselves from blacks by means of separate-but-equal religious institutions, or blacks making demands for "rights and power." In assigning equal blame to both whites and blacks, Nelson seeks to be an equal opportunity offender in the hope that both whites and blacks will then be more willing to participate in "'a new creation in Christ' of united conferences and united congregations and a united people with a united mission and a united love for a lost and disunited world."[10] But as will be discussed later, in the matter of racial prejudice and discrimination, blacks can hardly be said to have equal culpability. Furthermore, since when is it a moral failing to insist on one's equal rights and political parity, from those depriving you of both? On his central assertion that Regional Conferences constitute separate-but-equal structures, it should be noted that separate-but-equal was a legal term enshrined in the United States constitution, permitting enforced segregation. Since membership in these Regional Conferences is open to all ethnic groups, they do not deserve this label. Nelson appears to be happy to use the language of that bygone era, but not its history, since he derides its use as diversionary. Nelson then invokes a racially reconciled incident of two Baptist congregations, one black and one white, which he concludes is evidence that racial reconciliation is not a complicated process. One can only wonder if

---

[9] Nelson, 2001, 59-60.
[10] Nelson, 2001, 60.

racial reconciliation is so easy, why it has taken so long for some of the largest denominations in the country to achieve a modest form of it.[11]

In a sermon preached on January 16, 2010 to commemorate Martin Luther King, Jr.'s birthday, and entitled "The Truth in Black and White," Nelson returns to his anachronism and unity arguments by posing the question, Is the SDA Church in this country a color-coded church? Reading between the lines, he concludes that it is color-coded, and that the time for change has come. Change can occur, believes Nelson, if the final prayer of Christ (John 17:20-22) is adhered to, since unity was a significant criterion for global evangelistic success. Secondly, change is possible if Christians live as they should: with color-code-free minds and attitudes, attend multiracial congregations, and implore church leaders to discontinue a separate-but-equal system. His stance appears to have evolved, since he does not call for the wholesale elimination of Regional Conferences but that all conferences within the territory of Regional Conferences should be closed and a merged entity be formed, as in the Miracle in Memphis.[12] To his credit, Nelson calls on young white visionary leaders to take the first step in this process, even if it could eventually cost them their administrative positions.[13]

---

[11] He questions the standard rebuttal by Pragmatists of Regional Conferences, who often remark, "If you only knew the history of regional conferences, you would understand why we must continue to cling to them for representation and/or for separation." Nelson, 2001, 60, 61.

[12] The author invokes the racial reconciliation incident known as "the Miracle of Memphis," in which the mainly white Pentecostal Fellowship of North America merged with the black Pentecostal denominations to form the Pentecostal Charismatic Churches of North America, headed by black bishop Itheil Clemmons. Nelson, "The Truth in Black and White," 2010.

[13] In his dissertation on the subject, Russell West clarifies that the race relations effort called the Pentecostal Partners: A Racial Reconciliation Strategy for 21st Century Ministry, had 16 formal presentations by church leaders on the problem of racial divisions and ritualized conversation on the way forward. West concluded that while the Pentecostal proposals were commendable, it was impeded by its "intercultural symbol selection," because they had used language and themes from past race relations discourse without adaptation. Consequently, they experienced the same

In 1997, influential public health scholar and Harvard professor David R. Williams wrote an opinion piece for the *Adventist Review* in which he offers resolutions to the racial divisions in the SDA Church in the United States. He views Regional Conferences as a progressive response to the prevailing racial attitudes of conservative Christians like Adventists and, as such, maintaining these conferences makes sense.[14] Despite this reality, Williams sees a biblical mandate for corporate unity that is doctrinal, visible, and organizational. While acknowledging the successes of Regional Conferences, particularly in evangelism among blacks, he asserts that "Racially oriented evangelism can produce racially insensitive and even racially prejudiced congregations."[15] William's hopeful approach has him advocating the minimizing of human frailties and maximizing the possibility of change through the cross of Christ. Like Nelson, Williams' preferred option is ending all existing conferences and establishing new ones supported by new ways of thinking about race relations, in order to overcome centuries of prejudice and mistrust, including white flight.[16]

Fredrick Russell, a former president of Allegheny West Conference (a Regional Conference), who sees a generational shift in race relations with the political ascendancy of Barack Obama, argues that since the attitudes and actions of white leaders have changed for the better, it was time for the church to rid itself of "the last symbols of our historical divide — racially segregated conferences in the

---

"self-defeating problems that plague racial conflict resolution. But when they allowed their original race-transcending ideas to emerge, "their community-building aims seem to be more closely achieved." Russell W. West, "That His People May Be One: An Interpretative Study of the Pentecostal Leadership's Quest for Racial Unity" (Ph.D. diss., Regent University, Virginia, 1997).

[14] David R. Williams, "The Right Thing to Do: A divided church and what to do about it," *Adventist Review*, Feb 20, 1997. Williams cites Schuman and his colleagues, whose research finds that whites are more inclined to favor equality as a principle than in practice. Schuman et al., 138f.

[15] Williams, 1997, 25.

[16] Williams, 1997, 25.

United States."[17] Russell references as a model for Adventists the United Methodist Church's decision to eliminate its Central Jurisdiction as a means of healing black and white racial division. History, though, tells a different story. As with the United States and its sectional divide and subsequent reunion based largely on religion and race, historians have chronicled a similar movement within the Methodist church.[18] Methodism began in the United States in 1784, but by 1830 the Methodist Episcopal Church (the North) and the Methodist Protestant Church (the South) split because of slavery. The sectional divide was ended on April 23, 1939, with the merger of the northern and southern Methodist Episcopal Churches and the Methodist Protestant Church, forming the United Methodist Church. The United Methodist Church also established six jurisdictional conferences to elect bishops and other church officers. While five of these conferences were regional in scope, the sixth was race-based and was called the Central Jurisdiction. Significantly, Methodist historian Peter C. Murray notes that the newly created Methodist Church was "the most rigid and segregated church structure of any Protestant denomination."[19] However, the unity of the Methodist Church was achieved on the basis that black and white members could be separate but equal in the same denomination, and the Central Jurisdiction was the mechanism to achieve this separation.[20]

In his comparison of the growth and development of Regional Conferences and the Central Jurisdiction, Adventist historian Alfonso Greene's analysis suggests that in twenty-four years the membership growth of the latter was 8,363 (2.47 percent),

---

[17] Fredrick A. Russell, "The Obama Message," *Adventist Review*, Feb. 21, 2008: http://www.adventistreview.org/issue.php?issue=2008-1505&page=17 (accessed 8/18/10). Russell's article is rebutted by Rock months later. Rock, "Revisiting 'The Obama Message," *Adventist Review*, July 24, 2008: http://www.adventistreview.org/issue.php?issue=2008-1505&page=1991 (accessed 9/18/10).

[18] Greene; Peter C. Murray, *Methodists and the Crucible of Race 1930-1975* (Columbia, MO: The University of Missouri Press, 2004).

[19] Murray, 3.

[20] Murray is clear about the motivation to create the Central Jurisdiction. It "was not created out of any moral commitment, but was a compromise with racial prejudice and bigotry." Murray, 5.

compared to 4,476 (28.19 percent) for the former. Astonishingly, when the growth of black membership in overall denominational membership is assessed, the Central Jurisdiction percentage increase was 10.22 percent compared to 299.02 percent for Regional Conferences — a growth rate 29 times that of Central Jurisdiction. A similar contrast in both their income and tithe fund revealed a threefold increase in Regional Conferences over Central Jurisdiction.[21] Today, there are approximately 500,000 black Methodists in the U.S. — a number that should have been larger considering there were 373,327 members in 1964 — a 25 percent increase compared to a 94 percent increase in the Regional Conferences. It is possible that these statistics formed the basis for comments by Methodist theologian John Cobb to Adventist Ethicist David Larson during a chance encounter:

> My denomination, The United Methodist Church, has devastated its ministry in this country to Hispanics by insisting on integrating many structures in the name of 'inclusiveness.' Our Hispanic outreach was once vibrant and effective; now it is either sick or already dead. I hope other denominations don't make the same mistake we did. There is something important about cultural and racial clusters that we ignore at our peril.[22]

Like Nelson, Russell places his faith in the young, who are loath to accept old rationales for past racial hostilities, as the vehicle for creating a united church. However, his belief in a change in the country in the age of Obama may be excessively optimistic, considering some of the reversals in the president's political fortunes. Some examples are: the racial epithets and effigies hurled at black politicians, including President Obama, during the rampaging Tea Party marches of the 2009 healthcare debate, or the "otherness" insinuated in the demands of Birthers for the President's birth certificate, or the Tea Party lament, "I want my country back." Furthermore, as Russell had been in a position of power to follow

---

[21] Greene, 253-257.

[22] Alexander Carpenter, "Between a Rock and a Hard Race Question," *Spectrum,* July 27, 2008: http://www.spectrummagazine.org/ blog/2008/07/27/betweenrockandhardracequestion (accessed 8/18/ 10).

through on his noble aspiration to move the church forward, his crusading zeal for the abolition of Regional Conferences atrophied.

Another Idealist is Adventist educator David Penno, whose investigation into the perceptions of clergy and laity regarding Regional Conferences betrayed some degree of bias with the designation "race-based organizational segregation" to describe Regional Conferences. Unfortunately, Penno does not offer his working definition for "segregation." Today, Regional Conferences are not specifically race-based, since they include most ethnic groups that populate the other conferences. Also, Regional Conferences are not segregated, since segregation in the U.S. was a legal policy and practice of separating blacks from whites institutionally. However, a case could be made for a form of *de facto* segregation (homogeneous racial grouping), since Regional Conferences are dominated by blacks. Further, in his statement of the problem, Penno states that since all racial segregation has been removed from U.S. society, then the SDA Church has a moral responsibility to fall in line. No mention is made by Penno of the causes of segregation, namely individual, cultural and institutional racism. Penno's thinking on the subject is also exposed in his assertion that the first evidence of structural segregation within the SDA Church came in 1909 when the North American Negro Department was organized at the GC. As was previously stated, the North American Negro Department was a grudging concession to blacks by white church leaders, who had largely ignored pleas from Ellen White for a greater unbiased effort among blacks. Hence, the establishment of the North American Negro Department was evidence of failure by white church leaders to address the need of black members, who sought acceptance and full integration in the church.[23]

Penno is of the opinion that segregation is a significant aspect of the SDA Church, despite the fact that integrated congregations are no longer a hindrance to the proclamation of the gospel. He also believes that social pressure has moved in the direction of more, not less, integration as the dominant trend. The conclusion to his research also reinforces this perception about the church and Regional Conferences under the six measures tested. First, there was strong disagreement from respondents that the prevailing social

---

[23] Penno, 3-5, 23.

conditions that necessitated Regional Conferences remain relevant; neither did they believe that the church's mission would be impaired if Regional Conferences were discontinued. Second, respondents agreed that removing "segregation" (i.e., Regional Conferences) will improve the tarnished public image of the church—though no indication is given as to how widespread public knowledge of Regional Conferences is outside of U.S. Adventists. Third, on the perception of white flight, respondents felt that issues of leadership rather than worship style would be the cause for whites to leave if they were in the minority. Fourth, the majority opinion was that merging Regional Conferences with a conference geographically situated would be cost-effective and efficient, though doubts remained about equal distribution of resources. Fifth, options were mixed about how such a merger would impact the clergy, with apprehension about whether blacks would be given leadership opportunities. Finally, uncertainty prevailed over the current system remaining.[24]

Citing Russell, Penno appears to share the view that with the election of President Obama, the time for change had come, though he concedes that should the "segregated" system remain, members from both conference systems should attempt co-operative ventures to increase interethnic fellowship and church outreach. Penno's apprehension of any *kumbaya* moment anytime soon appears well founded. He cites a Facebook group called, *The Adventist Desegregation Coalition*, which was formulated following the election of President Obama to eliminate "segregation" in the form of Regional Conferences. A similar effort was launched in May 2010 in the form of a petition for *Racial and Ethnic Reconciliation in the Seventh-day Adventist Church*. Neither appears to have had much impact on the Adventist community; indeed, the petition was closed with only 205 signatures out of the million they sought.[25] These

---

24 Penno, 47, 168-170.

25 "The Adventist Desegregation Coalition," *Facebook*, February 1, 2009: http://www.facebook.com/group.php?gid=53734749401 (accessed 11/22/10); Racial and Ethnic Reconciliation in the Seventh-day Adventist Church," *Care 2: petitionsite*, 26 May 26, 2010: http://www.thepetitionsite. com/1/race-reconciliation-in-the-seventh-day-adventist-church/ (accessed 8/20/10).

grassroots efforts by Adventist members failed to generate support from church leaders, perhaps for reasons of self-interest.

However, a window into the thinking of the hierarchy of the SDA Church was opened, on matters of race, and the display was lamented by many of those present. The occasion was the election of President Obama on November 4, 2008. As the first black to achieve this position, his election was greeted nationally and internationally as historic. Writing in the *Adventist Review*, Alvin M. Kibble, a vice-president of the NAD, laments what he witnessed at the GC headquarters in Silver Spring, MD, a day after Obama's election. He intones, "To my disappointment, but not surprise, nothing was said. No formal reference was made. No statement. No observation. Only silence."[26] Despite Adventists being typically conservative, Republican (at least most whites), and apolitical, Kibble felt that a moment was missed by church leaders to reflect on how the Adventist community would be impacted by this change. Regardless of one's politics, it was difficult to see how the church hierarchy assumed a posture of silence; if nothing else, they are at least guilty of racial insensitivity, given the pride black members would have had, at the historic nature of the 2008 election.

As a conservative systematic theologian, Koranteng-Pipim articulates a theological view of racism as a denial of Christian teachings. Since racism is an ideology of supremacy, deeming blacks to be inferior to whites, Koranteng-Pipim conveys a view of a largely white church hierarchy oblivious to racism's insidious effects, with a belated statement of denunciation coming in 1985, a Race Summit in 1999, and an appeal to dismantle racism within the SDA Church. He theologizes racism by observing how it violates all Ten Commandments, how it contradicts Christ's teachings, and how it is an obstacle to unity. Like other Idealists, Koranteng-Pipim identifies the efforts cited above as the epitome of racism within the church, since they remain an embarrassment and threaten the credibility of Adventists. I note that Koranteng-Pipim does not blame the continued institutional, cultural and even individual racism as threatening the church's standing; rather, all blame is assigned to

---

[26] Alvin M. Kibble, "When Silence is Not Golden," *Adventist Review*, January 15, 2008: http://www.adventistreview.org/article. php?id=2360 (accessed 11/22/10).

Regional Conferences, as if their mere absence would address the racism that made them necessary. The fact that the church has not been involved in serious racial reconciliation efforts, and that there was no follow-up with the race summit (a matter that will be addressed later), is not for Koranteng-Pipim a matter of embarrassment or jeopardizing the church's credibility. Rather, their visibility makes Regional Conferences susceptible to this barrage of criticism.[27]

Koranteng-Pipim is optimistic about a resolution to the church's problem of racism. He grounds his optimism in a statement from Ellen White, and in the unique identity, mission, and name of the SDA Church. Racial harmony can be achieved by an acknowledgment of racial prejudices; confession of the sins of racism; seeking biblical solutions, one of which is reconciliation; developing interracial relationships, and taking a stand against racial injustice.[28] Punctuating his sanguinity on the church's ability to overcome the scourge of racism this quote from White is used to conclude his argument: "Walls of separation have been built up between the whites and the blacks. These walls of prejudice will tumble down of themselves as did the walls of Jericho when Christians obey the Word of God, which enjoins on them supreme love to their Maker and impartial love to their neighbor."[29]

Assessment of the Essential Arguments

It is clear from the above arguments calling for a fresh approach to race relations in the SDA Church in the U.S., that the central focus is the abolition of Regional Conferences, despite their significant successes since 1945. Such arguments are hinged on the anachronism of such structural accommodation for blacks, given that society no longer accepts "separate but equal" as a governing philosophy. And to some extent, the prevailing structures represent a strategic failure of Adventist leadership in establishing appropriate race relations between blacks and whites, in a country in which racism has historically been an organizing principle. Consequently, for many in the church, Regional Conferences are an ongoing source

---

[27] Koranteng-Pipim, 302, 312f, 342f, 346, 354,
[28] Koranteng-Pipim, 417f, 419-430.
[29] White, *The Southern Work*, 43.

of embarrassment and shame. Like other denominations, the SDA Church has tended to assume social norms with respect to racism until those norms have become untenable, at which point they conform to the socially acceptable.[30] However, the socially acceptable is seldom socially equitable. Perhaps, it is in this light, that a distillation of the three essential arguments made by Idealists — Love-Unity Ethic, Segregation, and the Age of Obama — should be viewed.

Love-Unity Ethic Argument

In assessing the history of schisms, H. Richard Niebuhr laments the fact that Christianity, which promised solidarity for a divided world, embraced and even championed the very conflicts it had hoped to transform. He presents his case as follows:

> The problem of the world is the problem of a synthesis of culture — of the building up of an organic whole in which the various interests and the separate nations and classes will be integrated into a harmonious, interacting society, serving one common end in diverse manners... And every civilization which has possessed... such a synthesis has received it from its religion... But the dilemma for the Western world lies in the fact that while it depends upon religion for the creation of a common mind and birth of a common loyalty, the only religion available seems incapable of establishing, even within its own structure, the desired harmony.[31]

The answer to this ineffectual religion, from Niebuhr's perspective, is a Christianity that is less a focus on ecclesiastical institutions and creeds, and more a realization of the child-parent relationship embodied in the Christian's relationship with God, and the brotherhood and sisterhood of each other. Such a religion would exhibit divine love, which seeks to harness the potential of all, "in self-sacrificing devotion to the Beloved Community" of God and all

---

[30] This form of Christianity is denounced by Niebuhr as just being a, "religion which merely adjusts itself to social conditions whether these make for union or for schism." H. Richard Niebuhr, *The Social Sources of Denominationalism*, 274.

[31] H. Richard Niebuhr, *The Social Sources of Denominationalism*, 267, 268.

believers.   The practical consequences of such love would be decreased self-interest and increased fellowship and harmony. But he warns that the path to unity, which love demands, is arduous; it demands repentance, and sacrifice.[32]

This portrait of a love-unity ethic is compelling, for it minimizes posturing and pretension, focusing instead on the wellbeing of all within the community while discouraging hasty solutions by increasing awareness of the complexity of achieving unity. It is not always clear that these elements of the love-unity ethic that are appealed to by Idealists are part of their formulation. The biblical warrant often used to underpin this argument is the part of the farewell discourse of Christ in John 17, considered by NT theologians to be a "High-Priestly Prayer."[33] The bulk of the prayer is addressed to the disciples, who have been designated to lead the church in its mission of proclaiming the saving message of Christ. As the church fulfils its mission "in the unity of divine love," citizens of the world community will be cognizant of the divine mission of Christ to this world. All those who embrace this salvific message of the disciples will exhibit the unity for which Christ prayed. NT scholar George R. Beasley-Murray saw this unity to be both "radical and fundamental," since it is centered in God and revealed in Christ, and his redemptive work.[34] As a consequence, the unity for which

---

[32] H. Richard Niebuhr, *The Social Sources of Denominationalism*, 279-280. He concludes that the unity odyssey requires jettisoning old loyalties, and learning "to look upon their separate establishments and exclusive creeds with contrition rather than with pride," 284.   Martin Luther King, Jr., viewed the "Beloved Community" as an "inclusive human community characterized by love and nonviolence." Kenneth L. Smith and Ira G. Zepp Jr., *Search for the Beloved Community: The Thinking of Martin Luther King Jr.* (Valley Forge, Pennsylvania: Judson Press, [1974] 1998), 129.

[33] From this standpoint, the prayer is considered to be "a supreme example of the intercession of the risen Lord alluded to in 1 John 2:1; Hebrews 7:25; 9:14; Rom 8:34." It is generally accepted that the prayer has three sections, Christ prays for himself (1-5), his disciples (6-19), and his Church (20-26).   George R. Beasley-Murray, *John*, gen. eds. David A. Hubbard and Glenn W. Barker, *Word Biblical Commentary* 36 (Waco, TX: Word Books Publisher, 1987), 294f.

[34] Beasley-Murray, *John*, 294, 298. The author goes on to explain that "the unity envisaged is possible only through the accomplished

Christ prayed is hardly the superficial "Can we all get along" unity that is often envisaged.

A question that is often posed by Pragmatists, in response to the chants of Idealists to get along is, "Does getting along, have anything to do with being in the same administrative structure?" Catholic theologian Hans Küng has been appropriated by Pragmatics to assert that the two are not specifically connected. In discussing unity in diversity, Küng first argues that God had willed that the Church (local and universal) be one, "incontrovertibly one," because it was born of "one saving event."[35] But Küng challenges a typical misconception of many Idealists by asserting that:

> The unity of the Church has nothing to do with the mythological magic of the number one and the intrinsic fascination of oneness. The unity of the Church is not simply a natural entity, is not simply moral unanimity and harmony, is not just sociological conformity and uniformity. To judge it by externals (canon law, ecclesiastical language, Church administration, etc.) is to misunderstand it completely. The unity of the Church is a spiritual entity. It is not chiefly a unit of members among themselves, it depends finally not on itself but on the unity of God, which is efficacious through Jesus Christ in the Holy Spirit.[36]

This spiritual context of the Church is understood within Adventist theology, despite its absence in the debate over Regional Conferences. Adventists believe in a visible and an invisible church. The visible church is involved in the operationalizing of the mission and ministry of Christ great commission (Matt. 28: 18-20); while the

---

redemptive action of God in Christ, while it yet calls for an appropriate ethical response from those drawn into it...[it is a unity that is] brought about in reciprocal love. The two belong together like the two sides of a coin." 302f.

[35] He clarifies that, "Christ has reconciled God and man, he has also removed all opposition between man and man; he is the basis of his Church's unity." Hans Küng, *The Church* (London: Burns & Oates, 1968), 271.

[36] Küng, 1968, 273.

invisible or universal church is constituted of God's people from around the world.[37]

Further, contrary to the view of realists, Küng's declares that

...the unity of the Church presupposes a multiplicity of Churches: the various Churches do not need to deny their origins of their specific situations; their languages, their history, their customs and traditions, their way of life and thought, their personal structure will differ fundamentally, and no one has the right to take this from them. The same thing is not suitable for everyone, at every time and in every place...It is not necessary for this diversity and variety to breed dissensions, enmity and strife. In certain cases, some characteristics or individual peculiarity can be sacrificed for the sake of peace and love, and mutual concessions made. As long as all have the one God, Lord, Spirit, and faith and not their own private God, Lord, Spirit, and faith, all is in order.[38]

The context of Küng's remarks is the diversity of Christian traditions and denominations, yet the sentiment can be ascribed to diversity within individual faith traditions. From Küng's perspective, not only must diversity be celebrated, it must be safeguarded. Yet if this diversity is injurious to the collective, then by mutual consent, individual difference can be forfeited for the sake of harmony. So, whether individual peculiarity triumphs over group harmony, it is the oneness of the Godhead that is to be guaranteed.

Expanding on this love-unity ethic, German theologian Dietrich Bonhoeffer defines love as the "reconciling of man with God in Jesus Christ," since men and women are in disunion with God and their fellow human beings. As a result of this alienation, love is

---

[37] Ministerial Association, *Seventh-day Adventists Believe: A Biblical Exposition of 27 Fundamental Doctrines* (Hagerstown, Maryland: Review and Herald Publishing Association, 1988), 142.

[38] Küng, 1968, 274-275. From Küng's perspective, co-existence should not jeopardize Church unity, rather "unity is only endangered by co-existence which is neither co-operation nor support, but basically a hostile confrontation," 276.

the vehicle used by God to surmount humanity's disunion.[39] This perspective on the love-unity ethic presents a challenge for Idealists because, in their estimation, these Regional Conferences are an eyesore in the twenty-first century and clear evidence of disunion. But if, as Bonhoeffer concludes, disunion is an ever-present state as a result of The Fall, with love as the only antidote, then whether Regional Conferences remain or are replaced, disunion can, and I dare say, will persist, if love is absent. Perhaps then, Idealists are misguided in their insistence that Regional Conferences are indicative of disunion. If the latter is true, then a focus on indications of love within the Adventist community, manifested in how difference and diversity are accommodated for example, maybe a more accurate marker of the love-unity ethic.

Love has been called by Bible scholar and clergy John Stott, "the preeminent Christian grace," and the unmatched characteristic of God's people, which seeks the welfare of others regardless of the cost to the individual.[40] Despite the fact that many forms of love exist,[41] even the one in question, *agape*, tends to be sanitized into a benign "God is love" motif. Like Stott, Bonhoeffer and other bible scholars have challenged this view of love, by insisting that it is costly. Bonhoeffer sees Christ view of love as an uncompromising demand to love one's enemies, with the intention to win them over.[42] Martin Luther King, Jr., called love "a supreme unifying principle of life," not "some sentimental and weak response," it is both active

---

[39] Importantly for this book, Bonhoeffer goes on to assert that, "This deed of God is Jesus Christ, is reconciliation. Dietrich Bonhoeffer, *Ethics* (New York: A Touchstone Book by Simon and Schuster, 1955), 55. The same conception of love is shared by Tillich who builds on Hegel's fragment on love with its dialectical scheme of "love as separation and reunion." Paul Tillich, *Love, Power, and Justice: Ontological Analyses and Ethical Applications* (Oxford: Oxford University Press, 1954), 22.

[40] John Stott, *The Contemporary Christian: An Urgent Plea for Double Listening* (Leicester, UK: Inter-Varsity Press, 1992), 146f.

[41] Tillich identified four types of love: *epithymia* or *libido* (desire), *philia* (mutual friendship), *erōs* (romantic attraction), and *agape* (ultimate reality that is transformative), with each one being incomplete without the other three. Tillich, 1954, 32f.

[42] Bonhoeffer, *The Cost of Discipleship* (London: SCM Press, 1948), 131.

and aggressive.[43] But he cautions, that in seeking to be the moral guardians of society, Christians must realize that history has shown that sincerity and conscientiousness, while noble virtues, can morph into horrendous vices.[44] When those who speak of the church's need to exhibit Christian love, in the context of the dissolution of Regional Conferences, the question may be asked, to what extent is the well-being of those whose institutions they seek to dismantle being considered? One does not get this impression from Rock's closing remark in response to Russell's article — a firm, if not indignant, "Why not leave them alone?"[45]

But, there is little doubt that Idealists are both sincere and conscientious in their belief that institutional relics, of an era this country would sooner forget, should be consigned to history where they belong. However, little is mentioned about the long and short-term consequences of such an outcome, including the perception within the black community of the demise of Regional Conferences. Since there is often little contact between blacks in Regional Conferences and white Adventists, a communication and communion challenge occurs; which Matsuoka describes as "a loss of speech across lines of difference and alienation."[46] It will not be too difficult for the black community to view such talk as nothing more than a white power grab. Compounding the communication challenge is the fact that in general, perceptions within the black and the white communities in the U.S. remain polar opposites on issues of racial equality, about which more will be said.[47] Further, in

---

[43] Martin Luther King, Jr., *Strength to Love* (Philadelphia: Fortress Press, 1981), 5.

[44] King, *Strength to Love*, 38, 43.

[45] Rock, "Revisiting 'The Obama Message," 2008.

[46] Importantly, the author observes that to remedy this distance, there is a need for a "way of speaking about estrangement across racial lines that neither undermines the advancement in opportunities and cooperation that has been achieved nor falsifies the enduring reality of the injustices and poverty that continue to haunt many." Matsuoka, 1998, 4, 5.

[47] In a 1995 Washington Post opinion poll, participants were asked, "How big a problem is racism in our society today?" Sixty-seven percent of surveyed blacks stated that racism was a big problem, while only 38 percent of whites agreed. "Race Relations Essays and Articles at Notes," http://www.enotes.com/race-relations-article (accessed 12/28/ 10).

defense and coping theory,[48] it is acknowledged that individuals deploy defenses or coping strategies to enable them to manage stress and emotional distress. As these coping skills can be either adaptive or maladaptive, clinicians working with a client must ensure that even a maladaptive coping skill is not removed without replacing it with one that is more efficient; otherwise greater harm may result. This same care is needed in any discussion on the future of Regional Conferences given the nature of their historical evolution and ongoing success.

Finally, as a corrective to the sentimentalization of love, this love has been rightly placed in dialectical tension with justice. Though not alone, Reinhold Niebuhr, one of twentieth century's premier theologians is celebrated for his love-justice dialectic – considered to be his all-encompassing social philosophy.[49] Niebuhr famously wrote, "Love as a substitute for justice is odious, but love as a supplement to justice is an absolute necessity."[50] For Niebuhr, love is a coercive influence on law enforcement, ill at ease with justice, yet each is in need of the other. Christians in general and Idealists, in particular, do an injustice to the love ethic by ignoring love's demands. Love demands equality and — evenhandedness; treating others as one would expect to be treated — the essence of the

---

[48] Individuals have biological, psychological and social defenses to enable them to cope with life, self and species-preserving actions. E. M. Pattison, "Defense and Coping Theory," in *Dictionary of Pastoral Care and Counseling*, 267-269.

[49] Charles C. Brown, *Niebuhr and His age: Reinhold Niebuhr's Prophetic Role and Legacy* (Harrisburg, Pennsylvania, 2002), 250; Roberts also linked love and justice together viewing them as interdependent and grounded in God, what he calls "lovingly just." J. Deotis Roberts, *Liberation and Reconciliation: A Black Theology* (Maryknoll, NY: Orbis Books, 1994), 46.

[50] Reinhold Niebuhr, "The Gospel in Future America," *Christian Century*, 75, 18 June, 1958, 714; Niebuhr, *The Nature and Destiny of Man: Human Destiny* (New York: Charles Scribner's Sons, 1943), 2: 246f; Niebuhr further contends that, "Religion will always leaven the idea of justice with the ideal of love. It will prevent the idea of justice, which is a politico-ethical ideal, from becoming a purely political one, with the ethical element washed out. The ethical ideal which threatens to become too purely religious must save the ethical idea which is in peril of becoming too political." Reinhold Niebuhr, *Moral Man and Immoral Society*, 2001, 80f.

Golden Rule. Black Adventists have labored against stiff opposition within and outside of the church to achieve a modicum of parity with white Adventists by means of Regional Conferences. With this achievement has come a measure of self-actualization[51] for the black SDA community. Therefore, the lovingly-just thing to do would appear to be a dialogue with blacks regarding, whether the very thing that has led to their empowerment, should now be placed on the altar of sacrifice in the name of unity. Clearly then, there is more at stake here than just a drive for unity – the collective dignity and self-determination of a people is on the line.

Segregation Argument

With the passing of Plessey vs. Ferguson in 1896, the U.S. Supreme Court legalized what was accepted practice North and South, namely "separate but equal." It would take fifty-eight years for this egregious decision to be overturned with the Brown vs. Board of Education decision. Yet, as history illustrates, a legal mandate does not always equate to behavioral compliance, as was the case in the formation of the White Citizens' Council, a white supremacist organization formed in 1956, to combat the passing of Brown vs. Board of Education, and lauded by former Republican president hopeful Governor Haley Barbour, before his inevitable recantation.[52] As Barbour's *faux pax* of misremembering the true

---

[51] As the apex of Abraham Maslow's hierarchy of needs, self-actualization has to do with self-exploration and action and conveys the sense of maximizing one's potential to the fullest extent.

[52] The Governor of Mississippi made the incredulous and revisionist remarks in an interview in a conservative rag: "You heard of the Citizens Councils? Up north they think it was like the KKK. Where I come from it was an organization of town leaders. In Yazoo City, they passed a resolution that said anybody who started a chapter of the Klan would get their ass run out of town. If you had a job, you'd lose it. If you had a store, they'd see nobody shopped there. We didn't have a problem with the Klan in Yazoo City." Andrew Ferguson, "The Boy from Yazoo City," *The Weekly Standard*, 16.15 (December 2010): http://www.weeklystandard.com /articles/boy-yazoo-city_523551.html (accessed 12/ 28/10). The remarks set off a political firestorm and within days Barbour was condemning the segregationist group with this statement: "When asked why my hometown in Mississippi did not suffer the same racial violence when I was a young

nature of the Citizens Council would suggest, some recollections and attitudes never die. So, when Idealists point to dramatic changes in U.S. society relative to "separate but equal," and they view it as indicative of the prevailing racial mood—hence the need to dismantle any vestige of the country's scandalous past—they ignore the continuing reality of racial attitudes of both blacks and whites.

In a Pew Research Center study in January 2010, U.S. blacks and whites continue to hold divergent opinions on anti-black discrimination, with 43 percent of blacks and only 13 percent of whites reporting more discrimination against blacks. These figures are reversed when the question is whether the country has done enough to give blacks equal rights, relative to whites. Fifty-four percent of whites say yes, and 36 percent say more is needed; while only 13 percent of blacks say yes, and 81 percent say more needs to be done. Importantly, the assessment of blacks on the state of their progress has increased dramatically during the last two years—the election of President Obama appears to be the catalyst for the spike in the numbers (more on this below).[53] Given these contrary views of race relations in the U.S., it should not be surprising that black Adventists desire to hold on to the gains they have made within the Regional Conference structure.

Regional Conferences are alleged to be institutions of segregation, and as such are *de facto* obstacles to the SDA Church advancing its outreach to the wider world without appearing hypocritical. As previously observed, Regional Conferences cannot

---

man that accompanied other towns' integration efforts, I accurately said the community leadership wouldn't tolerate it and helped prevent violence there. My point was my town rejected the Ku Klux Klan, but nobody should construe that to mean I think the town leadership were saints, either. Their vehicle, called the 'Citizens Council,' is totally indefensible, as is segregation. It was a difficult and painful era for Mississippi, the rest of the country, and especially African Americans who were persecuted in that time." Governor Haley Barbour's website, http://www.governorbarbour. com/ news/2010/dec/12.21.10govbarbourweeklystandard.html (accessed 12/ 28/10).

[53] "Blacks Upbeat about Black Progress, Prospects," *The Pew Research Center*, January 12, 2010: http://pewsocialtrends.org/2010/ 01/12/blacks-upbeat-about-black-progress-prospects/ (accessed 12/28/ 10).

be accurately classified as segregated, since admission is not restricted on any basis, including ethnic origins. Nevertheless, Idealists correctly identify Regional Conferences as the predominant domain of blacks. In their groundbreaking analysis of the black church in the United States, professors of religion C. Eric Lincoln and Lawrence H. Mamiya, establish that black religion, though integral to this country's history, is often ignored in religious studies, the result of which is a distorted view of religion. A consequence of ignoring the black religious tradition has been the realization that 80 percent of black worshipers attend seven of the major black denominations in this country; leaving the remaining 20 percent in Roman Catholic and Protestant Churches, except for a few in black sects. Importantly, they reveal that the overwhelming majority of blacks attending mainline white Protestant churches do so in congregations that are predominately black.[54] The fact that such a small percentage of blacks attend mainline white Protestant denominations is sobering and should be a factor in the current debate over Regional Conferences, since the racial divide may not simply be evidence of disunion. The segregation argument then may have less to do with administrative structures per se, and more to do with the historical racial divide — the painful legacy of slavery.

The question then arises, are black or any other ethnic institutions, segregated because they are homogeneously populated? In her provocatively titled book, *Why Are All the Black Kids Sitting Together in the Cafeteria*, university president and clinical psychologist Beverly Daniel Tatum explores racial identity development, and what it means to be a U.S. citizen living in a race-conscious society. She argues that subordinate groups existing in an asymmetrical environment must focus principally on survival; while the dominant group resists awareness of inequality, from which they largely benefit. In this environment, subordinate groups develop adaptive skills to avoid the ire of the dominant group — one of which is "self-segregation."[55] Pastoral theologians have made a similar observation, including the fact that whites can find respite from the

---

[54] C. Eric Lincoln and Lawrence H. Mamiya, *The Black Church in the African American Experience* (Durham: Duke University Press, 1990), xii.

[55] Beverly Daniel Tatum, *Why Are All the Black Kids Sitting Together in the Cafeteria?* (New York: BasicBooks, 1997), 24.

adverse effects of racism given their majority status in the United States; they can remain in their gated communities, send their children to all-white schools, and attend their all-white churches. However, beyond a black church or community, blacks "have minimal freedom to put race aside when they are tired of dealing with it."[56]

Using the racial identity formulation advanced by psychologist William Cross, Tatum illustrates how the five stages lead from assimilation to the dominant white culture, to finding ways to advance one's newly established racial identity for the good of the black community. In the midst of this identity development, and due to invalidation, blacks often disengage from whites, searching instead for those who share their perspective.[57] It can, therefore, be argued that Regional Conferences, like most other black institutions, represent to blacks a haven from the dominant white culture that they contend with throughout their lives. For this reason, if Regional Conferences were to be dissolved, black attendance at all or mainly all black churches will continue. Such is the case in local churches within the PUC, where there are no Regional Conferences.

With the field of psychology ably identifying and labeling racial identity development and other important phenomena, such as the acculturation process,[58] in comprehending how minorities

---

[56] Boyd and Bohler, 202.

[57] Tatum, *"Why are all the Black Kids Sitting Together in the Cafeteria?"* 59-60. Cross's five stages of racial identity development are pre-encounter: absorbing beliefs and values of whites; encounter: dealing with being a target of racism; immersion/emersion: desire to be surrounded with symbols of one's racial identity; internalization: a sense of security in one's racial identity; internalization-commitment: finding ways to translate one's racial identity. Cross later reduced the five stages down to four, omitting the internalization stage. William E. Cross, Jr., *Shades of Black: Diversity in African-American Identity* (Philadelphia: Temple University Press, 1991), 190-223.

[58] Acculturation has been defined as "a dynamic process of change that individuals undergo as they interact with and adapt to a new or different cultural environment; it is an interactive process that occurs along different life domains (e.g., language, values) at different rates of change." Different theories exist, including the unidimensional process: individuals

138

sustain emotional health within the dominant cultures, they have recently been joined by the field of SCPC in this important conversation. Pastoral psychologist Carroll A. Watkins Ali introduced to the field the pastoral function of survival and liberation, motivated by the need to frame the struggles of blacks from a non-white perspective. Since the history of blacks has been one of oppression and resistance, response to their communal need for deliverance has been largely absent from ministry outside of the black church. Ali views black liberation and womanist theologies, as well as black literary artists like Toni Morrison and James Baldwin, as sources for a black pastoral theology, which can best address communal survival for those lacking self-direction and self-determination. For the pastoral caregiver, Ali recommends three approaches in offering care in the black community: (1) understand the insidious nature of racism in self and society; (2) successful treatment is premised on the use of self in the therapeutic process; (3) alliances with the black community involve negotiating beliefs and values. Further guidelines include responding to the urgent needs and being an active advocate for the black community.[59]

Since offering care is the business of any religious community, such care should always be premised on the betterment of the care-seeker. Hiltner challenged caregivers to exhibit the characteristics inherent in the primitive biblical imagery of shepherding, which is "the exercise of tender and solicitous concern."[60] In offering this level of care for the black community,

---

relinquish aspects of their culture to embrace the dominant culture; the Berry's Acculturation Model: assimilation, separation, marginalization, and integration; the Interactive Acculturation Model: integration, assimilation, separation, anomie, and individualism; and the Relative Acculturation Extended Model: acculturation is assessed along seven domains (religious beliefs, principles and values, social relations, family relations, economics, work, and politics and government) in the private and public arena. Lourdes M. Rivera, "Acculturation: Theories, Measurement, and Research," in *Handbook of Multicultural Counseling*, ed. Joseph G. Ponterotto, J. Manuel Casas, Lisa A Suzuki, and Charlene M. Alexander (Thousand Oaks, CA: Sage Publications, Inc., 2010), 331-334.

[59] Ali, 2, 42-61, 72-84, 92f, 137.

[60] Seward Hiltner, *Preface to Pastoral Theology* (New York: Abingdon Press, 1958), 15.

James Poling urges the dominant white community to "practice goodness," in a society racked by the evil of racism. He lists six responses in the art of goodness: "develop a spirituality of resistance... live in solidarity with resistance communities... take moral and material inventory... confront the abuser within... confront persons of power... [and] negotiate with institutions..."[61] These practical measures are foundational in offering care, particularly in the context of this current debate within Adventism. Consequently, when Idealists argue for the dismantling of Regional Conferences — resulting in the removal of a significant pillar that serves to bolster the agency of the black Adventist community — without thoughtful consideration of the psychosocial ramifications of what they seek, this could be a case of caregiving malpractice.

Perhaps a final word should be reserved for the very act of resisting the evil of racism. In the context of this text, resistance gave birth to Regional Conferences, but now these conferences are viewed as dated, embarrassing, and an obstacle to unity and outreach efforts. History has shown that when advocating for their rights, blacks are typically viewed by whites and some blacks as agitators, militants, trouble-makers, and radicals — a derivative of the "angry black man syndrome." This syndrome conveys the perception that black men are prone to become indignant when they feel they have been treated as second-class citizens. The term is often used by white racists to describe black men who protested against racism and oppression, and as a pejorative. It is also used to dismiss expression of legitimate grievances.[62] Additionally, resistance is often perceived as aggression, and aggression, in turn, is generally viewed negatively.

Practical theologian Kathleen J. Greider challenges the prevailing misconception of aggression as solely a negative force. She emphasizes its ambiguity and relationality and insists that aggression must be reckoned with since failure to do so creates

---

61 Poling, 175-177.
62 "Angry Black Man Syndrome," Wikibin website, http://wikibin.org/articles/angry-black-man-syndrome.html (accessed 12/28/10).

distortions of aggression.[63] The main cause of distorted aggression Greider argues "is the trauma of personal and social relationships of domination and subjugation that suppress constructive aggressiveness in individuals and in groups."[64] This keen insight on aggression offers a way of understanding the name-calling associated with resistance, since the walls of separation erected by racism are designed to deter fellowship and community, and any hope of transformative protest displayed by the constructive use of aggression, is nullified. Though aggression is often solely viewed as injurious, its ambiguous quality means that it can lead to both the cause and the cessation of violence, Greider illuminates. It is this latter aspect of aggression that coheres with resistance — a nondestructive aggression. A defense against this nondestructive aggression is the name-and-shame approach used by some whites in the United States. So, being "too militant," says Greider "is one of the major weapons in the extermination program against women's aggression."[65] Though in this work Greider is referencing aggression directed against women, her sentiments are just as relevant for any group having to cope with the silencing of their nondestructive aggression.

Militancy against oppressive forces in the form of nondestructive aggression is an integral part of the Christian tradition. In her reflection on Christ's aggressive outbursts in the Temple recorded in three of the Gospels (Matt. 21:11-13; Mark 11:14-16; John 2:14-16), Ellen White describes how he was repulsed at how the secular had invaded the sacred in the fraudulent and abusive activities of religious leaders, and how the poor were distressed by

---

[63] Kathleen J. Greider, *Reckoning with Aggression: Theology, Violence, and Vitality* (Louisville, KY: Westminster John Knox Press, 1997), 6, 13.

[64] Greider, *Reckoning with Aggression*, 48.

[65] Kathleen J. Greider "Too Militant"? Aggression, Gender, and the Construction of Justice," in *Through the Eyes of Women: Insights for Pastoral Care*, ed. Jeanne Stevenson Moessner (Minneapolis: Fortress Press, 1996), 13. Greider eloquently expresses the relevance of militancy in faith communities as follows: "For people and communities of faith, militancy is sometimes necessary not only as an expression of psychological self-esteem but of spiritual 'faith-esteem,' making people more able to stand by their prayerfully considered beliefs," Greider, "Too Militant"? Aggression, Gender, and the Construction of Justice," 137.

the underhandedness in which their piety was being perverted. Her graphic portrayal reads as follows:

> With searching glance, Christ takes in the scene before Him as He stands upon the steps of the temple court. With prophetic eye He looks into futurity, and sees not only years, but centuries and ages. He sees how priests and rulers will turn the needy from their right, and forbid that the gospel shall be preached to the poor. He sees how the love of God will be concealed from sinners, and men will make merchandise of His grace. As He beholds the scene, indignation, authority, and power are expressed in His countenance. The attention of the people is attracted to Him. The eyes of those engaged in their unholy traffic are riveted upon His face. They cannot withdraw their gaze. They feel that this Man reads their inmost thoughts, and discovers their hidden motives. Some attempt to conceal their faces, as if their evil deeds were written upon their countenances, to be scanned by those searching eyes. The confusion is hushed. The sound of traffic and bargaining has ceased. The silence becomes painful. A sense of awe overpowers the assembly. It is as if they were arraigned before the tribunal of God to answer for their deeds.[66]

Importantly, White portrays Christ as prophetically gazing past the religious sacrilege in the Jerusalem temple of his day, to centuries of oppression, intolerance, and other human indignities, all of which cause him immense anguish, which he displaces onto the violators before him. This articulation of a present and future epiphany is the embodiment of White's writings, a fact generally embraced by Adventists. Hence, this passage conveys to Adventists the pathos with which Christ regards all human suffering, and the consternation and ultimate retribution perpetrators of such suffering will have to endure. Christ's example of nondestructive aggression is a reminder that such a posture is still required wherever forces of oppression lurk. Though it should not be deduced that all who pose the question regarding the appropriateness of Regional Conferences post-segregation are being necessarily oppressive; rather it is a call

---

[66] White, *Desire of Ages* (Mountain View, CA: Pacific Press Publishing Association, 1940), 157f.

for sensitivity surrounding all the issues and nuances inherent in such discourse.

Age of Obama Argument

British Prime Minister Harold Wilson notably remarked that "A week is a long time in politics," a fact that all politicians ignore at their peril. On November 4, 2008, the world witnessed a historic event of immense proportion, with the election of Barack Obama as the 44th president of the United States. As the first person of color to assume the post, the essence of newspaper headlines that followed declared his to be a post-racial presidency, but two years later was there buyer's remorse? In his article entitled "White Flight," nationally acclaimed journalist Ronald Brownstein analyzed exit polls from the Nov 2, 2010, mid-term elections. His opening sentence is revealing: "By any standard, white voters' rejection of Democrats in November's elections was daunting and even historic."[67] Brownstein reports that 60 percent of whites nationally voted for Republicans (43 percent in 2008) and only 37 percent for Democrats, the president's party, and these numbers may even understate the level of white flight. Alarmingly for President Obama, most white voters expressed profound disappointment with his performance and hostility towards his policies, including the new healthcare law. Minority voters shared precisely opposite opinions. Ironically, minority voters expressed more optimism about the future and the government than did white voters, even though their communities were more impacted by the recession.[68] To rephrase the proverbial words of Cornell West, "Race Still Matters!"[69]

Further evidence that President Obama has not ushered in a post-racial era is the fact that 60 percent of whites have racist views of blacks and believe that blacks are lazier than other groups. When given three ways to consider the causes of racial inequality — racism and discrimination by whites, inherent inferiority of blacks, and

---

[67] Ronald Brownstein, "White Flight," *The National Journal online* ed. http://nationaljournal.com/magazine/in-2012-obama-may-need-a-new-coalition-20110105?page=1 (accessed 1/7/11).
[68] Brownstein, "White Flight."
[69] Cornel West, *Race Matters* (New York: Vintage Books, 1994), xvi.

black character and behavioral flaws — whites overwhelmingly chose the latter, reaffirming centuries-old myths, stereotypes and false science used to justify slavery.[70] These differing perceptions of race have led lawyer and professor Roy L. Brooks to emphatically declare, "The Age of Obama is not, in my view, postracial. It is racial."[71]

What the previous statistics reveal is a less than glowing depiction of the state of race relations in the United States. It would also suggest that those who argue for change to the administrative structures of the SDA Church in the United States, using the Obama presidency as a rationale, may be premature, if not misguided. There is no doubt that this country is a much different place than it was after the gains of the Civil Rights Movement, but neither can it be said to be free of the legacy and cost of the past. Antiracism scholar Tim Wise argues that the then-and-now difference of the Obama presidency is the ending of Racism 1.0 (racial hatred that led to acts of aggression like lynching) and the beginning of Racism 2.0 (where the exceptional black is permitted to ascend the social and political structures to ease white fears). Brooks and Wise diverge as they diagnose the racial divide that challenges this country. For Wise, white people need to take responsibility for addressing their

---

[70] Tim Wise, *Between Barack and a Hard Place: Racism and White Denial in the Age of Obama* (San Francisco: City Lights Books, 2009), 93-95. Others view the age of Obama through the lens of his speech on race, with its post-racial tone; claiming that he offered a sanitized version of the history of racial injustice in the United States and used harmful racist stereotypes. Amy L. Heyse and Ebony A. Uley, "Barack Obama's (Im)Perfect Union: An Analysis of the Strategic Success and Failures of His Speech on Race," *The Western Journal of Black Studies* 33.3 (2009): 153-163. Christopher Metzler interprets the speech as a Faustian bargain of placating whites, while pandering to blacks. Christopher J. Metzler, "Barack Obama's Faustian Bargain and the Fight for America's Racial Soul," *Journal of Black Studies* 40.3 (Jan. 2010): 395-410.

[71] His assertion is based on the many disparate resources that the black community must contend with, including income, employment, health, education, housing, and criminal justice disparities. These capital deficiencies have led to a racial dynamic of contrast – racial success and racial despair. Roy L. Brooks, *Racial Justice in the Age of Obama* (Princeton: Princeton University Press, 2009), xiii.

racism and white privilege. They must learn to listen to, and believe, what ethnic minorities say about racism, and they must be willing to cope with the disturbing history of this nation on matters of race. Brooks, on the other hand, argues that it is the capital deficiencies faced by blacks in net household income, housing, health, the judicial system, and education, more than white racism, which is at the root of the race problem. Brooks does not dismiss the power of structure and culture in perpetuating racism but is convinced that both internal (values and behaviors) and external (racism) factors contribute to this disparity in resources.[72]

Significant to this debate, Brooks' four racial justice theories of Traditionalism, Reformism, Limited Separation and Critical Race Theory in assessing the conflicting racial dynamics of racial success and despair in the Age of Obama, offer insight into why Pragmatists are intent on keeping Regional Conferences. Traditionalism sees danger in a society that celebrates racial differences over racial similarities, and it contends that capital deficiencies in today's black community persist because of circumstances for which blacks themselves are solely responsible. Since traditionalists do not accept that external factors sustain disparate resources, they offer few external prescriptions. Reformists view race as still mattering in post-civil-rights America since a history of discrimination and stereotyping contribute to uneven resource distribution, and internal factors outweigh external ones in sustaining this disparity. They believe in ongoing civil rights reform and economic remedies from the government, as well as self-help programs operating in the black community.

Limited separation is voluntary, racial, non-exclusive isolation, which presents blacks with the option of living and working in their own communities and institutions or in mainstream ones – it is racial solidarity without nation building. It is grounded in black liberation theology, where one can be both black and Christian. It also believes that an undue burden has been placed on racial integration and assimilation since whites are more reluctant to concede power on the basis of self-interest than they are racists. Limited separatists assert that it is illusionary to invest excessive energy pursuing racial integration since it has been deleterious to

---

[72] Wise, *Between Barack and a Hard Place*, 116-136; Brooks, xiv.

blacks. They also contend that scarce resources have been transferred out of black communities, as stable black families exit them, and with their exit have come urban blight, isolation, disaffection, and disease. Limited separatists favor black self-help institutions like black businesses, historically black colleges and universities, aided by federal funds.[73]

In my view, Regional Conferences, with some qualification, fall under the rubric of the limited separation model of racial justice theory, because of fierce independence and self-determination efforts of blacks to remain within the SDA Church structure, while at the same time retaining self-governance. While Regional Conferences have significant degrees of autonomy, they nevertheless are a part of the church's organizational hierarchy to which they have fiduciary, doctrinal, and church polity obligations — to the Unions they are located in, the NAD, and ultimately to the GC. So, while limited separatism does not completely capture the structural essence of Regional Conferences, it does, however, offer a useful interpretative framework through which they can best be understood in this post-civil rights era.

It should be noted that while he was perhaps not thinking of Brooks' limited separation formulation, Rock emphatically rejects such a characterization: "Black Conferences are not separatist."[74] However, in a book edited by Rock, one author embraces the term "separatist." The author notes that given the racism of church leaders in the 1940s, blacks "accepted a partial separatist status as a means of working successfully for the Lord among their own people."[75] I see Pragmatists as are vulnerable on this point since they are far too defensive in denouncing as inaccurate any use of the word "segregation" to define Regional Conferences. As earlier stated, Regional Conferences are not segregated, but they are populated predominantly by blacks. So, while calling Regional Conferences segregated is wholly inaccurate, they are nevertheless

---

[73] Brooks, 14-21; 35-43; 63-73.

[74] He continues: Regional Conferences "are united with their union offices and local sister conferences by doctrine and policy, are highly productive, and generously integrated." Rock, "Revisiting 'The Obama Message.'"

[75] Rock, *Perspectives*, 136.

separate or distinct from any other SDA administrative structure. Du Bois argued that blacks should not resist the word segregation: "there should never be an opposition to segregation pure and simple unless that segregation does involve discrimination."[76] This resistance to words like "separate" and "separatist" may be due in part to black Adventists not wishing to be labeled with a word that has such a negative connotation in U.S. history, and perhaps not being willing to be linked to an Adventist form of Black Nationalism of the 1960s. Limited separatists have no such qualms with the use of the word "segregated." They advance a "black nationalism" of racial solidarity, absent of nation building. The religious motto often associated with this thinking is that of being "unapologetically black and Christian at the same time."[77]

Furthermore, similar to Limited Separatists, Pragmatists also have difficulty with the claims of integration. Indeed, a mantra of Pragmatists is a clarification of what integration actually is, a version of which is echoed by Rock: "The opposite of segregation (exclusion from fellowship) is de-segregation (open access), not cultural blending [integration] or amalgamation."[78] Additionally, Pragmatists share a burden for the wider black community plagued by deficits in resources and disempowered by institutional racism. These communities are viewed by black Adventists as mission fields into which they have been sent, and in which many of them still reside. To some extent, Pragmatists also believe, like Limited Separatists, that it will take maximum effort by the blacks for their community to overcome the external and internal elements of racism. At the epicenter of this fight for social justice within the black community has always been the black church. Historically, the black church has been regarded as the most successful of all black

---

[76] David Levering Lewis, *W. E. B. Du Bois: A Reader* (New York: Henry Holt and Company, 1866), 557.

[77] Brooks, 64f. A subtle form of Black Nationalism could be implied in Rock's rationale for a black Adventist theology, since "black leadership is greatly restricted with respect to the harmonizing of theoretical proclamation and social practice." Rock, *Institutional Loyalty versus Racial Freedom*, 160.

[78] Calvin B. Rock, "Regional Conferences: An Exhibition of Unity in Diversity," *The Regional Voice Magazine*, 2010 Special General Conference Issue, 8.

programs and institutions designed to address the needs of blacks. Brooks argues that this success has been essentially due to the black church's undiluted focus under the weight of racial integration. Ever since its formation, the black church has been left unscathed at the end of Jim Crow, and both Pragmatists and Limited Separatists see no need for it not to continue its regenerative work within the black community.[79]

The fourth racial justice theory approach outlined by Brooks is critical race theory, which utilizes narrative form to convey difficult messages and raise racial awareness. It focuses on racial domination and disparity, enforced by white hegemony and privileged positions. The theory comports with a less prescriptive and more diagnostic view of racial power differentials, believing that simply exposing these relationships is sufficient. Theorists of this model agree that the major external determinant for the maintenance of disparity of resources for blacks is the absence of advocates from outside of the black community. The black-white binary is rejected by critical race theorists, as all disenfranchised groups with their own civil rights challenges are clustered into one. Brooks believes that this approach has some merit, but its approach towards racism in society is deficient. To deliver the more lasting impact, Brooks envisages an amalgam of all four post-civil rights theories.[80]

I return to Brooks's limited separation to highlight the fact that advocates of this model regard themselves as no more Balkanized in U.S. society than are ethnic groupings such as a Koreatown and Chinatown in Los Angeles, California. Also, because they view integration as optional, few solutions are offered to racial subordination and the restricted access faced in integrated structures. According to Brooks, no solutions are offered because, given the potency of the "interest convergence principle," no solutions are possible; otherwise, there would be no need for limited separation in the first place. In the context of this book, this belief that no amount of problem-solving will cure society's racial inequities is a troubling aspect of the Pragmatists' position.

---

[79] Brooks, 75, 78f, 77.
[80] Brooks, 89-108.

However, history, the failed efforts of many, and the intransigent nature of humankind appear to be on their side.[81]

As will be argued in the next chapter, Pragmatists have an almost fatalistic approach to ongoing racism – little is ever going to change! A biblical warrant for such a stance is found in Christ's response to Judas' outcry that the alabaster box of perfume should have been put to a more humanitarian use, rather than be squandered in a feet-washing ritual: "The poor you will always have with you" (Matt. 26:11, NIV). Since poverty is one of many social ills, including racism, that plague human society, Christ's words affirm the presence of the poor as well as racism and presumably, the ongoing fight to eradicate both.

Summary

I have attempted to present the central arguments of Idealists in their effort to dissolve Regional Conferences since they are anachronistic. The legitimacy of their quest is bolstered by the fact that in general, institutions must constantly reinvent themselves if they are to remain relevant in an ever-changing world. But 'the more things change, the more they stay the same,' which I take to mean external change taking place around us may not necessarily lead to attitudinal change, which in the end is at the heart of the debate. Can the ethic of love and unity overcome centuries of

---

[81] The fight against racism has been pursued with no more vigor than was reflected in the life and work of W. E. B. Du Bois. Yet, a Pulitzer-winning historian concludes this about Du Bois' life: "In the course of his long turbulent career, then, W. E. B. Du Bois attempted virtually every possible solution to the problem of twentieth-century racism – scholarship, propaganda, integration, cultural and economic separatism, politics, international communism, expatriation, third-world solidarity. First had come culture and education for the elites; then the ballot for the masses; then economic democracy; and finally all these solutions in the service of global racial parity and economic justice. An extraordinary mind of color in a racialized century, Du Bois was possessed of a principled impatience with what he saw as the egregious failings of American democracy that drove him, decade by decade, to the paradox of defending totalitarianism in the service of a global ideal of economic and social justice." David Levering Lewis, *W. E.B. Du Bois: The Fight for Equality and the American Century 1919-1963* (New York: Henry Holt and Company, 2000), 571.

bigotry and dehumanization of blacks by whites without justice? Can the end of legal segregation displace discrimination and white privilege without ongoing effort by whites to join in the liberation efforts of blacks? Finally, can the election of the first black president of the United States possibly turn the page of racism making the country post-racial? Perhaps limited separation may have to suffice until serious efforts at racial reconciliation are undertaken.

Arguments for Preserving the Current Regional Conference Structure in the SDA Church in the United States

The dominant group in a society is often shocked to find that subordinate groups remember the harms done to them, which often resurface as the primary basis of their attitudes and behaviors toward the dominant group.[1]

Arguments of Church Leaders and Administrators

Winston Churchill reportedly once remarked that "There is nothing wrong with change, if it is in the right direction."[2] The challenge of Churchill's statement lies in the all-important question of who is determining the "right direction." For Idealists, the right direction is change to a more integrated administrative structure, though parity in all levels of the administrative hierarchy may be harder to achieve. For Pragmatists, change is more administrative parity, while structural accommodation is maintained. This stance of Pragmatists will be outlined through three essential arguments: Cultural Pluralism, Blaming the Victim, and White Privilege. There is a plurality of voices among Pragmatists in defense of Regional Conferences, but none have joined the debate with more persuasive rhetoric than Calvin B. Rock. His D.Min. and Ph.D. dissertations, as well as articles in church publications, have sought to advance a rationale for the presence and preservation of Regional Conferences, even as a chorus beckoning for change has been building to a crescendo. Rock's response to this call for change is the most cogent of either side of the debate; but as will be argued, it is not without critics.

Despite Rock's impressive articulation of the need for Regional Conferences as a form of structural accommodation to

---

[1] Ronald W. Walter, *The Price of Racial Reconciliation* (Ann Arbor, MI: The University of Michigan Press, 2008), 5.

[2] "Change Quotes," http://thinkexist.com/quotations/change/ (accessed 1/7/11).

blacks, as a means of fulfilling the competing demands of institutional loyalty over against racial freedom, the arc of his successful professional career within the SDA Church has left one question unanswered. As previously observed, Rock's voice of protest was pronounced in the 1970s' debate over continued structural accommodation in the form of Regional Unions, which ultimately failed to materialize. Having served the GC, first as president of Oakwood College, and later until his retirement as a Vice-president of the GC, his voice of protest was largely muted. As a Niebuhrian, Rock would likely explain his lack of protest while serving at the GC as "politics being the art of the possible."[3] Since retirement, however, Rock was at the forefront of a failed attempt by black members to establish the first Regional Conference on the West Coast. On November 19, 2003, a two-person delegation of Charlie Joe Morgan and Reginald Robinson, members of the newly minted Regional Fellowship, had their request for a feasibility study on establishing a Regional Conference declined by the PUC executive committee.

During the late 1970s push for Regional Unions in the NAD, Rock was distilling his thoughts in his Ph.D. dissertation, the thesis of which was to disconfirm any notion that black demands for further autonomy within Adventism were due to the redressing of racial grievances. Instead, argues Rock, the request for increased self-governance was enshrined in the sociological and moral imperatives of the "cultural pluralism" principle, in order that blacks could be at ease within the largely white denomination of Adventism in the United States. Rock defines cultural pluralism as "one of the three major theories or models of assimilation at work in American society"; the other two are Anglo-conformity and the melting pot.[4] His usage conveys a conventional rendition of a

---

[3] The full quote reads as follows: "This life of ours is like politics more than it is like art, and politics is the art of the possible." H. Richard Niebuhr, *The Responsible Self: An Essay in Christian Moral Philosophy* (New York: Harper & Row Publishers, 1963), 52.

[4] It should be noted that modern acculturation models, as previously cited, no longer reference cultural pluralism or the melting pot. Calvin B. Rock, "Cultural Pluralism (A Sociological Reality) and Black Unions" (D.Min. diss., Divinity School of Vanderbilt University, 1978), 1f, 55.

minority living within a majority culture while preserving their cultural distinctiveness and having their ethnic heritage and traditions accepted by the majority population. Rock reviews the history of black protest and resistance within Adventism covered previously, and which he summarizes in three distinct periods: 1909 to 1929, fighting for participation; 1929-1944, fighting for accommodation; 1969-1978, fighting for autonomy.[5]

As a form of assimilation, Rock believes that cultural pluralism best describes what people of color face in actuality. He writes: "for racial minorities, pluralism is not occasional; it is the overwhelming reality, and the darker the skin, the more obvious that reality becomes."[6] This social reality of being identified by one's skin color results in boundary enforcement that leads to structural separation, fewer primary contacts (in social settings like church) and more secondary contacts (meeting the postal worker, for example). Rock then deduces that since primary contact is the basis for the assimilation process, including Anglo-conformity and the melting pot, a lack of such contact makes pluralism inevitable. This negative push towards structural separation is countered, argues Rock, with a positive attraction toward group attachment, a point acknowledged by Tatum in the previous chapter. Rock reinforces his insistence on the inevitability of pluralism by quoting The Kerner Commission Report, which was charged with investigating the motivations for the race riots of 1967 in the U.S.[7] The report concluded that the United States is "moving towards two societies, one black, one white — separate and unequal."[8] This sociological phenomenon is a pivotal argument used by Rock in most of his writings in defense of Regional Conferences.

Rock references some of the same statements by Ellen White quoted earlier in this book to illustrate her pragmatic approach in addressing a deteriorating racial climate when she finally sanctioned segregated congregations — what Rock calls "structural peculiarity."

---

[5] Rock, "Cultural Pluralism," 14.
[6] Rock, "Cultural Pluralism," 62.
[7] Rock, "Cultural Pluralism," 63, 64f.
[8] "Report of the National Advisory Commission on Civil Disorders," http://www.eisenhowerfoundation.org/docs/kerner.pdf (accessed 1/7/11).

He then reasons that it is too much to ask a faith tradition or individual within that tradition to swim against the tide of social norms. As he asserts: "it is not reasonable to expect the Christian religion or any one of its segments to reverse the tide that time has fashioned."[9] Rock's conclusion that the church is incapable of effecting a course correction in the midst of social inequities is unnecessarily fatalistic since it undermines a central Christian tenet: "With man this is impossible; but with God all things are possible" (Matt. 19:26, NIV). Niebuhr speaks to this sense of fear of the impossible when he writes:

> Furthermore, there must always be a religious element in the hope of a just society. Without the ultrarational hopes and passions of religion no society will ever have the courage to conquer despair and attempt the impossible; for the vision of a just society is an impossible one, which can be approximated only by those who do not regard it as impossible. The truest visions of religion are illusions, which may be partially realised by being resolutely believed. For what religion believes to be true is not wholly true but ought to be true; and may become true if its truth is not doubted.[10]

Finally, Rock appeals to scriptural mandates as validation for the cultural pluralism model and the embrace of Regional Unions. The Apostle Paul's problem-solving is invoked, as illustrated by his mediation of ethnic tensions between Jews and Gentiles. Rock observes the outcome to be one in which Jews and Gentiles remained "separate and autonomous culturally and... structurally while yet maintaining consensus and unity in doctrine and brotherhood."[11] Given this example, Rock states that black Adventists who are members of Regional Conferences have no reason to be ashamed. Furthermore, Rock argues, since the church is a mere reflection of

---

[9] Rock, "Cultural Pluralism," 84. He expands further by noting that "Such a conclusion in my opinion is not a negative statement about Christianity or its founder. It is, as I think the case of Ellen White demonstrates, a commentary on the inability of the church to formulate aggressive social policy in a sociological and political vacuum." Rock, "Cultural Pluralism," 92.

[10] Reinhold Niebuhr, *Moral Man Immoral Society*, 81.

[11] Rock, "Cultural Pluralism," 97.

society, it is not unreasonable to find structural accommodation in its midst, since they proliferate in society, and to think otherwise is to delude oneself.[12]

Since Rock's Ph.D. dissertation arguments have previously been enunciated, I will summarize his more recent arguments which bear resemblance to his previous writings, with few exceptions. In an article entitled, "Black Seventh-day Adventists and Structural Accommodations," published in 1996, Rock essentially gave a précis of his 1978 D.Min., dissertation without updating his literature review.[13] Such an update would have provided him with a more informed view of the current thinking on acculturation models and their connection to social identity and cognition. For example, based on the most widely utilized acculturation model by J. W. Berry, Rock's focus on "cultural pluralism" could be replaced with Berry's fourth acculturation strategy of integration, which is akin to biculturalism, in which the individual holds in tension both his/her own culture while engaging and adapting aspects of the prevailing culture. Social scientists like Amado Padilla and William Perez take the position that decades of research into acculturation models are limited since they have an overreliance on: 1) an inert view of intergroup relations; 2) a principle of a uniform acculturation process among all out-groups; 3) a reliance on self-report language, practices and patterns.[14]

In his 2010 article in defense of Regional Conferences, Rock continues some of his now-familiar themes, such as cultural pluralism, unchanged racial attitudes of whites towards blacks, the Kerner Commission Report, the absence of social integration, and Hans Küng's reference to unity over uniformity, but he adds new rationales. He illustrates the challenge of social distance, which

---

[12] To those who are Pollyannaish, Rock offers this sardonic response: "Those whites and blacks who wish to hold on to their dreams are entitled to the privilege, but must the work of God suffer while we vainly work and wait for the structure of a whole society to change?" Rock, "Cultural Pluralism," 113.

[13] Rock, *Perspectives*, 119-25.

[14] Amado M. Padilla and William Perez, "Acculturation, Social Identity, and Social Cognition: A New Perspective," *Hispanic Journal of Behavioral Sciences* 25.1 (February 2003): 50, http://www.stanford.edu/~apadilla/PadillaPerez03a.pdf (accessed 1/7/11).

results in blacks being educated in all-black schools, fewer mixed marriages involving blacks, and the pervasive pattern of white flight. Rock sees merit in the homogeneous unity principle, the belief that converts to Christianity prefer not to cross cultural and ethnic barriers to become members. He sees no contradiction in being self-determined and being loyal to the denomination. Rock then draws the comparison between Regional Conferences and the United Methodist Church's Central Jurisdiction to illustrate the tremendous strides made by the former over the latter. He also reaffirms the importance of not dissolving a structure that exists for the health and wellbeing of a minority, in order to conform to social mores.[15]

Writing in the area of diversity, Leslie Pollard — clergyman, church administrator, and president of Oakwood University — poses the following question in an address at the October 1999 NAD Summit on Race, "What Do We Do with Differences?"[16] This question has been answered in three ways: by "reject-the-idea," being "difference-blind," and affirming that "difference-doesn't-matter." From Pollard's perspective, diversity explores difference in the context of inequality. He urges an ethno-sensitive approach as the Christian norm rather than the ethnocentrism of society. Such an approach will view difference as an opportunity and not an obstacle; it would embrace the celebration of difference, and it charts a path towards cross-cultural competence.[17] In an earlier article, Pollard, who is a Pragmatist, favoring the continuation of Regional Conferences, posed some practical diversity-related questions. He shows concern for how successful ethnic groups will be in balancing the desire for mission particularity, while being cross-cultural in outreach. Another question goes to the heart of the current debate, namely, what forms of structure will be tolerated and how will their effectiveness be determined?[18]

---

[15] Rock, "Regional Conferences," 8-10.

[16] Les Pollard, "What Do We Do With Differences?" *Adventist Review* (November 2, 2000): http://www.adventistreview.org/2000-1549/story1.html (accessed 8/17/10).

[17] Pollard, "What Do We Do With Differences?"

[18] Les Pollard, "The Cross-Culture: Challenging a church as it begins a new millennium," *Adventist Review*, February 2000, 24.

Like Rock, church administrator Joseph McCoy also responded to Johnsson's "Four Big Questions," and his arguments in favor of Regional Conferences are not dissimilar. It should be noted that McCoy was a former Regional Conference president, and he presently serves as an administrator in the Office of Regional Conference Ministry, which no doubt influences his thinking on the subject. McCoy first acknowledges the racialized nature of U.S. society, though he concedes that the majority are not racist. He punctuates the commonly held view among Pragmatists that Regional Conferences are not segregated, but are a part of the church's organizational hierarchy. He is suspicious of the Idealists' argument for more "togetherness," which he views as code for dismantling Regional Conferences. McCoy even accuses church leaders of being bent on pursuing a divide and conquer strategy, pitting black members against their leaders in these Regional Conferences. Pulling no punches, McCoy concludes that church leaders in general and Johnsson's article in particular, seek to undermine Regional Conferences by questioning their relevance, while at the same time assuring black leaders that they have no hidden agenda to dismantle their institutions. This approach of church leaders, thinks McCoy, is disingenuous, for while it "may be well-intentioned…it can be disarming, intoxicating, deceptive, and counter-productive if the issue and the implications are only considered in a cursory manner."[19]

The final pragmatist to be considered is the revered church administrator and former NAD president Charles Bradford, who graciously offered a confidential draft document for use in this book. As the only person of color to serve as president of the NAD, Bradford is in a unique position to offer a critique of those who seek to dissolve Regional Conferences since, as discussed previously, he was a major beneficiary of black protest in the 1970s. His election as president of the NAD in 1979 effectively nullified further voices of protest after the GC failed to approve Regional Unions the previous year. In his article, Bradford appeals to church leaders to engage in an honest and transparent debate over the future of Regional Conferences. Bradford asserts that the discussion is surreptitious

---

[19] Joseph W. McCoy, "Adventist Review: Readers Respond to Four Big Questions."

and suggestive, leaving the false impression that "their regional brethren [black leaders] are guilty of troubling Israel, sustainers of a separatist movement."[20]

To counter this victim-blaming approach of church leaders, Bradford reviews the history of the mission to Southern blacks, the "church's glacial progress in race relations," and the historic 1944 Spring Meeting of the GC, in which approval was given to formulate Regional Conferences.[21] As he assesses this history, Bradford insists that:

> Regional conferences are not a protest movement. They are not organized in 'a fit of pique'... [they] grew out of this experience of trial and error, of searching for 'a better way'... Decisions were not made in a dark corner but at the highest level of Church governance, the General Conference Committee. There was plenty of sunshine. The formation of regional conferences cannot be called a separatist movement... Leaders must tell it like it is: Regional Conferences were recommended by the General Conference... But now after 60 years of progress and growth it seems that our leaders want to revise history.[22]

His frustration at the tone and tenor in which the debate is being framed is evident. In Bradford's view, church leaders are attempting to whitewash the historical record concerning these conferences, and as a consequence, place the blame for disunion on black members who constitute Regional Conferences. This elder statesman returns to his administrative moorings to remind Idealists that each organizational entity has autonomy to orchestrate and implement strategies in pursuit of the church's mission, so long as it is done with respect and collegiality. Moreover, each organizational

---

[20] Bradford alludes to the biblical encounter in which King Ahab of Israel accuses the prophet Elijah of being a trouble maker, following years of drought, which the prophet had predicted (1 King 18:16-18). The author expands by observing that "when young people ask church leaders about regional conferences the leader leaves the impression that the regional brethren pulled out and they may return at any time." Charles E. Bradford, "Dissolution of Regional Conferences," letter to church administrators, June 19, 2010, 1.

[21] Bradford, "Dissolution of Regional Conferences," 2.

[22] Bradford, "Dissolution of Regional Conferences," 5.

entity is entitled to the recognition and support due to all other duly authorized entities, and this includes Regional Conferences.[23]

Assessment of the Essential Arguments

Having marshalled the different arguments made by some Pragmatists in defense of the continuation of Regional Conferences, it may be wise to recall the second rule of negotiation, namely, "When you are explaining you are losing."[24] In recent years, Pragmatists have found themselves in the spotlight, fielding questions on the relevance and necessity of Regional Conferences, which were an antidote for an ailing country diagnosed with the terminal disease of racism. To a large extent, United States society has led the charge in righting some of the more egregious legacies of this country's historic racial injury. Lagging some distance behind has been the Christian church. My previous assertion on this matter is in keeping with the sentiment of Rosado, who laments the fact that, "To stay relevant, the church must not only respond to change; it must also anticipate change, for change challenges leadership to deal more effectively with differences."[25]

This deficiency in anticipating change is not the exclusive domain of Pragmatists and Idealists but is one of the perennial blights that afflict church leaders in particular and organizational leadership in general. The historical successes of Regional Conferences are beyond dispute. It is no small feat to transform the SDA Church's mission among blacks in the U.S. from its humble beginnings to where it stands today. For this achievement, the countless leaders of the nine Regional Conferences over the period of their existence must be celebrated. But, surely some of these leaders currently serving, or those who are no longer in office must have at least anticipated a clamor for change, a dialogue about the next step forward, or a conversation regarding the most effective structure for a multicultural society. Yet, what is true of the black leaders in these

---

[23] Bradford, "Dissolution of Regional Conferences," 5.

[24] Zillow Mortgage Marketplace, "When you are Explaining You are Losing," http://www.zillow.com/blog/mortgage/2009/05/22/zillow-mortgage-marketplace-when-you-are-explaining-you-are-losing/ (accessed 12/17/10).

[25] Rosado, 120.

Regional Conferences is also applicable to church leaders up and down the organizational hierarchy of the SDA Church.

This anticipatory deficiency is, for Old Testament theologian Walter Brueggemann, a lack of prophetic imagination. Among the prophetic tasks, writes Brueggemann is the requirement to "bring to expression the new realities against the more visible ones of the old order."[26] Creative expression of what might be, over against what is, is an indispensable trait of religious leaders. To this end, the SCPC field regards the prophetic as one of the pastoral functions, despite Hiltner's surprising exclusion of it in his original formulation, particularly as it played a prominent role in ancient times. Howard Clinebell and Carroll Watkins Ali can be credited with rehabilitating the prophetic function within the field of SCPC, by situating it within the social action arm of pastoral ministry.[27] It is this prophetic function that is needed as the debate over Regional Conferences ensues. In this debate, Pragmatists advance three essential arguments for persisting with Regional Conferences — Cultural Pluralism, Victim-blaming, and White Privilege, to which we now turn.

Cultural Pluralism Argument

This psychosocial argument of amicable coexistence of different cultures, with their oft-competing values in a postmodern society, is the most utilized rationale by Pragmatists for the continuance of Regional Conferences. What is being inferred by cultural pluralism is the need for black Adventists to orient themselves within their own subculture for the preservation of their

---

[26] Walter Brueggemann, *The Prophetic Imagination* (Minneapolis: Fortress Press, 2001), 14.

[27] Clinebell envisaged the prophetic ministry as seeking "to change a community and its institutions so that they will support not stifle wholeness in all persons." Howard Clinebell, *Basic Types of Pastoral Care & Counseling: Resources for the Ministry of Healing and Growth* (Nashville: Abingdon Press, 1992), 40. It should be noted that Wayne Oates also saw the viability of the pastoral care field as a force in addressing social ills (e.g. racism) in a prophetic manner. Wayne Oates, *Pastoral Counseling in Social Problems: Extremism, Race, Sex, Divorce* (Philadelphia: The Westminster Press, 1966), 12.

collective ethnic identity, as they discharge their mission by proclaiming the church's message largely within the wider black community. It is this understanding that is implicit in the question posed by Rock in his Ph.D. dissertation, namely, "Can blacks be contented and faithful members of a majority white denomination [in the United States] and true to their racial commitments and identity at the same time?"[28] Pragmatists answer Rock's question in the affirmative, by referencing the Regional Conference as the antidote to this duality. Pragmatists are not alone in their assessment of the need for some form of cultural pluralism for blacks to nurture their faith and identity. Time magazine journalist David Van Biema reaffirmed this view in his assessment of religion in the United States. Biema views this cultural tension as dating back to the period of Reconstruction when blacks were either discouraged or took flight from white churches.[29]

Yet as Tillich reminds us, "no human relation exists in an empty space."[30] That empty space of limited interaction between black and white members has been a pronounced feature within the SDA Church—a fact that is often lamented by church members as they engage in this debate. Whether exacerbated or not by the Regional Conference structure, there remains a void in the nurturing of meaningful relationships within Adventist subcultures in the United States, and the current debate is but a symptom of a wider problem—one of a lack of community between blacks and whites within the Adventist faith. Indeed, if the current debate accomplishes nothing more than an increased awareness of the importance of formulating and maintaining relationships across the Adventist subcultures, then it would have accomplished much.

While social distance is a phenomenon of a racialized society, it need not be the prevailing custom of religious communities like the SDA Church. In his acclaimed book, *I and Thou*, Martin Buber

---

[28] Rock, "Institutional Loyalty Versus Racial Freedom," 3.

[29] Biema notes that "people attend the church they are used to; many minorities have scant desire to attend a white church, seeing their faith as an important vessel of cultural identity." David Van Biema, "The Color of Faith," *Time* (January 11, 2010): http://www.time.com/time/printout/0,8816,1950943,00.html (accessed 1/3/10).

[30] Tillich, 1954, 91.

offered a formulation for community relations.[31] He argues that relationships are not formed by individuals simply being enamored with each other; rather they must stand in a right relationship with God as their center, and this should invariably lead to mutually fulfilling relations with each other. Buber acknowledges that "The community is built up out of living mutual relations, but the builder is the living effective Centre."[32] Echoing Buber's call for mutually satisfying communal relations, pastoral psychotherapist Margaret Kornfeld envisages true communities to be "works in progress... always changing... always 'becoming.'"[33] This understanding of the evolving nature of community is instructive to all communities, be they secular or sacred. Within the Adventist context, particularly in the ongoing debate, evolving communities could have timely resonance, when models of collective racial identity are factored into the equation.

The racial salience — the degree to which one's race is a part of one's self-understanding and function in one's daily interpersonal exchanges — blacks achieve, through the development of a racial identity similar to the ones advanced by either Cross or Janet Helms (as discussed elsewhere), particularly during the latter stages, allows them to navigate ambiguous situations.[34] These latter stages of racial identity development assume that the individual has a positive sense

---

[31] Martin Buber, *Between Man and Man* (New York: The Macmillan Company, 1968), 15.

[32] Buber, *Between Man and Man* (New York: The Macmillan Company, 1968), 45.

[33] Kornfeld suggests that what distinguishes real from pseudo communities is their ability to communicate honestly, problem-solve effectively, and have a healthy degree of self-love so they can love others. Margaret Zipse Kornfeld, *Cultivating Wholeness: A Guide to Care and Counseling in Faith Communities* (New York: Continuum, 2000), 19, 20.

[34] A discussion of the theories of identity development by William E. Cross and Janet E. Helms can be found on pages 136 and 168 respectively. Cross and Helms have collaborated in expanding Cross' 1971 nigrescene model (the process of becoming black) of the stages of black identity development. William E. Cross, Jr., Thomas A. Parham, and Janet Helms, "The Stages of Black Identity Development: Nigrescence Models," in *Black Psychology*, ed. Reginald L. Jones (Berkley, CA: Cobb & Henry Publishers, 1991), 319-38.

of his or her racial identity, so that they now can be more accepting of their own racial identity and that of others.[35] Since racial identity is intertwined with the cultural pluralism argument, then as each successive generation of black Adventists develops such an identity, they are better able to occupy space outside of their comfort zone and live with the ambiguous nature of life's circumstances in forming community. However, the corollary to this aspect of racial identity maturation is that black institutions will still play a role in the development of racial identities for the next generation. In addition, if this process of racial identity development is true of all, if not most, ethnicities, including white identity, the burden cannot be placed on a single ethnic group to cope with life's ambiguities in community. That is to say, in the context of this debate, it should not be encumbered upon blacks solely to bear responsibility for community building or disunion within Adventism, as a focus on Regional Conferences tends to do.

Another element of the cultural pluralism argument is the belief that since racial attitudes in the country have not changed appreciably over the decades, it is divorcing oneself from reality to believe that they wills anytime soon; hence attempting to fix what is not broken [i.e., dismantle Regional Conferences] is a fool's errand. This dose of realism borders on fatalism since the Christian faith has at its center a transformational ethic in the salvific process: "Therefore, if anyone is in Christ, the new creation has come; the old has gone, the new is here!" (2 Cor. 5:17 NIV). The stock-in-trade for the Christian is the belief that re-creation is not only possible but is a present ongoing reality. I believe that this re-creation goes some way to explain (outside of Wise's racism 2.0) the election of President Barack Obama, given the prevailing racial attitudes in the country. Indeed, prior to the 2007 Iowa caucus, most blacks had serious reservations about his viability as a presidential candidate on the basis that a major white electorate was not ready to permit a black man to occupy the White House! But it happened!

---

[35] Tina Q. Richardson, Angela R. Bethea, Charlayne C. Hayling, and Claudette Williamson-Taylor, "African and Afro-Caribbean American Identity Development: Theory and Practice," *Handbook of Multicultural Counseling*, 227-39.

Furthermore, as "salt of the earth" (Matt. 5:13, NIV), Christians are supposed to be catalysts for change, depending on the degree of engagement they have in society. Perhaps no theologian has better captured the verities in this dynamic of engagement than H. Richard Niebuhr, in his classic, *Christ and Culture*. Niebuhr first states the problem: "A many-sided debate about the relations of Christianity and civilization is being carried on in our time."[36] Yet he is clear that the debate is both confusing and ambiguous, with many permutations as to what exactly is meant by "Christ" and "culture." Importantly, he sees both Christ and culture in a symbiotic relationship, as his familiar fivefold typology on the nature of this engagement indicates.[37] Niebuhr ends the book by stating that the enduring problem remains "unconcluded and inconclusive," leaving today's religious thinkers to explore the validity of this typology in a largely non-Christian and postmodern world.

However, Niebuhr has been criticized by John H. Yoder and D. M. Yeager for offering what they argue is a reductionistic approach to this Christ-culture engagement. Yoder and Yeager contend that the five approaches do not work in reality, since they make certain assumptions about culture and ignore the fact that Christ did embrace, as well as condemn, certain aspects of culture. Instead, these authors advance an approach in which the church can

---

[36] Niebuhr views the debate taking place in many arenas, one of which is the "broad questions of the church's responsibility for social order or of the need for a new separation of Christ's followers from the world." H. Richard Niebuhr, *Christ and Culture* (New York: Harper & Row Publishers, 1951), 1.

[37] Christ against culture: the most uncompromising view of culture, since it rejects culture's claims to loyalty and is isolationist in nature; the Christ of Culture: Jesus is viewed as society's savior, akin to the social gospel movement; Christ above Culture: a battle between God and humanity, and culture is amoral since God orders it, which creates a mysterious linkage between God's grace and human culture; Christ and Culture in Paradox: loyalty to Christ and responsibility to culture is advocated in an uneasy tension; and, his preferred, though by no means conclusive, option — Christ the Transformer of Culture: a hopeful view of culture, since in the cross human culture can be transformed. H. Richard Niebuhr, *Christ and Culture*, 45-229.

become a transformative agent within society, in mediating faith and social justice in what they call "Authentic Transformation."[38] More recently, NT theologian D. A. Carson also has revisioned Niebuhr's project in *Christ and Culture*, but his approach is not to argue for a specific kind of relationship between Christ and culture; rather, he assesses different positions and poses other relevant questions. Interestingly, Carson advocates that Niebuhr's typology should be viewed collectively as a single biblical, theological approach. He further observes that, while Christians are obligated to interact in society in healing and helpful ways, the church's mandate is primarily one of evangelism and discipleship.[39] Despite these criticisms, there is a general acceptance that Niebuhr correctly argues for the type of engagement in society by transformed Christians, which leads "from faithlessness and self-service to the knowledge and service of God."[40]

Sadly, this transformative participation in society has not always been displayed by Christian believers. On the contrary, while the history of the Christian church has been marked by "forgiveness and faithfulness," remarks Glen Stassen, it has also been plagued with "defensiveness and evasion." Stassen continues: "In many imaginative and often unconscious ways, we have diluted, distorted, reshaped and revised the patterns of faithfulness that are God's will in order to conform them to our unfaithful practices, or at least to tame them, so they do not confront our unfaithful practices

---

[38] The authors share Stassen's authentically transformationist relation between Christ and culture, which is simply defined as conversion. "It means the transformation of faith from distrust and idolatry to integrative faith in God." Stassen offers seven concrete practices that comport to authentic transformation and cohere with Niebuhr's historical realism and faith in God's sovereignty. They are: Jesus' love manifested in loyalty and caring; mutual servanthood; prayer; evangelism, forgiveness and inclusion; and deliverance, justice and nonviolent transforming initiatives. Glen Stassen, "A New Vision," in Stassen, in *Authentic Transformation: A New Vision of Christ and Culture*, in Stassen, Yeager, and Yoder, 191, 207-08.

[39] D. A. Carson, *Christ and Culture Revisited* (Grand Rapids, MI: William B. Eerdmans Publishing Company, 2008).

[40] H. Richard Niebuhr, *Christ and Culture*, 228.

so forcefully."[41] Stassen's critique of Christianity is relevant for Adventists as this debate continues since it was unfaithful practices that led to the formation of Regional Conferences at the outset. Even the debate itself is distorted, with its exclusive focus on Regional Conferences at the expense of the far weightier matter of racial reconciliation. So, while Pragmatists advance cultural pluralism as a basis for the continuation of Regional Conferences, they may wish to reflect on their theology of societal engagement. Is it sufficient simply to seek the betterment of the black Adventist and wider black community, or do Regional Conferences have a responsibility to society as a whole? Similarly, should they concern themselves with how the SDA Church is represented in the wider society? Rock concedes the point that God's love does transcend culture, but he adds the important caveat that this transformation of culture does not occur miraculously with dissolved cultural differences; rather, it is a time-sensitive occurrence, "often centuries," he writes ominously.[42]

Blaming the Victim Argument

The DPCC defines victimization as "an individual or group of individuals (especially one identified by a distinctive characteristic, such as race, sex, and socioeconomic background) is unjustly harmed or has their rights violated," and powerlessness is a primary feature of victimhood.[43] Philosopher Marilyn Nissim-Sabat observes that "One of the most pervasive ways in which collusion with oppression is enacted is through victim blaming."[44] In his classic text, William Ryan coined the phrase "blaming the victim" to

---

[41] Stassen, Yeager, and Yoder, 206.

[42] Rock continues: "It does so by equipping varied cultures to hold identical doctrinal beliefs while employing differing methodologies for mission." Rock, "Region Conferences," 9.

[43] D. E. Miller, "Victimization," in *Dictionary of Pastoral Care and Counseling*, 1301.

[44] Nissim-Sabat notes that "Even when oppression is acknowledged, victim blaming denies any relation between, on the one hand, oppression originating in society, such as racism, and on the other hand, inner oppression, such as self-blame or other psychic compulsions." Marilyn Nissim-Sabat, *Neither Victim nor Survivor: Thinking Towards a New Humanity* (Lanham, MD: Lexington Books, 2009), 112.

counter erroneous charges regarding the causes of poverty advanced by Daniel Patrick Moynihan in his book *The Negro Family*. Ryan defined "blaming the victim" as "applying exceptionalistic explanation to universalistic problems."[45] He notes that victim blamers often exhibit genuine regard for those they blame, and he identifies this quality as one of two rationales for a psychological understanding of the phenomenon. Blaming the victim, suggests Ryan, is an unconscious concession which gratifies the blamer's self-interest over against the interest of the victim.[46] More recently, this phenomenon has received some attention by social psychologists in their attempt to address social ills.[47]

The self-blame that Nissim-Sabat references as characteristic of individuals who are subjected to blaming the victim was explored by psychiatrist Frantz Fanon in his books *Black Skin White Masks* and *The Wretched of the Earth*. In these books, Fanon uses psychoanalytical theory to explain how the black experience of living in a white world is fraught with feelings of inadequacy and dependency. Consequently, he argues for a re-identification process from whiteness to blackness, which can lead to blacks freeing themselves from both the inferiority that their colonizers forced on

---

[45] William Ryan, *Blaming The Victim* (New York: Pantheon Books, 1971), 19, 5,

[46] Ryan, 6, 26.

[47] Their studies reveal two distinctive forms of victim blaming. One is victim blaming which is understood to be "an internal attribution; individuals who suffer are held responsible for their own predicaments." The second distinction is society blaming, defined as "an external attribution; societal conditions are held accountable for the sufferings of an individual." Charles L. Mulford, Motoko Y. Lee, and Stephen C. Sapp, "Victim-Blaming and Society-Blaming Scales for Social Problems," *Journal of Applied Social Psychology* 26.15 (1996): 1324. The attribution theory of social psychologist F. Heider, from which the notion of victim blaming has been studied, posits that "individuals make internal attributions when they identify a person's supposed personal characteristics as the cause of her or his behavior or circumstances and external attributions when they identify the environment and the situation as causes for a person's behavior or circumstances." Lee M. Johnson, Rehan Mullick, and Charles Mulford, "General versus Specific Victim Blaming," *The Journal of Social Psychology* 142.2 (2002): 249.

them, as well as from the self-blaming and self-victimization motivated by oppression.[48] I can see Pragmatists argue that Fanon's re-identification process took place within and among black Adventists as they fought for the right to organize themselves into Regional Conferences, and hence they are generally free of the internal consequences of blaming the victim, yet the external consequences remain.

Pragmatists contend that implicit in the current debate is a victim-blaming strategy, whereby blacks are held responsible for the current state of racial separation within the SDA church in the United States. The upshot is that whites are therefore absolved of any culpability for the past or present actions of whites that may have contributed to reinforcing racial separation. With the arguments and language used by Idealists, including some degree of historical revisionism and minimizing, Pragmatists detect a scapegoating of Regional Conferences. Pastoral theologian and psychotherapist Pamela Cooper-White acknowledges that the tendency of perpetrators to blame their victims is a standard defense against assuming responsibility for the perpetration.[49] Consequently, Pragmatists believe that a way to resist this blaming-the-victim tactic is to challenge current church leaders to acknowledge the church's record of racial discrimination, to avoid minimizing the history of Regional Conferences, and perhaps to take responsibility vicariously for these past wrongs. However, Pragmatists stop short of any form of public ritual or racial

---

[48] Fanon notes that, "The Negro makes himself inferior. But the truth is that he is made inferior... The Negro recognizes the unreality of many of the beliefs that he has adopted with reference to the subjective attitude of the white man." This state of "being for other," while not present when "the black man is among his own," is an ever-present reality. "For not only must the black man be black; he must be black in relation to the white man." What Fanon proposes is "nothing short of the liberation of the man of color from himself." Frantz Fanon, *Black Skin, White Masks* (New York: Grove Press, 1967), 149, 110, 8.

[49] Additionally, Cooper-White notes that the characteristic use of minimization, denial, and blaming is rooted in the need of offenders to maintain power, control, and domination. Pamela Cooper-White, *The Cry of Tamar: Violence Against Women and the Churches' Response* (Minneapolis: Fortress Press, 1995), 208.

reconciliation process that could advance the debate to a mutually agreed upon terminus.

White Privilege Argument

In challenging the limits of power and the hubris of democratic governance in his book, *Moral Man and Immoral Society*, Reinhold Niebuhr insightfully observed that "The most common form of hypocrisy among the privileged classes is to assume that their privileges are the just payments with which society rewards specially useful or meritorious functions."[50] Niebuhr's words have an understandable resonance wherever one is located, and in whatever era. The span of human history is largely a story of the powerful dominating the defenseless, and the privileged exercising their sense of entitlement over the disadvantaged, while unwittingly or not, believing all this to be their right. Despite its repeated recurrence, privilege remains innocuously underexposed, and therein lies its potency. Though this final argument is not invoked explicitly by Pragmatists in defense of maintaining Regional Conferences, it is implied. References to social distancing, white flight, a "Black America" remaining despite social progress, and whites being generally not disposed to what blacks propose by way of racial redress – all these are indicative of white privilege.[51] I will briefly assess white privilege beyond what has already been mentioned, in terms of white racial identity, the power and resistance of white privilege, and how it shapes the current debate.

The study of whiteness and white racial identity is a relatively new field of study despite the fact that it was referenced by Du Bois in 1935.[52] The post-civil rights era provided the impetus for

---

[50] Reinhold Niebuhr, *Moral Man and Immoral Society*, 117.

[51] These words are more accurately described as follows: white supremacy – the belief that the white people are superior to nonwhites, which drives the unjustified treatment of nonwhites; whiteness – physical features are lighter skin tones, though it is associated with a default standard or signifier of other races; white racism – superiority that is expressed individually, institutionally, and culturally by whites over nonwhites; and white privilege – the result of an insidious supposition of the racial superiority of whiteness.

[52] Du Bois writes, "It must be remembered that the white group of laborers, while they received a low wage, were compensated in part by a

169

blacks, to explore how being white affects white people, but white scholars were initially less impelled. This initial reluctance to engage in a discourse on whiteness and white racial identity is largely due to the fact that whites are oblivious to the fact that they are an ethnic group. Psychologist Janet Helms observes that a lack of awareness of their racial identity causes whites to feel threatened by those who have no such qualms, and the result is an unhealthy perception of themselves. On the other hand, incorporating a healthy white racial identity leads to an increased awareness of issues related to ethnicity, including ethnicity-based entitlement, and guilt and shame from generational abuses that are assiduously avoided.[53] Clergywoman and theologian Thandeka, who explores the intersection of race and class in the development of whiteness, addresses this internal conflict faced by whites grappling with their racial identity, and labels it "white shame." She defines white shame as the "deeply private feeling of not being at home in one's own white community."[54] From Thandeka's perspective, this sense of alienation reinforces the need to maintain the imperceptibility of a white racial identity, with its reliance on the perception of superiority, while accenting the racial identity of others.

In developing a white racial identity model, Helms sought to increase the awareness of institutional racism and white privilege, dismiss racism as a trait, and advocate for ending racism and its legacy costs. Helms' model includes a three-step, two-phase approach. It starts with Contact, during which, along with maintenance of the status quo, one is unaware of white privilege.

---

sort of public and psychological wage. They were compensated in part by a sort of public and psychological wage. They were given public deference and titles of courtesy because they were white." W. E. B. Du Bois, *Black Reconstruction in America, 1860-1880* (New York: Free Press, 1935), 700.

[53] Janet E. Helms, *A Race is a Nice Thing to Have: A Guide to Being a White Person or Understanding the White Person in Your Life* (Topeka, KS: Content Communications, 1992), i, ii,

[54] The author locates the origin of this shame in childhood, during which the white child becomes a victim of its own community since the child is forced to suppress such feelings of shame and, through a modeling process, the child now acts in ways expected by its white community. Thandeka, *Learning to Be White: Money, Race and God in America* (New York: Continuum, 2000), 12f.

Next is Disintegration, in which awareness of racism, and being challenged to choose between ethnic loyalties over moral mandates, produce anxiety and shame. Reintegration occurs as conflicted emotions from the previous steps are managed by the idealizing of their white racial identity and intolerance for other ethnic groups. Moving out of this stage requires some type of transformative event or personal contact that challenges assumptions of superiority and inferiority. Whites remain at this stage for the longest period of time, which perhaps explains the enduring racial attitudes they hold towards persons of color, as reflected in previously cited surveys.[55]

Helms' second phase reflects the evolution of a healthy white identity, beginning with Pseudo-independence, where racial issues are intellectualized. Here the individual maintains a wholesome view of whiteness, minus the superior attitude. This stage is also characterized by elements of liberal guilt and paternalism as whites seek to understand and help blacks overcome the effects of racism through, for example, affirmative action and special education programs. This stage could be extremely challenging for a country that is now so polarized in the age of Obama that just the mention of words like "liberal" and "conservative" is enough to rally those who hold competing views. This is particularly so in conservative evangelical traditions, among which the SDA Church is numbered, and they would most likely fall in Brooks' traditionalism theory of racial justice.

The Immersion-Emersion stage is typified by an increased effort to understand better the reality of U.S. history and the role played by white racism to shape the lives of minority groups. This desire for an unsanitized version of history by whites would appeal to Pragmatists, who allege revisionism when it comes to the history of racism in the SDA Church and the formation of Regional Conferences. This stage is also illustrative of a greater show of personal responsibility by whites for racism and of motivation to increase awareness of the liabilities and assets of white privilege. Finally, during the Autonomy stage, whites are weaned of their privilege and often adopt an antiracist stance, as they establish security in their white racial identity.[56]

---

[55] Helms, 24, 30-32.
[56] Helms, 33f.

171

About white privilege, sociologist George Lipsitz is categorical: it is a social reality that whites are encouraged to profit from, by adhering to an identity that makes them beneficiaries of financial, personal, and social capital. Yet it is also "a delusion, a scientific and cultural fiction that, like all racial identities, has no valid foundation in biology or anthropology."[57] Lipsitz identifies how power, possessions, and racial politics, have been sustained by an unwitting adherence to white supremacy. In this regard, what Du Bois dubbed a "Negro problem" is essentially a white problem. Lipsitz chronicles how whites have systematically hoarded their privilege by excluding black communities from housing, education, employment, health and wealth opportunities and at the same time claiming that blacks suffer for failing to seize their chances when offered. Disturbingly, to illustrate the nexus between race and health, Lipsitz quotes a national study that places 60 percent of Blacks' and Latinos' communities within sites of uncontrolled toxic waste. Lipsitz even argues that even civil rights laws have reinforced the possessive investment in white privilege since whites contend that problems in the black community no longer stem from discrimination, but from the flawed character of blacks. And when adversely impacted by some laws like affirmative action, whites cry foul, using phrases like reverse discrimination.[58]

As Lipsitz moves towards the end of his text, he insightfully observes that a common rhetorical move of "defenders of white privilege... [is to] relegate black grievances against whites to the past while situating white complaints about blacks in the present."[59] I suspect that most Pragmatists would affirm this assertion of Lipsitz; since in the current debate, Idealists are almost dismissive of the history of Regional Conferences, concerning themselves instead with the aesthetics of the current reality (i.e., these Regional Conferences make the SDA Church look racist). Using Lipsitz' language, Pragmatists and some Idealists would agree that the possessive investment in white privilege is a reality, evidenced by the racial disparity in representation throughout the institutional organization of the SDA Church. And where there is minority representation, it is

---

[57] Lipsitz, 2006, vii.
[58] Lipsitz, 2006, xviii, 19, 9, 24, 105
[59] Lipsitz, 2006, 224.

often no more than tokenism at best. In this context, blacks often report feeling that they must be several times more qualified than their white counterparts in order to have received their seat at the proverbial table. Interestingly, sociological research confirms that "White persons are disproportionately in positions of power and influence in our country."[60]

Of white privilege, one can rightly ask, how can resistance be offered to a phenomenon that remains oblivious to most? Cloaked in invisibility and shielded by a conspiracy of silence, white privilege is difficult to detect and even harder to confront. In his book *The Racial Contract*, black philosopher Charles W. Mills approaches the issue of white privilege from a legal perspective. "In effect, on matters related to race, the Racial Contract prescribes for its signatories an inverted epistemology, an epistemology of ignorance, a particular pattern of localized and global cognitive dysfunctions (which are psychologically and socially functional), producing the ironic outcome that whites will, in general, be unable to understand the world they themselves have made."[61] This unknowing and unsaid aspect of white privilege perplexes the best minds, with many whites asking questions like: What does the country's racial past have to do with me? I'm not even from this country, I'm a nationalized citizen; how have I contributed to the plight of minorities? The tasks of overcoming something so enormous and yet so ethereal is daunting; where do I start? What can I do, I feel so helpless? Is doing nothing an option? These represent just some of the questions I have heard expressed by some whites in response to awareness of white privilege. Perhaps it is this sense of anguish that now represents the sentiment in historian Winthrop Jordan's famed text, *The White Man's Burden*.

---

[60] Constantine and Sue, 253, sources for references are: J. J. Scheurich, "Toward a Discourse on White Racism," *Educational Researcher* 22.5 (1993): 5-10; J. J. Scheurich & M. D. Young, "Coloring Epistemologies: Are Our Research Epistemologies Racially Biased?" *Educational Researcher* 26.4 (1997): 4-16.

[61] The author views the "Racial Contract" as an agreement between whites to categorize nonwhites as morally and legally inferior to them. Charles W. Mills, *The Racial Contract* (Ithaca, NY: Cornell University Press, 1997), 18.

In his seminal work on the origin of racism in the United States, Jordan concludes by describing intrapsychic tensions between "the best and worst in the white man's nature." This tension arises from a perpetual duality of the white man's conscience, as Jordan notes as follows:

> ... his Christianity, his humanitarianism, his ideology of liberty and equality–demanded that he regard and treat the Negro as his brother and his country-man, as his equal. At the same moment, however, many of his most profound urges, especially to maintain the identity of his folk, his passion for domination, his sheer avarice, and his sexual desire, impelled him toward conceiving and treating the Negro as inferior to himself, as an American leper.[62]

Further, this tension born of principle and praxis is of such a nature that it is not easily placated, and as Jordan observes, the peace of mind sought by whites comes at the expense of the rights, privileges, and freedoms of blacks. As a consequence, Jordan proffers that in a desperate attempt to evade the beast within, whites have projected onto blacks the qualities they most despise about themselves, furthering their own debasement. Jordan expresses this circular dilemma facing whites in rather ominous tones:

> Conceivably there was a way out from the vicious cycle of degradation, an opening of better hope demanding an unprecedented and perhaps impossible measure of courage, honesty, and sheer nerve. If the white man turned to stare at the beast within him, if he once admitted unashamedly that the beast was there, he might see that the old foe was a friend as well, that his best and his worst derived from the same deep well of energy. If he once fully acknowledged the powerful forces which drove his being, the necessity of imputing them to others would drastically diminish. If he came to recognize what had happened and was still happening with himself and the African in America, if he faced the unpalatable realities of the tragedy unflinchingly, if he were willing to call the beast no more the Negro's than his own, then conceivably

---

[62] Winthrop D. Jordan, *The White Man's Burden: Historical Origins of Racism in the United States* (London: Oxford University Press, 1974), 225.

he might set foot on a better road. Common charity and his special faith demanded that he make the attempt. But there was little in his historical experience to indicate that he would succeed.[63]

Jordan's description of the psychic contortions that whites undergo in their struggle with the internal equilibrium of balancing their principles and practice has some resonance with the psychoanalytic theory of "splitting" and ambivalent living.[64] Despite Jordan's despair as to a positive outcome to this introspection of staring down the beast within, the field of SCPC, as well as social psychology, is more hopeful, but realistically so. Indeed, the thesis of Poling's book strikes an optimistic note in the belief that "a liberated and critical consciousness that has been tested and proven over many generations of struggle enables some individuals and groups to resist and survive the power of evil."[65] Clearly, Poling is not hopeful that all will experience the joy of successful resistance since his thesis is premised on an intergenerational collective consciousness, bequeathed to those resisting evil. Yet the community of faith must hold fast to the gospel with its message of hope and transformation.

Further, Poling's statement implies that, should those who resist evil lack this historical collective consciousness in their narrative, they should seek out the wisdom of those with such experiences. In fact, his second of six responses offered to individuals in the dominant group who desire to resist evil, requires developing camaraderie with the group engaged in the act of resistance.[66] I believe that this solidarity realignment is vital in

---

[63] Jordan, 226.

[64] "Splitting" describes an inability to hold opposing thoughts, beliefs or feelings about self or others cohesively in consciousness, a kind of all-or-nothing thinking. Freud viewed splitting as a defense mechanism to protect the ego and to resolve ambivalent feelings. Melanie Klein is credited with advancing the concept of splitting with her theory of object relations; she posits that infants' separate consciousness from their experiences of good and bad aspects of their caregivers, and also must struggle to integrate opposite drives like love and hate.

[65] Poling, xiii.

[66] Poling, 176. Poling's other six responses for resisting white privilege has previously been mentioned.

forging the mental toughness that is required of whites in their resistance of white privilege. Contextually, then, white Adventists in general, and those in the Idealists' camp in particular may derive some benefit in their fight to resist white privilege by establishing meaningful alliances with black Adventists both within and outside of Regional Conferences, since these blacks have a history of being a community of resistance. Any such alliances by white Adventists would hopefully be met by gratitude and mutual solidarity by black Adventists. In actuality, all believers are heirs to Christ's legacy of suffering and can rightly be viewed as members of a community of resistance—a reality that should make forming alliances with those who suffer more achievable.

Poling engages in a thoughtful reflection upon his privileged standing as a white middle-class male, offering insight on what it would take to achieve a "liberated and criticized consciousness" in order to resist the prevailing social order of race, class, and gender bias. He speaks of the damage this life of privilege has inflicted on him, his relationships with others, his sexuality; all this damage diminished his commitment not to benefit from the system. Yet, he remains convinced that as he addresses his moral culpability, and his suffering as one fighting against oppressive systems, he "can come to new forms of forgiveness, healing, and shared action for justice."[67] Additionally, he cautions that resistance to the evil of white privilege is often complicated by the use of oppressive language (such as misconceptions of servanthood).[68] Since the use of language sets the terms of any debate, it can be argued that the rhetoric used by Idealists in characterizing Regional Conferences as "segregated," "race-based," and "anachronistic," is yet another form of oppression and a demonstration of the power of privilege. Framing the debate with such historically emotive language places Pragmatists in the defensive crouch, from which attack invariably becomes the best form of defense.

In a feminist critique of whiteness and social justice, Jacqueline Battalora, a public-interest lawyer, utilizes critical race theory to frame how resistance is achieved. Battalora argues for a critical white racial ethic as a response to racial domination. This

---

[67] Poling, 108.
[68] Poling, 144.

approach principally addresses the way racial classification shapes our experiences. In particular, the belief is that as whiteness is racialized, it becomes more culturally visible and privileges gained from it become neutralized. Resistance to this exposé will lead to some asserting that they did not seek this privilege, while others may be overcome with debilitating white guilt. Skill will be required to increase self-awareness so that responsibility for, and the dismantlement of, white privilege can begin.[69] Typical of most critical race theory approaches, Battalora emphasizes the use of language over practical interventions. Yet, as with most resistance strategies for white privilege, the process of deconstruction can only begin when the cloak of invisibility is lifted.

Tim Wise's approach to de-centering the power of white privilege has resonance with those previously mentioned. He first calls for white people to shoulder responsibility for dealing with racism and the privileges they derive from it, in alliance with people of color. Wise points out the irony of this recommendation, since "taking responsibility" is often a charged leveled at blacks. As Wise frames it, whites need to view responsibility not as a bludgeon, but as a tool of liberation. However, he is not optimistic that the apparatus of racism will grind to a halt any time soon. Second, whites need to actively listen to, and believe in, the narratives of the oppressed – and not selectively, either. Wise notes that whites tend to accuse those resisting oppression as "playing the race card," to shield themselves from confronting their own inadequacies. Finally, whites need to educate themselves, their children, and the wider society about how blacks were treated by white forebears. Failing to re-educate themselves simply prolongs ignorance, denial and their continued complicity in oppression.[70]

I conclude this section with some of the approaches developed for resisting white privilege, by briefly reviewing, in

---

[69] Battalora defines critical white racial ethics as "a process of self-conscious racial reformation, guided by a commitment to the dismantling of racial hierarchy." Jacqueline Battalora, "Whiteness: The Working of an Ideology in American Society and Culture," *Gender, Ethnicity, and Religion: Views from the Other Side* (ed. Rosemary Radford Ruether; Minneapolis: Fortress Press, 2002), 11, 12-17.

[70] Wise, *Between Barack and a Hard Place*, 116-34.

chronological order, four randomly selected sociological and psychological journal articles from Psychinfo, to detect any change in theory and practice. With a focus on disproportionate minority incarceration, two researchers in the field of social work evaluate the impact of white privilege on unprecedented and unequal detention. Tracing the roots of white privilege to the colonization of the country, they establish it as a barrier to achieving solidarity and the cause of racist practices in the criminal justice system, for which there are no easy solutions. They offer a two-fold view of resistance: (1) consciousness-raising, to expose how white privilege influences detention policies and practices that disproportionately affect blacks and Latinos; (2) the need for personal, professional and political action to shape policies that consider the multicultural needs of society.[71]

Psychologists Danica Hays and Catherine Chang explore the implications for clinical supervision of white privilege oppression and racial identity. They observe that mental health professionals are predominantly white despite the ethnic diversity of the United States, and since supervisors are the gatekeepers to the profession, they have a responsibility to explore issues of race with their trainees. Part of this exploration should include an awareness of racial identity models, which has been shown to have a salutary effect on training culturally competent clinicians and improve the supervisory relationship. They conclude that the preferred approach in addressing white privilege is to increase awareness of its existence; this, in turn, should result in more insight into ethnic group membership. Observing group dynamics in supervision, role-playing, the empty chair technique, journaling, sharing narratives of different ethnic backgrounds, have all been found to be effective in dealing with oppression and privilege.[72]

---

[71] Nocona Pewewardy and Margaret Severson, "A Threat to Liberty: White Privilege and Disproportionate Minority Incarceration," *Journal of Progressive Human Services* 14.2 (2003): 53-74.

[72] Danica G. Hays and Catherine Y. Chang, "White Privilege, Oppression, and Racial Identity Development: Implications for Supervision," *Counselor Education and Supervision* 43 (December 2003): 134-45.

One qualitative analysis conducted in battered women's homes by a group of social scientists investigated the impact of white privilege and the belief in colorblindness on the services women of color received from white staff. Southern states (AL, GA, and MS) were chosen in order to access more black women and because of the South's racial history, and interviews were conducted with the executive directors of these agencies. The study was structured around a three-dimensional view of white privilege: structural benefit; a position from which self and others are viewed; and unnoticed and anonymous cultural practices that are assumed to be normal. Talk of color-blind norms, they argue, has become code for white norms. From this study, three themes emerged: the fiction of color blindness, of everyone being treated the same; use of stereotypes to make women of color "the other"; and practices developed according to white norms, thus maintaining the status quo. The study concluded that white privilege impacts all areas of social life, including battered women's shelters, with whites as the beneficiaries and blacks disadvantaged. Further, even though the language of color-blindness is used to promote equality, it is but another guise for white privilege in which whiteness is the signifier.[73]

The final article consulted, developed, and piloted an attitude scale for assessing white privilege in four areas using undergraduate and graduate students: preparation to challenge white privilege; ability to judge the consequence of dealing with white privilege; the level of awareness of white privilege; and regrets over white privilege. The researchers identified white privilege attitudes in terms of three types of reactions that come from an awareness of white privilege: affective (fear, guilt, shame and anger); cognitive (from denial to critical consciousness); and behavioral (from avoidance to acting to dissembling. The research revealed detachment from the socially acceptable self-presentation and white privilege attitudes. The study validated the White Privilege Attitude Scale (WPAS) as the first such measure to assess white privilege, and

---

[73] Denise A. Donnelly, Kimberley J. Cook, Debra van Ausdale and Lara Foley, "White Privilege, Color Blindness, and Services to Battered Women," *Violence Against Women* 11.6 (2005): 6-37.

the formulation of interventions to overcome it would be the goal of future research.[74]

From this perusal of four approaches available to those who choose to resist white privilege, there are clear overlaps. However, significant effort will be required, if the desired outcome of transitioning through Helms' stages of white racial identity is to be attained – particularly breaking out of her Reintegration stage. From a spiritual care perspective, her assertion that a transformative event is required has appeal, since this is arguably the exact terrain Christianity occupies. The "new creation" of which the Apostle Paul speaks in 2 Cor. 5:17, embraces the totality of the individual, and no area of the human experience is beyond the power of the gospel to transform and sanctify. In this regard, Ashby's insight into the need for a rediscovery of a "black spiritual heritage," which has allowed blacks to survive racism, can also be true for whites. Despite the exploitative nature of white missionary efforts through the centuries, there remains a rich "white spiritual heritage" to which whites have ready access, and which many have assumed may assist them in establishing communities of resistance. Specifically, for white Adventists, there is the visionary leadership and inspirational insights of Ellen White that can serve as the basis for a "white spiritual heritage." White was decades ahead of her time in understanding the issues of race relations, for she courageously led a single-handed effort against the white racism of her day. Despite the fact that White acquiesced to the prevailing structural accommodation, she nevertheless anticipated a day when God would lead his people to a more inclusive "better way!"

A final, but important word on the concept of privilege is necessary as I conclude this chapter. Much of the discussion thus far has centered on the issue of white privilege, but the reality is that while privilege is accorded to whites, it is also accorded to males. Allan Johnson, a sociology professor, has defined this basic form of privilege as operant "when one group has something that is systematically denied to others not because of who they are or what they've done or not done, but because of the social category they

---

[74] E. Janie Pinterits, Lisa B. Spanierman, and V. Paul Poteat, "The White Privilege Attitudes Scale: Development and Initial Validation," *Journal of Counseling Psychology* 56.3 (2009): 417-29.

belong to."[75] This distinction is an important one since all individuals or groups can be accorded the power of privilege, even when such an individual or group is a part of an oppressed community. In the case of black leaders in Regional Conferences, it is possible to detect an element of the form of privilege that McIntosh calls "unearned entitlement," where strength is, in reality, socially sanctioned permission to dominate subordinates in order to hold on to what they have achieved, given their lack of race privilege.

It could be argued that such signs of dominance construed as strength have been in evidence during the early 1960s through early 1990s in Regional Conferences. One area is the tenure of a few presidents of these conferences, in particular, the "unprecedented 31 years" (1962-1993) of Charles E. Dudley, as president of South Central Conference, a feat that earned him the unofficial title of "dean' of the Regional work."[76] He had unquestionable success, for under his leadership the conference grew from 4,200 members in 55 churches to over 25,000 members in 137 churches.[77] Despite his successes, many Adventists would contend that Dudley outstayed his welcome. One can only wonder how many black clergy had their administrative leadership potential either stymied or delayed by such an extended tenure in office. Privilege was also exercised by black leaders in their often-subjective hire of ministerial graduates from Oakwood University on the basis of patronage and name recognition, and less so on scholarship, talent, and merit. This dynamic of privilege ensures that beneficiaries of privilege maintain an affinity with the privileged group, thus perpetuating privilege.

Evidence of the manifestation of privilege is arguably on display in the leadership style of the two prominent black leaders in the BUC over the past thirty years. As beneficiaries of the Pierson Package, Pastors Cecil Perry and Don McFarlane were part of a large contingent of black clergy from the Caribbean who were invited to

---

[75] Allan G. Johnson, *Privilege, Power, and Difference* (New York: McGraw Hill Higher Education, 2001), 138.

[76] "Regional Voice Founder Passes," *The Regional Voice Magazine*, 2010 Special General Conference Issue, 6.

[77] *The Regional Voice Magazine*, 2010 Special General Conference Issue, 6.

the United Kingdom to bolster the black work. Their rise to the pinnacle of church administration was not unexpected, given the dearth of black leaders, and their successes have been significant, based on the standard Adventist metrics of increased tithes and baptisms.[78] Both men have served as president of the South England Conference (SEC) and the BUC for a combined, though not concurrent, 40-year period, beginning in 1985 to 2011. At the time of writing there are approximately 177 clergypersons employed by the BUC, and based on conversations with ministerial colleagues in England there have been approximately 40 clergypersons who have left the United Kingdom over the last twenty years – a 23 percent turn-over for a relatively small organization. Most of these individuals have successful careers in the United States and Canada, particularly given the competitive nature of ministry in these countries. It could be argued that this unexpected exodus of talented clergy is indicative of the true legacy of Perry's and McFarlane's tenure – a legacy of a lost generation of potential leaders to the BUC. This argument is bolstered by the fact that in 2011, at the BUC Nominating Committee meeting, McFarlane lost re-election to Pastor Ian Sweeny a significantly younger man, who at the time was two years into his tenure as the new President of the North England Conference. Since then, Perry has retired, and McFarlane left the country for the U.S. soon after his defeat, and both leave behind a complicated legacy to say the least. As Johnson reminds us:

> Privilege increases the odds of having things your own way, of being able to set the agenda in a social situation and determine the rules and standards and how they're applied…Privilege means being able to decide who gets taken seriously, who receives attention, who is accountable to whom and for what. And it grants a presumption of superiority and social permission to act on that

---

[78] Figures readily available from the SEC, BUC, and GC websites reveal that from 1986 the membership of the SEC was 9,637 and total contributions were £4,024,528 ($6,036,792); and in the BUC 16,065 membership, and £6,268,923 ($9,403,384) total contributions. By 2010 membership in the SEC had risen to over 20,000 with £11,691,922 ($17,537,883) in tithe; and at the BUC 31,662 members with £17,812,064 ($26,718,096) of income.

presumption without having to worry about being challenged.[79]

Summary

Pragmatists contend that the basis for the preservation of Regional Conferences is one of cultural solidarity, and their case has been outlined in this chapter. Convinced that the weight of history is on their side, Pragmatists suggest that while changes in racial attitudes may be possible, it is highly unlikely. Therefore the structural accommodation by church administrators for blacks, need not be tampered with. Consequently, their cultural pluralism argument does not accommodate the possibility of a divinely transformed community, where even entrenched human failings such as racism, can adequately be surmounted. Next, the authentic nature of their victim blaming argument may impede their desire to pursue reconciliation. Finally, their white privilege argument, which rightly requires that whites become more conscious of its debilitating effects on all minorities, and the constant attention required to mitigate its impact, both indicate how challenging, achieving a constructive outcome is, hence the pessimism of the Pragmatists.

---

[79] Allan G. Johnson, 33f.

A Spiritual Care and Pastoral Counseling
Formulation of Mandate and Methods
in Racial Reconciliation

Reconciliation becomes the main idea in which Christian theology is set. Reconciliation is not posited in a dialectical tension with liberation, but rather liberation becomes the motive force that empowers the community in its quest for a restored community.[1]

Beyond the Idealists' and Pragmatists' Rhetoric

Reinhold Niebuhr once wrote, "The fact is that any commitment, religious, political or cultural, can lead to intolerance if there is not a residual awareness of the possibility of error in the truth in which we believe, and of the possibility of truth in the error against which we contend."[2] Here Niebuhr appeals for tolerance, humility and an open mind as essential ingredients in any disputation, including the current one in which both sides are to engage honestly without harming their relationship because of a lack of empathy, perspective, and self-criticism. Having assessed some of the central arguments made by Idealists and Pragmatists for the closure or continuance of Regional Conferences, I feel that Niebuhr's sage advice has resonance. Both sides acknowledge the success of Regional Conferences. But, Idealists contend that they have passed their shelf-life since U.S. society is no longer segregated, while Pragmatists retort that racial attitudes have not changed significantly and, hence, their dissolution would be counterproductive. Both sides agree that the debate has merit. Yet, Idealists are distinctly uncomfortable with the negative attention they receive when Regional Conferences are discussed while Pragmatists loathe the fact that Regional Conferences are in the "eye of the storm," since there is

---

[1] Noel Leo Erskine, *King among the Theologians* (Cleveland, OH: The Pilgrim Press, 1994), 155.

[2] Reinhold Niebuhr Papers, LC, Box 17, quoted in Richard Crouter, *Reinhold Niebuhr on Politics, Religion, and Christian Faith* (Oxford: Oxford University Press, 2010), 134.

never talk of conferences adjacent to Regional Conferences being dismantled or amalgamating with Regional Conferences. Both sides also agree that there is a lack of intercultural dialogue between blacks and whites. But Idealists attribute this to the "segregated" organizational structures while Pragmatists counter that the problem is relational, not structural–there is inbuilt social distance in society. All the while, the error in each side's truth is blithely ignored, and a mutual "better way" remains elusive.

This book contends that fundamental to understanding the inertia of the current debate about the existing form of structural accommodation is the inexplicable silence by Idealists and Pragmatists on the issue of racial reconciliation. To reiterate, I understand racial reconciliation to be a dimension of the ongoing divine mandate to overcome alienation, in this case between ethnic groups, through identification and in solidarity with each other, which can result in peacemaking and restored relationships. Since there are no overtly observable hostilities between black and white Adventists, the issue of peacemaking is perhaps moot, but restoring relationships or building community is certainly relevant. As the history of the SDA Church's work among blacks in the United States indicates, the racial disparity and discrimination that predominated in society were also reflected in the church. The outgrowth of these discriminatory practices was both the defection of some prominent black church leaders and the birth of Regional Conferences. Pragmatists insist that there are no lasting resentments stemming from this history (a questionable stance at best); consequently, talk of racial reconciliation will only lead to white guilt. The view of Idealists on the merits of racial reconciliation is less clear, but they are certainly not clamoring for it. Surely, a denial or lack of commitment to reconciliation is an affront to Christ's very mission and message.

This important four-part chapter will explore what it will take to move beyond the rhetoric of the Idealists and the Pragmatists by starting with examination of the 1999 Race Summit, the U.S. church's only foray into racial healing, incorporating models that utilize Gordon Allport's Contact Hypothesis as a basis for minimizing bias and stereotypes, and recent studies that explore the efficacy of diversity. The chapter then moves to spiritual reflections on reconciliation with considerations from the Apostle Paul and insights from the SCPC field. Practices of reconciliation will then be discussed using the example of the South African Truth and Reconciliation Commission and practices of reconciliation from the perspective of the peace and justice movements. Finally, the pioneering work of Eric Yamamoto in racial justice will be appraised, and his fourfold Interracial Justice model adapted to offer the SCPC field in general, and Adventism in particular, a viable approach to racial healing.

The 1999 Race Summit

While the evangelical community in the United States initiated racial reconciliation efforts in the late 1980s, Adventists entered this arena a decade later when NAD hosted a Race Summit on October 27-30, 1999. There is some indication that Adventists may have been prompted more by events in the political world to engage in this racial dialogue than any moral imperative. In a church article, Richard Osborn, the then vice-president for education at the NAD, hinted at this possibility. Osborn stated that two years earlier, he and three notable ethnic minority members were part of a religious delegation invited to the White House by President Clinton to explore how religious communities could assist in improving race relations in the United States. The presidential assignment was discomfiting to Osborn as he questioned whether Adventists could authentically contribute to the discourse given "the fragile nature of race relations" in its midst.[3]

The four-day Race Summit was held at the church's headquarters in Silver Springs, Maryland, with over 300 administrators and institutional leaders in attendance. The Summit was convened by national church administrators from the North American Division (NAD) of the SDA Church. Participants for this event were chosen by Union and Conferences officials in the NAD, and a report of the Summit was published in the official church organ, the *Advent Review*. The purpose of the Race Relations Summit was

---

[3] Richard Osborn, "Floppy Disc Event or Revolutionary Summit," *Adventist Review* (December 2, 2000): http://www.adventistreview.org/9948/story1-2.htm (accessed 1/3/10).

...to bring leaders of the Seventh-day Adventist Church in North America together, not in confrontation but in trust, to tackle our most critical issues; to listen carefully and respectfully to one another and to the whole faith community; to search for solutions, focusing on what is right rather than on who is right; and to hold ourselves and the Church accountable in areas in which change is needed.[4]

This rationale is laudable in several areas. First, church leaders were prepared to have a candid dialogue about the problem of racial divisions within the church. Second, church leaders were taking ownership of the problem. Third, solutions were being sought based upon the justice of the cause. Finally, church leaders were holding themselves accountable to the national membership for remedying the problem.

However, two salient elements were missing from the Summit's stated purpose. Absent was the willingness by church leaders to take responsibility for the egregious manner in which blacks were discriminated against by church leaders at that time. Although Alfred C. McClure, NAD president, performed a sincere and surprising personal apology at the conclusion of the summit, noticeably absent was any formal apology from the organizational body he led.[5] Despite McClure's laudable effort, it is important to note that while the ministry of reconciliation has a personal element, in that it is individuals that reconcile, it is also attentive to institutional issues. As Czechoslovakian theologian, Jan Milič Lochman writes, "It is also concerned with *conditions and systems...*

---

[4] "Goals and Recommendations," *Adventist Review* (December 2, 2000), http://www.adventistreview.org/9948/story1-3.htm (accessed 12/20/10).

[5] Importantly, McClure informed the delegation that he would commission all staff at the NAD "to make race relations a top priority. I'm going to ask them to develop a curriculum of understanding and make it available to all congregations in the NAD." It remains unclear if such a curriculum was developed and distributed to local congregations, since no one at the NAD's Human Rights department could recall one being developed. "An Expression of Sorrow and Apology," *Adventist Review* (December 2, 2000): http://www.adventistreview.org/9948/story1-4.htm (accessed 12/20/10).

the individual is a member of the community. The question of personal salvation is concerned with relationships in family, community and society."[6] Also, Summit organizers issued a preamble in which they refused to attribute culpability to those at the time who permitted such discriminatory practices or who gave tacit approval by their silence. Even though the history of Regional Conferences was reviewed, it focused on what happened rather than seeking insight into why it happened, and how the continued racial divide could be overcome.

In the opening lines of her important text, psychiatrist Judith Herman observes a dialectic in the human response to trauma. Herman remarks that the typical reaction to traumatic events is to dismiss them from our conscious mind, but traumas are obstinate and disdain obscurity. The futility of denial in resolving trauma is inherent in the fact that recollecting and truth-telling are prerequisites to healing and restoring personal relationships. When secrecy is the prescribed method of coping with traumatic events, concludes Herman, "the story of the traumatic event surfaces not as a verbal narrative but as a symptom."[7] Is it possible that one symptom of SDA failure to address racial trauma is the continued social distance practiced by black and white Adventists? Among the many recommendations of the Race Summit was a plan to hold a second Race Relations Summit in 2001.[8] This 2001 Summit never

---

[6] Providing a further context for his thinking, Lochman writes that "The reconciling event also has liberating consequences for the structure of the Christian community, for its 'church order'. In the long-run the Church of Christ can never be content to establish itself as a permanently structured and self-enclosed entity based on the divisions of race, nationality, culture and sex. It is the body of Christ, an organic unity composed of many members." Jan Milič Lochman, *Reconciliation and Liberation: Challenging a One-Dimensional View of Salvation* (tr. David Lewis; Philadelphia: Fortress Press, 1977), 108-09.

[7] Judith Herman, *Trauma and Recovery* (New York: BasicBooks, 1992), 1.

[8] Another recommendation was the establishment of a Race Relations Committee whose terms of reference included: (1) Identifying racial barriers within the church that contribute to distrust and disunity; (2) Identifying Christian methods of resolving racial conflict and preventing cultural tension through education, love, and diplomacy; (3) Identifying

materialized, and neither did the subsequently approved 2002 Summit. One speaker at the summit expressed the opinion that it was little more than a "floppy disk event: easily put in and just as quickly taken out."[9]

That the SDA Church in the past has approached the issue of racial reconciliation in such an unsatisfactory manner may serve to hinder more meaningful social contact between blacks and whites in the future. This would mirror a prevailing societal phenomenon in which unsuccessful efforts at social change lead to further distrust, lingering suspicion, and reinforcement of stereotypes. Social psychologists confirm that the basis for positive intergroup relations that ensure the safety, self-respect, and welfare of group members is mutual trust and acceptance. Indeed, they have identified three psychosocial processes that contribute to intergroup bias, distrust, and conflict. The first is social categorization, the means by which individuals comprehend their environment by simplifying the complexity of social reality through the grouping of objects. The generalizing that takes place through this process often results in stereotyping, which leads to individuals identifying themselves as "in-group" or "out-group" relative to these categories — "them" and "us." The second is intergroup competition, which emerges from the social categorization process to produce the urge to cohere within an in-group as a means of identity and protection. Yet it is this exact process that produces other in-groups, resulting in intergroup competition. Since the level of competitiveness is higher for group-to-group interaction than for individual-to-individual, it gives rise to the phenomenon social psychologists call individual-group discontinuity (the tendency to be more competitive and less

---

specific manifestations of racism in the church (personally, culturally, and institutionally); (4) Recommending specific strategies for dismantling racism through consciousness raising, education, advocacy, or activism; (5) Recommending a replicable methodology for social change with specific, manageable, and realistic goals that will encourage a new level of unity within the North American Division; (6) Recommending ongoing strategies for improving race relations within the Seventh-day Adventist Church. Office of Human Relations [the official North American Division website]; "Race Relations Committee;" http://www.nadadventist.org/human relations/about/racecom.html (accessed 5/2/10).

[9] Osborn.

cooperative). The third is intergroup threat (real or imagined) and distrust, with the perception of a threat playing a crucial role in interracial prejudice, while trust increases among members of the same in-group.[10] Consequently, any further race summits organized by the SDA Church will have to reckon with at least these three intergroup dynamics, working to mitigate any meaningful racial reconciliation attempts.

Countering Bias and Social Distance with Contact Theory

The aforementioned findings reflect the reality that racial reconciliation is an arduous task for any organization, let alone one as multiethnic as the SDA Church. Yet within this diagnostic of intergroup bias lies the basis for approaches that may improve relations between blacks and whites. Intergroup contact is acknowledged by social psychologists as the antecedent of intergroup reconciliation. Gordon Allport's Contact Hypothesis has been the bedrock of much of the research designed to improve intergroup relations. It posits that changes in racial attitudes are affected by intergroup contact, provided that these four conditions are met: there is cooperative interaction, equal status among the participants, individualized contact, and institutional support for the contact.[11] The theory was focused not on the past to determine causation but on the present. Researchers have since extended Allport's model to address the issue of causation and the psychology of reducing bias, rightly believing that as individuals change, so does society.[12] Others have appropriated Social Identity Theory and Self-Categorization Theory to establish other models for contact, arguing that, given changing situations, individuals oscillate between personal and collective identity, and these shifts impact intergroup interactions.

---

[10] Arie Nadler, Thomas E. Malloy, and Jeffrey D. Fisher, *The Social Psychology of Intergroup Reconciliation* (Oxford: Oxford University Press, 2008), 16, 228-32.

[11] Gordon W. Allport, *The Nature of Prejudice* (Reading, MA: Addison-Wesley Publishing Company, Inc., 1979), 281.

[12] See Walter G. Stephan and Cookie White Stephan, *Intergroup Relations* (Colorado: Westview Press, 1996), 71-74. Their model of the contact hypothesis is as follows: Societal Context, Situational Context,

Other models built on Allport's intergroup research are used by social psychologists. One is the Decategorization model which occurs when intergroup contact is conducted on the basis of personal information and characteristics rather than by categories. This creates occasions for increased familiarity with out-group members and decreased bias toward them. Another model, Recategorization, also known as the Common In-Group Identity Model, reduce intergroup bias by transferring individual identities into a shared common inclusive identity, such as a religious affiliation. This model could appeal to black and white Adventists because they share a common religious heritage. However, a drawback of these two models is that they do not adequately address the motivation of individuals to exclude and differentiate–the very basis for establishing boundaries and social categories. Still, another, is the Mutual Intergroup Differentiation Model, which attempts to address these limitations by having different groups participate in complementary superordinate objectives without adjustment to the in-group/out-group differentiation–groups within a larger group.[13] It is argued that "this strategy allows group members to maintain their social identities and positive distinctiveness while avoiding insidious intergroup comparisons... [It] does not seek to change the basic category structure of the intergroup contact situation, but rather it attempts to change the intergroup affect from negative to positive by creating intergroup interdependence and mutual respect."[14]

The Mutual Intergroup Differentiation Model has resonance, to some extent, with the Regional Conference structure. Blacks and whites preserve their distinctiveness while operating under the same policies and practices of the SDA Church to advance its mission and message. In this regard, it can be argued that, in this uniquely Adventist solution to the race problem, leaders of the SDA Church in the 1940s were socially progressive and innovative in arriving at this psychosocial model of intergroup interaction, creating a structure that social psychologists are only now studying and naming. What

---

Personal Factors, Mediators, Personal Consequences, and Societal Consequences.
[13] Nadler, et al., 259-63.
[14] Nadler, et al., 264.

clearly is absent, however, is the notion that this Adventist form of mutual intergroup differentiation was designed to reduce bias, mitigate stereotypes, eliminate leadership and power differentials, and establish meaningful exchanges between blacks and whites–all these challenges remain. Furthermore, the ultimate objective of this model is reconciliation and the forging of a common identity, not simply fostering an acceptable working environment and professional relationships.

Diversity Works

As the SDA Church continues to overlook the merits of a formalized approach to racial reconciliation, not only is the level of social distance between its black and white members in the United States maintained and even exacerbated, but it could also be failing to maximize the benefit of the cultural and ethnic diversity within its ranks. In 2007, Robert D. Putnam, political science professor at Harvard, and Scott E. Page, professor of complex systems, political science and economics at the University of Michigan, came to seemingly different conclusions from their independent studies on the issue of diversity.[15] Putnam arrived at the following three deductions: (1) immigration will be the cause of significant ethnic diversity in all modern societies and will create both challenges and possibilities for social capital; (2) ethnic diversity, in the short-term, challenges social solidarity and hinders social capital because diversity tends to promote in-group solidarity and out-group distrust, social isolation, and discomfort; (3) in the long-term, ethnic diversity forms new types of social solidarity, depressing the negative effects of diversity because, as trust increases, social

---

[15] It must be noted that Putnam and Page had different definitions for diversity. By diversity Putnam means ethnic diversity, while for Page it is "differences in how people see, categorize, understand, and go about improving the world." Robert D. Putnam, "E Pluribus Unum: Diversity and Community in the Twenty-first Century," *Scandinavian Political Studies* 30.2 (2007): http://www3.interscience.wiley.com/cgi-bin/fulltext/ 11851 0920/PDFSTART (accessed 7/22/10); and Scott E. Page, *The Difference: How the Power of Diversity Creates Better Groups, Firms, Schools, and Societies* (Princeton: Princeton University Press, 2007), xiv.

distance is minimized.[16]   Putnam concludes that the "central challenge of modern, diversifying societies is to create a new, broader sense of 'we.'"[17]

While Putnam views diversity as initially problematic, a "no-pain- no-gain" perspective, Page sees diversity as a fundamental ingredient in problem-solving–the power of the whole over the sum of the parts. It is important to remember that Page is thinking about the cognitive merits of diversity as he constructed a theoretical model while Putnam used field research.   Page's central claim, presented in a mathematical formulation, is that "collective ability equals individual ability plus diversity" and that "diversity trumps ability."[18]   Page's research leads him to three conclusions about diversity: "(1) diverse perspectives and tools enable collections of people to find more and better solutions and contribute to overall productivity; (2) diverse predictive models enable crowds of people to predict values accurately, and (3) diverse fundamental preferences frustrate the process of making choices."[19]   Among his supporting arguments are assertions that different perspectives classify knowledge, thus simplifying problem-solving; an array of experiences, education, and identities in either a group or individual can improve decision-making; and that diversity results in more diversity.[20] Page concludes, "What each of us has to offer, what we can contribute to the vibrancy of our world, depends on our being different in some way, in having combinations of perspectives, interpretations, heuristics, and predictive models that differ from those of others. These differences aggregate into a collective ability that exceeds what we possess individually."[21]

What Putnam and Page demonstrate from their research is that diversity works when diversity is honored, despite the accompanying growing pains. Yet their diversity research reaffirms

---

[16] By "social capital" Putnam means "social networks and the associated norms of reciprocity and trustworthiness." Putnam, 137-138, 142, 149, 158, 159.

[17] Putnam, 139.

[18] Page, xiv.

[19] Page, 13.

[20] Page, 50, 173, 234, 295.

[21] Page, 374.

biblical wisdom, particularly in the words of Solomon, regarding the virtue of collective wisdom of others (Prov. 11:14; 15:22; 24:6). In view of the fact that there was no follow-up to the Race Summit of 1999, which might have facilitated fresh thinking about multiethnic interactions within the SDA Church (particularly between blacks and whites) and exploration of an organizational realignment for a twenty-first century church, the need for thoughtful reflections on racial reconciliation is in order. In this section, I have discussed the salutary effect of models utilizing Allport's Contact Hypothesis to improve intergroup interactions and research that validates potential values of diversity. I will next establish the theological imperative for the church to engage in racial reconciliation.

Spiritual Reflections on Racial Reconciliation

Methodist theologian Vincent Taylor notes that forgiveness and reconciliation have rightly been viewed as the summation of the Christian experience, as long as the terms are appropriately defined. Both forgiveness and reconciliation are aspects of humanity's restored relationship with God. Since forgiveness implies annulment of sins, any investigation of forgiveness and reconciliation necessitates an explanation of the doctrine of Atonement with which they are inextricably connected.[22] The doctrine of the Atonement addresses the question of how sinners are made right before a holy God and how—in the life, suffering and substitutionary death of Christ—humanity is liberated and given the answer to the problem of evil.

Reconciliation is largely a New Testament concept, the Old Testament version of which is atonement. Atonement is concerned with a breach in the relationship between God and humankind that God assumes the responsibility to repair.[23] This reparative work is transacted in the suffering of Christ on the cross. Thornton claims the cross "names suffering for what it is and [it] can be a means for radically critiquing all attempts to camouflage, minimize, or distort

---

[22] Vincent Taylor, *Forgiveness and Reconciliation: A Study in New Testament Theology* (London: MacMillan and Company, Ltd, 1941), xv.

[23] "Reconcile, Reconciliation," *The International Standard Bible Encyclopedia* (gen. ed. Geoffrey W. Bromiley; Grand Rapids, Michigan: William B. Eerdmans Publishing Company), 4: 55.

the truth of its reality. The cross names reality and unmasks false optimism in all its forms."[24] Thornton speaks of the tendency to minimize suffering and to trivialize the price of restoration, affirming that both are antithetical to the cross of Christ. In the debate over Regional Conferences, the tendency on both sides to minimize the suffering of black Adventists, and the minimalistic efforts at restoration are in evidence. An investigation of the Pauline and SCPC perspectives on reconciliation will reveal the ongoing and urgent reality of re-establishing fractured relationships, reuniting divinity with broken humanity, and humankind with each other.

Pauline Approach to Reconciliation

The Apostle Paul is not alone among New Testament writers in using the concept of reconciliation, but he is the only one to appropriate much of its language. Ralph Martin, a NT theologian, has demonstrated that the trajectory of Paul's use of reconciliation as shown in biblical texts is due in part to Jewish and Greek predecessors, his own interpretative effort, and the influence of later Pauline disciples.[25] The five Greek words used for the concept of reconciliation convey the meaning of exchanging place with the other and being in solidarity with and not against the other.[26] This conceptualization, argues social justice theologian John W. de Gruchy, "is fundamental to the Christian understanding of reconciliation, to its process and practice, and to the notion of vicarious representation which lies at the heart of the gospel."[27] Literally, reconciliation concerns itself with how God relates to us as "the other," and how we relate to "the other." It is, says de Gruchy, "the process of overcoming alienation through identification and in solidarity with 'the other,' thus making peace and restoring relationships."[28] Therefore, it is problematic to speak of reconciliation without the notion of community and fellowship; since community is prefaced on regrouping of the alienated, and this regrouping is impossible without reconciliation.

---

[24] Thornton, 3.

[25] Ralph P. Martin, *Reconciliation: A Study of Paul's Theology* (Atlanta: John Knox Press, 1981), 81.

[26] The four Greek verbs and a noun are: *diallássō, synallássō, katallássō, apokatallássō,* and *katallágé.* The root of all these words, *allássō,*

Paul is credited with developing the doctrine of reconciliation, though the idea is inherent whenever estrangement or hostility is to be surmounted and unity restored. Indeed, Martin postulates that reconciliation is "an interpretative key to Paul's theology," and that it has relevance "to social and racial issues in Western society today."[29]   The New Testament usage of reconciliation divides into human relations and divine-human relations. There are several references to the interpersonal nature of reconciliation. In Matt. 5:23-24, an individual thought to be guilty has to shoulder the responsibility of repairing the frayed relationships ahead of church attendance. In Acts 7:26, Stephen's defense includes Moses' failed attempt to reconcile a dispute between two Jewish men; and in 1 Cor. 7:10f, the advice offered to married couples in conflict is a co-operative effort in bringing about resolution.   Women are not to be passive (or even passive-aggressive), as was the cultural expectation, and men are not to be aggressive in leveraging their power as was the norm, rather both must work in a mutually beneficial manner for the health of their marriage. In Eph. 2:14-16, Paul uses violent imagery of two once-warring factions divided by a barricade being reconciled by means of the event of the cross, a text most NT theologians acknowledge as foundational to Paul's reconciliation theology. Lochman's insights on these verses are useful:

> How often the Church has been structured as a racial church, a class church, a cultural church and a national church, and in addition gone on to seal itself off from

means "to exchange," and the derived *állos* means "another," or "the other." G. W. Bromiley, "Reconcile; Reconciliation," 55-57. Büchsel, "*katallasso*," Gerhard Kittel, *Theological Dictionary of the New Testament* (ed. tr. Geoffrey Bromiley; Grand Rapids: Eerdmans, 1977), 1: 255-9; H. Vorländer and C. Brown, "Reconciliation, Restoration, Propitiation, Atonement," *New International Dictionary of New Testament Theology* (ed. Colin Brown; Exeter: Paternoster Press, 1978), 3: 145-76.

[27] De Gruchy, 51.

[28] De Gruchy, 51.

[29] Martin goes on to assert that "the word reconciliation will be the 'chief theme' or 'centre' of his missionary and pastoral thought and practice. But 'reconciliation' is a word with a range of meanings." Martin, 5.

others behind these illegitimate walls. Yet the fundamental and inalienable dynamic of the Gospel of reconciliation constrains Christians again and again, despite all their inertia, to join in the liberating movement leading to awareness of the reconciling unity and to its practical achievement.[30]

Lochman reaffirms the central theme of these passages, showing that having accepted Christ's reconciliation efforts at the cross, the believer as an individual and in community with others should engage in a reciprocal process ending division.[31]

The more significant aspect of reconciliation, in Paul's view, is the divine-human relationship, as expressed in the key passages of Rom. 5 and 2 Cor. 5, from which emerge at least five themes. First, Paul is clear that the reconciler is God (2 Cor. 5:19), and Christ is God's agent for achieving reconciliation. Second, fellowship with God is restored since the obstacle to fellowship is removed–hostility gets displaced by communion. Third, reconciliation is accomplished through Christ's vicarious death on the cross, making things right with God for all who believe (Rom. 5:8). Fourth, all who are reconciled to God are changed, and maintaining distance from God is no longer desirable (Rom. 5:11). By accepting reconciliation as a divine bridge building initiative, believers are to walk across that bridge by faith expecting that improved interpersonal relationships will result. Finally, out of a sense of freedom from continued alienation, believers will be motivated to lead others to a similar state of well-being (2 Cor. 5:18). This final element of reconciliation

---

[30] Lochman, 110.

[31] Lochman sees believers engaging in an expansive work of reconciliation. "…we sinners who accept God's reconciliation should realize that this implies reconciliation with one another in all the estrangements of human life. We are thus to devote ourselves actively to the task of mutual reconciliation." Lochman, 110. G. W. Bromiley, "Reconcile; Reconciliation," *The International Standard Bible Encyclopedia* (gen. ed. Geoffrey W. Bromiley; Grand Rapids, MI: William B. Eerdmans Publishing Company, 1988), 4: 55; Taylor, 85; Martin, 162; Jarvis uses Eph 2:16 as his thesis, observes the declarative voice of Paul who "emphatically states that Jesus' death has accomplished it [reconciliation] for the believing community of faith." Jarvis J. Williams, *One New Man: The Cross and Racial Reconciliation in Pauline Theology* (Nashville: B & H Academic, 2010), 126f.

is fundamentally important, for, although God has completed the act of reconciliation at the cross, reconciliation must continuously be embodied. Martin sees in Paul's ministry of reconciliation a concrete example of how believers are to conduct themselves. Since the believers in Corinth were suspicious of Paul's work among them and his qualifications to engage in such work, he appeals to them to accept his hand in friendship once more, for reconciliation "must be applied to concrete human situations."[32]

If Paul's theology of reconciliation could be distilled down to its core element, De Gruchy asserts that it would probably sound like this: "the love of God in Jesus Christ turns enemies into friends, thereby creating peace."[33] This distillation by De Gruchy is important, for it conveys the fact that God's incomprehensible love is rooted in personal relationships and, consequently, this love seeks to end estrangement. This discomfort with separation and alienation is the antidote with which God seeks, through Christ, to inoculate believers. When released into the blood stream, this antidote infuses the believer with a strong case of Buber's "I-Thou" overcoming the "I-It." This transformation produced in the believer is the basis for Paul's ministry of reconciliation, a reconciliation that leads to community.

Yet, establishing community on the basis of a ministry of reconciliation is far from easy, as Buber long ago observed. Exploring what it takes for a group that seeks to attain a higher purpose beyond societal norms, Buber writes that such a "feeling of community... reigns where the fight that is fought takes place from the position of a community struggling for its own reality as a community... [Such a community] experiences everywhere a turning to, a dynamic facing of, the other, a flowing from *I* to *Thou*."[34] The difficulty of establishing reconciled relationships beyond the "Thou" of our social network is a task, to be sure. But as Buber acknowledges, nothing is more beneficial to the Divine-human exchange than "an unsentimental and unreserved exchange of

---

[32] Martin, 93. Similar observations are made by Williams, 108f; Taylor, 90; and G. W. Bromiley, "Reconcile; Reconciliation."

[33] De Gruchy, 52.

[34] Martin Buber, *Between Man and Man* (New York: The Macmillan Company, 1968), 31.

glances between two men in an alien place."[35] For all religious traditions, where racial challenges remain, a mutually shared glance and a determination to fight for community, will at least begin the process towards a reconciled outcome. On this point, Buber is succinct: "Community is where community happens."[36]

Spiritual Care and Pastoral Counseling Approaches to Reconciliation

In their analysis of the pastoral functions, as previously noted, Clebsch and Jaekle observe that the relevance of each function is circumstantially rather than concretely determined. This measure of adaptability of these functions provided the clergy throughout history with both challenges and opportunities for providing contemporaneously contextual ministries to those they served in their personal and social lives. Since the needs of individuals have continued to vary qualitatively, revisioning those needs and, more specifically, reconciling them has meant, as Thornton puts it, wading into "the waters of justice and streams of mercy to dress wounds and bind up deep scars."[37] Consequently, reconciling has taken center stage in a world steeped in alienation, hatred, and violence. The silencing of voices in *extremis* is no longer possible; hence, the end of the twentieth century and the dawn of the twenty-first century have seen the thirst for freedom and the explosion of liberative movements. The aftermath often has been reconciliatory and mediatory efforts, of which the Christian church and other religious traditions have, and sometimes have not, been at the forefront (e.g. the Civil Rights Movement saw Christianity on both sides of the issue) Whether actively involved or passively observant, the church has seen many of its traditional functions, chief among which is reconciliation, assumed by secular organizations as these entities grapple with the age-old problem of hostility and the alienation it causes. Since Christianity typically enjoys religious tolerance in the United States, victimhood is hard to embrace; not surprising, then, Catholic theologian Robert J. Schreiter rightly acknowledges that the

---

[35] Buber, 37.
[36] Buber, 31.
[37] Thornton, 147.

process of reconciliation "is initiated by the victim, not the oppressor."[38]

The process of reconciliation briefly sketched out by Clebsch and Jaekle includes, but clearly is not limited to, two modes of operation. The first is forgiveness, which seeks to reestablish the relationship with confession and repentance as precursors. The second is discipline as in correction, admonition, or harsher measures leading to confession and a change of behavior. They also reflected on the mental health of those who are burdened by the guilt of alienation from others, concluding that such alienation can be viewed as alienation from God.[39] From Clebsch and Jaekle's perspective, a valid question which arises is who is the one to extend such forgiveness and discipline, particularly as oppressor are seldom willing to initiate such a conversation. The African proverb, "He who feels it, knows it,"[40] is instructive here, validating Schreiter's acknowledgment that unless the aggrieved have an advocate, they invariably must become their own agents of change.

In his examination of Martin Luther King, Jr's writings on matters of social justice, pastoral theologian Donald M. Chinula, who views the SCPC field as "hyperindividualistic" (perhaps less so today), fashions a fourfold pastoral approach designed to communalize pastoral care and its functions. His schema has some useful elements that can serve as a template for an SCPC process of reconciliation. First, *reclamation* is necessary because key symptoms of oppression–a fractured identity and low self-esteem–are explored so that they can be relieved and remediated to restore the divine heritage stolen by coercion. Second, *conciliation*, he argues, goes beyond reconciliation by seeking friendship with one's former oppressor; but it also encourages the embracing of the worst in ourselves and in others. Third, *transformation* takes place when old or outdated issues of personal and social ethics are replaced by relevant and mutually beneficial ones. However, this transformation is best achieved when the individual, society, and institutions are

---

[38] Schreiter, 45.

[39] Clebsch and Jaekle, 56f, 81.

[40] "African Proverbs," *Inspirational Proverbs and Sayings*: http://www.inspirationalstories.com/proverbs/african-he-who-feels-it-knows-it/ (accessed 2/15/13)

transformed, thus mitigating psychic injury. Lastly, Chinula lists *transcendence*, which, when paired with immanence, reveals God's nearness and distance and ability to be impacted by suffering yet remote enough to do something about it.[41] It is this "inexhaustibility of divine reality, which infuses the human spirit… [that] can provide the norm for the self in its quest for healing and meaningful living."[42]

Despite the fact that Chinula's four-task approach to a more communal caregiving, seeks to displace the four foundational pastoral functions (healing, sustaining, guiding and reconciling), it nevertheless incorporates reconciliation within one of the tasks– Conciliation. Of his four tasks, three have definite appeal for racial reconciliation. Owing to the fact that he identifies within the Reclamation task the psychological dynamic of oppression as manifested in a loss of self and low self-confidence, I find it extremely cogent. What he fails to address, however, is the psychological dynamic of the oppressor, which, for the purpose of this book, is the manifestation of white privilege. Yet the emphasis in his Conciliation task of establishing friendships and not just on restoring relationships, while challenging, coheres with King's vision of the "Beloved Community." The difficulty of constructing such a community in the midst of the modern manifestations of evil may lie beyond the bounds of this present world–though it remains a noteworthy aspiration. His Transformation task challenges some contemporary religious experience and theology because of a lack of certitude about the divine operating in the human. For Adventists, belief in the regenerative power of God in the life of the "born again believer" remains a central feature of their theology. They still retain confidence in Paul's words in 2 Cor. 5:17 (NIV): "Therefore, if anyone is in Christ, he is a new creation; the old has gone, the new has come!"

In articulating the intersection between the Christian tradition and contemporary situations that are routinely experienced, pastoral theologian Charles Gerkin appeals for ministry that is more imaginative to traverse this divide. He constructs a valuable formula that offers a pastoral care perspective and praxis to

---

[41] Chinula, 56-57.
[42] Chinula, 58.

use in racial reconciliation. First, there must be an understanding that under normal circumstances, the application of the prophetic ministry can spring from the unexpected. Second, it is a timely response to human suffering and conflict. Third, the suffering and conflict, and the subsequent cry for relief are transformative in the mind of the imaginative prophetic pastor. Fourth, as the situation begins to unfold, the imaginative prophetic pastor displays astuteness. Fifth, rather than confront, the imaginative prophetic pastor adopts a conciliatory stance, allowing the issues to surface in a communal context. And sixth, the imaginative prophetic pastor creatively seeks occasion to relate the narrative of the situation with the larger Christian narrative to bring about fusion and resolution.[43] There is much utility in Gerkin's formulation that can have resonance in establishing an SCPC approach to reconciliation.

Though not specifically a pastoral theologian, Catholic theologian Robert J. Schreiter is of interest because of his work in the field of social change and peacemaking. His perspective on reconciliation is that it is an almost unattainable task since it fosters forgiveness, heals memories, and changes to societal structures that sustain alienation. In his global travels exploring conflict areas, he distills his findings by noting that one of the most challenging elements of the reconciliation process is dealing with victims of violence. Along with physical violence, racism is another virulent strain of violence because of the psychic injury it inflicts. Since violence is a destructive force on the meaning-making and narrative of individuals and their identities, it must first be overcome in the mind. For Schreiter, the first step in the process of overcoming violent suffering is to attend to the construction of a redeeming narrative that liberates one from the power of falsehood. Next is finding the best way to endure suffering and in so doing regain the lost humanity stolen by violence. So, as the core of the human essence is being restored, trust begins to develop. Since the violent memory remains potent, it must be disassociated from the actual violent act, and by retelling the story of violence in a trauma

---

[43] Charles V. Gerkin, *Prophetic Pastoral Practice: A Christian Vision of Life Together* (Nashville: Abingdon Press, 1991), 74-84

narrative, the violence itself is diminished.[44] The salutary effects of a placing suffering in a redemptive context be it violence to the body through armed struggle or violence to the psyche through racism, is very much a part of the arch of the black history in the U.S., through music and Negro spirituals in particular.

In some respects, Schreiter's approach to addressing the trauma of violence shares some characteristics of the popular Trauma Focused Cognitive Behavioral Therapy (TF-CBT), a short-term evidence-based psychotherapy approach to alleviating significant emotional and behavioral symptoms relating to a traumatic event. TF-CBT has several components which are designed to include cognitive behavioral and trauma-sensitive interventions to enable the traumatized to process their thoughts, feelings and behavior leading to increased safety, growth and interpersonal communications. The acronym "PRACTICE" outlines the sequential components of this treatment modality.[45] At the center of both approaches to trauma recovery is the power of the narrative — no matter how painful, the story must emerge. Similarly, it is difficult to have an effective racial reconciliation process unless the story of the adverse impact of racial injustice is retold.

---

[44] He concludes his book by delineating a Christian understanding of reconciliation, which includes some of the familiar conclusions derived from Pauline theology; 1) it is God who initiates and brings about reconciliation; 2) reconciliation is more a spiritual stance than a strategy; 3) reconciliation makes both the victim and the oppressor a new creation; 4) the new narrative that overcomes the narrative of the lie is the story of the passion and resurrection of Christ; 5) reconciliation is a multidimensional reality. Schreiter, 1, 30, 34-39, 59-62.

[45] The acronym "PRACTICE" represents: Psychoeducation is used to normalize and accurately explore thoughts and actions in response a trauma event. Relaxation techniques are taught to help manage trauma symptoms, and Affective Modulation manages feelings. Cognitive Coping and Processing challenges inaccurate cognition, and a Trauma Narrative is established to disconnect the overwhelming negative emotions from the traumatic event. In Vivo Mastery of Trauma Reminders, serve to mitigate generalized avoidant actions, which interfere with daily functioning. Conjoint Child-Parent sessions serve to improve communication skills, and finally Enhancing Future Safety and Development through skills training to increase self-efficacy and preparedness. Judith A. Cohen, Anthony P. Mannarino, and Esther Deblinger, Treating Trauma and Traumatic Grief in

In spite of the fact that approaches to racial reconciliation from the SCPC field are evolving, it is not difficult to extract general themes from which a methodological framework [see the final chapter] can be structured to assist spiritual caregivers in general and Adventist church leaders in particular to navigate this difficult terrain. Beginning with the initial contributions from Clebsch and Jaekle, it is heartening to see that their prophetic call for the proliferation of the pastoral function of reconciling has been heeded, with this text being no exception. Clebsch and Jaekle would no doubt be surprised that it has been in the secular arena, and to a lesser extent in the Christian Church, that reconciling has found its niche. This underutilization of the ministry of reconciliation should be alarming to all religious traditions, though it is not unpredictable. In Luke 16:8 (NIV), Christ laments the fact that "the people of this world are more shrewd in dealing with their own kind than are the people of the light."

Reinhold Niebuhr observes that the distinction between the "children of light" and the "children of darkness" is "self-interest." The former are oblivious of its power, while the latter are alert to it. However, the children of light are not foolish only because they misjudge how powerful self-interest is in their opposite number. Rather, they fail to appreciate its power in their own lives.[46] The challenge to the children of light is a simple one: they "must be armed with the wisdom of the children of darkness but refrain from their malice. They must know the power of self-interest in human society without giving it moral justification. They must have this wisdom in order that they beguile, deflect, harness and restrain self-interest, individual and collective, for the sake of the community."[47] These are challenging words indeed to all but more so to a religious tradition whose self-identification is that of the Remnant.

Children and Adolescents (New York: The Guilford Press, 2006), 32-45. Several websites are available to access more information about TF-CBT: http://academicdepartments.musc.edu/projectbest/tfcbt/tfcbt.htm; and http://tfcbt.musc.edu/ (accessed 1/23/11).

[46] Reinhold Niebuhr, *The Children of Light and the Children of Darkness*, 10-11.

[47] Reinhold Niebuhr, *The Children of Light and the Children of Darkness*, 41.

Ironically, this appropriation of "reconciling" by the secular world (including the Peace and Justice Movement) harmonizes with Thornton's view of these pastoral functions as "practices" because many in these secular organizations utilize some of the same language and theological principles enunciated by the Apostle Paul, as will be demonstrated. It should be stated that the probability of some of the same language being used in mediating conflicts around the globe may in part be due to the religious convictions of those who engage in this work of socially healing fractured relationships. These individuals have in their professional tool-kit religious practices that serve as their moral compass in the "soul" work of uniting and reuniting "souls!"

Practices of Racial Reconciliation
Progress and Pitfalls of the Truth and Reconciliation Commission
Perhaps no experience is more emblematic of racial reconciliation than the South African Truth and Reconciliation Commission (TRC), stemming from the Promotion of National Unity and Reconciliation Act signed into law by President Nelson Mandela on July 19, 1995. The racist system of Apartheid (Afrikaans for "apartness"), which mandated racial segregation between blacks and whites from 1948 to 1993, was to face a final reckoning after all manner of unspeakable atrocities and acts of indiscriminate violence were perpetrated by the white minority on the largely black population. Ominously, De Gruchy writes, "Only time will tell the extent to which the TRC did in fact get at the truth about apartheid's murky past and promote national reconciliation."[48] Lyn S. Graybill, at the time a South African humanities studies student, recalls the events in her book intriguingly entitled, *Truth and Reconciliation in South Africa: Miracle or Model?* She observed that the professionally diverse, seventeen-person, multiethnic commission moved with dispatch despite opposition from all the main political parties. The mainly white National Party (NP) contended that it was to be nothing more than a "witch hunt." The Inkatha Freedom Party (IFP) suggested that the African National Congress (ANC) would be the

---

[48] De Gruchy, 12.

sole beneficiary, while some in the ANC felt that they had sacrificed too much with the amnesty prerequisite.[49]

The goals of the TRC were to create a narrative of the human rights violations, to assist victims in restoring their dignity through storytelling, and review appeals for amnesty for repentant perpetrators. Perhaps because of a lack of cooperation from the Apartheid government officials, the TRC favored subjective forms of truth like personal and social truth over objective forms of truth like factual and restorative truth.[50] Using three subcommittees to achieve the goals, the TRC took six years to complete their work, at a cost of $30 million. They visited 61 towns to hold 140 hearings and took 22,000 victims' testimonies, spanning 37,000 violations; and over 7,000 perpetrators sought amnesty. Despite these resources, time and effort, the conclusions of the TRC report have been panned by many who observed and studied the commission's work. The TRC report was published on October 1998. It began by decrying the uncooperative nature of the Apartheid government. Inkatha also came in for criticism since it was claimed by the report to have been used as a tool of the NP in a divide-and-conquer strategy to infiltrate and wage war against the ANC.[51] Both the NP and IFP were said by

---

[49] Lyn Graybill, 2002, 5.

[50] Chapman and van der Merwe observe that this storytelling approach to accessing truth is problematic since the stories can only reflect the victim's perspective, and their interpretation of the facts. Furthermore, the data amassed by the TRC appears to not have been applied to "new understandings, interpretations, or recommendations." Chapman and van der Merwe, 244-45. The four notions of truth defined are: Factual truth — the evidence obtained and corroborated through reliable procedures; Personal truth — the many stories that individuals tell about their experiences; Social truth — established interaction, discussion and debate; and Restorative truth — the truth that places facts and their meaning within the context of human relationships. Dr. Weitekamp, "Restorative Justice for Victims of Mass Violence," paper delivered on December 3, 2009: http://www.victim-participation.org/files/Weitekamp-presentation.pdf (accessed 12/12/11).

[51] *Truth and Reconciliation Commission of South Africa Report*, 5: 196-97.

the report to be guilty of inciting hatred with violent rhetoric which triggered violent responses by the military and paramilitary.[52]

One of the toughest questions among many asked by theologians and ethicists at the time was this: Is there a moral equivalence between the defensive violence of the oppressed liberation movement of the ANC and the offensive violence of the perpetrators in the form of Apartheid government? The TRC's answer was unpalatable for many to hear as the TRC report concluded that the ends did not justify the means used by the ANC to resist oppression. Archbishop Desmond Tutu expressed this position succinctly, "A gross violation is a gross violation, whoever commits it and for whatever reason."[53] As a spiritual leader Tutu was expressing the futility of violence no matter its justification. As a consequence, the ANC was also held responsible for its acts of aggression in its efforts to counterattack. As Graybill notes, the ANC were the most hostile to the findings of the TRC, accusing it of "criminalizing the antiapartheid struggle" and calling its findings "capricious and arbitrary." The report of the TRC was met with ambivalence, according to historian and journalist Martin Meredith who encapsulates the sense of indifference with this pithy comment, "Thus the TRC ended its task, assailed from all sides, praised by few."[54]

Common wisdom assumes that when all sides of a conflict have difficulty with a particular outcome, it generally validates the outcome, but a review of much of the literature is mixed on this issue. An indication of this fact is the use of bipolar pairings of words such as "miracle or evil compromise," "achievement and shortfalls," "Holy Grail or secular pact," and "contributions and

---

[52] The TRC's work took six years, because the amnesty hearings did not conclude until May 2001. Lyn Graybill, 8, 145-58.

[53] Tutu continues that "There is thus legal equivalence between all perpetrators. Their political affiliation is irrelevant." *Truth and Reconciliation Commission of South Africa Report* (London: MacMillan Reference Limited, 1998), 12.

[54] Meredith writes of Tutu's more hopeful reflections thus: "The pain of facing the truth about past horrors was an unavoidable price to pay for reconciliation, he said. 'Now we are facing it. It is going to be horrible. But maybe the worst is already past." Meredith, 307.

limitations."[55] Hugo van der Merwe, an expert in the study of violence and reconciliation, has written extensively on the TRC, offering a critical evaluation of the commission. There was an understandable reluctance of white South Africans to participate in the process, with many of them believing there to be an in-built bias. An enormous amount of official and classified documents was destroyed by National Party officials, and the capacity to thoroughly investigate acts of violence was impeded by a lack of resources and reluctance to use subpoena power. Despite its dual mandate to establish truth and facilitate reconciliation, the former was subjugated by the latter, evidence of which was the overrepresentation of white victims' testimonies and the individualizing and not institutionalizing of the crimes committed. White overrepresentation was the TRC's way of mitigating white hostilities toward the process, as well as the sense of guilt and shame among the white minorities. The TRC failed to offer a substantive critique of the Apartheid system, leaving in place the disturbing notion held by a majority of South Africans – that its ideas were principled.[56]

Since the TRC never clarified what was meant by reconciliation or established goals to accomplish it, the commissioners disagreed on the value of interpersonal reconciliation when national reconciliation was the target. Consequently, the confession by perpetrators and the forgiveness of them by victims had mixed results as many perpetrators were no-shows at the meetings to face their victims. Van der Merwe does credit the TRC with facilitating political reconciliation despite the fact that it led to the resurfacing of uncomfortable truths and renewed tensions. Regarding racial reconciliation, the TRC was generally hesitant to broach the subject, missing an opportunity to address decades of racial animus under Apartheid, and centuries of colonial rule built

---

[55] The references are listed in the order that the phrases appear: Lyn Graybill 2002, 177; Hugo van der Merwe, "Reconciliation and Justice in South Africa," *Reconciliation, Justice and Coexistence: Theory and Practice*, 195; De Gruchy, 14; and Audrey R. Chapman and Hugo van der Merwe, *Truth and Reconciliation in South Africa: Did the TRC Deliver?* (Philadelphia: University of Pennsylvania Press, 2008), 241.

[56] Chapman and van der Merwe, 245-54.

on the inferiority of blacks. Chapman and van der Merwe observed, after one study in 1998 and follow-up studies years later confirmed that distrust between black and white South Africans will remain and never improve, this was a lost opportunity indeed–though racial attitudes are changing among the young.[57]

On matters of justice, observe Chapman and van der Merwe, the TRC was more a process of accessing truth at the expense of justice but achieving neither. They also note that calls for restorative justice from the populace were inadequately addressed because the concept, though initially ignored by the commission, was reframed to include the shared narratives, hearings, reconciling former foes, reparations, and even amnesty.[58] In the case of amnesty, while there was a sense among South Africans that perpetrators were being let off the hook, there was a quiet admission that it was democracy's price. There was a limited amount of retributive justice since it could only be applied to those seeking amnesty, but very few perpetrators sought amnesty.[59] The lack of retributive justice, the granting of amnesty, and the better access to legal assistance enjoyed by perpetrators, understandably led to great dissatisfaction among survivors as to the justice that the TRC had delivered. As the TRC was not established to deal with past economic and social injustices of the Apartheid era, its focus on the thousands of recognized victims of Apartheid and not the millions of blacks who were victimized by privileged white South Africans, led to a lack of awareness and accountability for the enormous socioeconomic disparities that blacks experienced. But van der Merwe concludes that while the TRC underperformed, it did nevertheless assist in creating an orderly process toward democratic, inclusive and responsible governance.[60] He ends by stating that, "As the first major institution shared by all South Africans, the TRC symbolized the national unity of a new rainbow nation."[61]

In his coverage of the TRC, Martin Meredith reports that the narrative approach of the TRC in the hearings and in written

---

[57] Chapman and van der Merwe, 260-61.
[58] Chapman and van der Merwe, 264.
[59] Chapman and van der Merwe, 266.
[60] Chapman and van der Merwe, 263-73.
[61] Chapman and van der Merwe, 279.

testimonials is in keeping with current psychotherapeutic trauma interventions, but it is disappointing that these narratives were never framed in the wider narrative of the oppressive and dehumanizing system of apartheid. This approach, observes Meredith, was clearly intended to mitigate and deflect blame from social, cultural, and institutional forces that erected such a system. In some respects, transferring institutional responsibility onto individuals who worked within these institutions may have had the desired effect of maintaining the integrity of these institutions at a time of immense volatility as the country transitioned from minority to majority rule. However, it may have also left victims unsatisfied, rightly suspicious of a government apparatus that once engaged in a reign of terror against them. Also troubling was the uncooperativeness and disdain that white South Africans had for the TRC, as Meredith reports.[62] With those who benefited most from the Apartheid system in many respects on the sideline, it is difficult to see how the TRC was anything but a means of minimizing of atrocities committed during the Apartheid regime since, as Chapman and van der Merwe conclude, it failed "to place the abuses in a more systemic context."[63] Yet they believe that while "the TRC did not deliver satisfactorily on specific assignments, it does not mean that it did not contribute to South Africa's transition from apartheid to a more democratic, inclusive, and responsible form of government."[64] Perhaps the lesson of transition from a bleak past to a brighter future is one that offers Adventists hope with respect to racial reconciliation.

Further, what reconciliation meant to the TRC in South Africa was not static but evolving as the process meandered beyond the scheduled eighteen months' allocation. What reconciliation meant in South Africa is best summarized by then President Nelson Mandela, who reportedly said as he took receipt of the TRC report, it was a "search for a nation at peace with itself and the building of a better life for all."[65] Perhaps acknowledging the outsized task it was set, Mandela added, "The wounds of the period of repression and

---

[62] Meredith, 289.
[63] Chapman and van der Merwe, 276.
[64] Chapman and van der Merwe, 278.
[65] De Gruchy, 25.

resistance are too deep to have been healed by the TRC alone."[66] Thus, reconciliation was a way of talking about past hostilities and atrocities without allowing such discourse to get in the way of forging a new nation's future. This perspective was incredibly optimistic at the time since the black majority with its hands on the reins of power could have exacted harsh vengeance on their largely white oppressors; but in Mandela and co-chair of the TRC, Archbishop Tutu, humanity and theology, prefaced on forbearance and forgiveness, provided the leadership that their people and the country needed to make a flawed process work. Approaching reconciliation as a process, argues De Gruchy, is reflective of Christian theology with its "already" (present) and "not yet" (future) tension; in this way, final reconciliation is always beyond reach.[67] As South Africa has continued down the path of peaceful coexistence, it is difficult to counter Mandela's future focus and easier to affirm that reconciliation is indeed an expedition from an alienated place to a future in communion with one's former foes.

Reconciliation in the Peace and Justice Movement

With the relative success of the TRC in establishing peaceful coexistence, it has in the process lent credibility to conflict resolution strategies with the increasing prominence of global peace and reconciliation movements. Of course, truces, treaties, mediations, and negotiations have long been a part of warfare and intergroup conflict. Now social science, philosophy, international law, international relations, political science, economics, social anthropology, ethics and religious thought are being amalgamated in order to bring about postconflict societies. Two of these eclectic approaches to reconciliation will be assessed by exploring their underlying theory or philosophy, the specific interventions used to achieve the desired outcome, and any common critiques of these approaches aimed at achieving lasting peace. The precursors to the study of conflict as a psychosocial phenomenon were Charles Darwin with his theory of survival of the fittest, Karl Marx with his

---

[66] "1998: Apartheid report accuses SA leaders," BBC Online, http://news.bbc.co.uk/onthisday/hi/dates/stories/october/29/newsid_2 468000/2468007.stm (accessed 1/12/11).
[67] De Gruchy, 28.

emphasis on class struggles, and Sigmund Freud with his psychosexual stages and the psychic struggles involving the Id, Ego, and Superego.

The contemporary social psychology field has attempted to address several questions regarding conflict resolution, and five of those questions are vital in establishing a theory of conflict resolution.[68] A central theory governing conflict resolution is that the outcome is determined by the cooperative or competitive nature of the individuals involved. The theory of cooperation and competition, developed by Morton Deutsch, is premised on the interdependence among goals of those in conflict and the actions they take; either they sink or swim together, or one sinks and the other swims. Other elements of this theory are that the conflict must be reframed as a mutual challenge to be resolved collaboratively. Such reframing is not possible unless the parties engage in behaviors and shared values of reciprocity, equality, fallibility, and nonviolence that tend to fosters cooperation. An understanding of the theory must then be coupled with skills training that addresses three areas: 1) establishing rapport between the conflicting parties by reducing suspicions, overcoming resistance, and fostering optimism; 2) building a sustaining conflict resolution process that is cooperative by identifying the form of conflict, framing issues as mutually solvable problems, practicing positive communication

---

[68] The five questions are: (1) What are the essential elements of productive and unproductive conflict management? (2) What causes one side in a conflict to fare better than the other? (3) What leads to a successful outcome following a conflict, if an agreement is achieved? (4) What role can third parties play in de-escalating and resolving conflict? (5) Does conflict resolution education enable individuals to manage their conflicts more effectively? In addition to these questions, others are now being asked, including how to understand the protracted and destructive nature of ethnic, religious and identity conflicts? Morton Deutsch, "Introduction," *The Handbook of Conflict Resolution: Theory and Practice* (eds. Morton Deutsch, Peter T. Coleman, and Eric C. Marcus; San Francisco: Jossey-Bass, 2006), 13-19. The field of social conflict management has several established journals, including *Annual Review of Conflict Knowledge and Conflict Resolution, International Journal of Conflict Management, International Social Movement Research, Peace and Conflict,* and *Research in Social Movements, Conflicts and Change,* to name just a few.

skills, acknowledging the needs of all sides, identifying shared interests and values and factoring in cultural differences; and 3) establishing a dynamic group problem-solving and decision-making process.[69]

This theory of conflict resolution understandably addresses issues of ethics and morality, given that to be effective in mediating interethnic disputes, one is required to deal with retributive and reparative justice, reconciliation, and the role of forgiveness in facilitating psychological and spiritual healing. Here, reconciliation is seen as the terminus of a process, initiated by forgiveness, at which point re-established relationships in community are achieved. As trust and distrust are essential elements of human interaction, they must be creatively managed within the conflict resolution process.   One conflict resolution model using an integrative approach is the Problem-solving and Decision-making (PSDM) model. It is a four-stage process of identifying the nature of the conflict, exploring solutions, assessing and selecting an agreed-upon solution, and obligating the parties to execute the plan. Stages one and two are for problem-solving and stages three and four for decision making although there is generally overlap.[70] Conditions that foster increased motivation to engage in this process are "a psychological climate characterized by cohesion, fairness, recognition of success, and openness to innovation."[71]

There are some notable criticisms of the conflict resolution theory, including those who prefer to use the phrase "conflict transformation" since conflict resolution conveys a promise that may be both undeliverable and/or undesirable. As peace and justice student Estheranna Stäuble writes, "While not always seeking to end conflict, conflict transformation aims at altering a given conflict in order to find nonviolent ways of communication and to create solutions."[72]   While this is a laudable criticism, conflict

---

[69] Chapman and van der Merwe, 24-39.

[70] Chapman and van der Merwe, 51-63, 94-97; 197-217.

[71] Chapman and van der Merwe, 218.

[72] Estheranna Stäuble, "Nonviolent Direct Action, Conflict Transformation, and the Global Justice Movement: The Aubonne Bridge Case" (M.A. thesis., University of Bradford, 2004), 10, http://www.aubonnebridge.net/data/aubonne_single_space.pdf (accessed 12/12/10).

transformation arguably suffers from the same flaw since it is heavily invested in psycho-education and techniques of peacemaking while knowledge and techniques are only as good as the individuals who utilize them. More importantly, they are contingent on the "transformation of the disputants' perceptions of each other and of the conflict. What remains totally untouched is the dimension of the underlying structures that have allowed the conflict to rise in first place."[73]

Ignoring oppressive structures as the TRC did, in favor of reestablishing relationships, means that those structures may continue to oppress long after the parties are reconciled. Additionally, because conflict resolution theory is a knowledge and skills-based approach, it could be guilty of assuming violent conflicts can rationally and objectively be known; hence, gaining mastery over it is just one intervention away.[74] This reasoning is flawed since a complete knowledge of human nature remains in the "not yet!" As the scripture reminds us, "The heart is deceitful above all things and beyond cure. Who can understand it?" (Jer. 17:9, NIV). Finally, conflict resolution theory places great stock in the skill, neutrality, and respect of the mediator from both sides. Yet decades of unsuccessful mediation attempts by the U.S. government in facilitating peace between Israel and Palestine, demonstrate the improbability of having such an effective mediator. Also, inherent in the theory is the assumption that warring factions will "play-nice" when decades or even centuries of embedded hostilities, prejudices, and acts against humanity can and will be displaced with the use of conventional interpersonal problem-solving skills. As one critic observes, a "multi-track" approach is perhaps preferable so that conflict resolution is but one approach to reconciling; others can include negotiations, diplomacy, and arbitration.[75]

---

[73] Here the author acknowledges the legitimate criticism of Conflict Resolution theory, while seeing value in the evolution of the theory. Marta Martinelli Quille, "A Response to Recent Critiques of Conflict Resolution: Is Critical Theory the Answer?" *Copenhagen Peace Research Institute* (August 2000): http://www.ciaonet.org/wps/qum01/ (accessed 12/12/10).

[74] Stäuble.

[75] Stäuble.

Given the complexity of any reconciliation process with its array of systemic, structural, interethnic and intercultural issues that must be grappled with, it is easy to forget that in the end, conflicts are between human beings at both the interpersonal and intrapsychic level; and it is here that conflict resolutions battles are won and lost. Social psychology is ideally situated to broach this subject since this is the terrain with which they are most familiar, given the established nexus between thoughts (cognition), feelings (affect) and actions (behavior). These three domains are fundamental to a psychological understanding of reconciliation since it can lead to a better understanding of and preparation for their exhibition, while interventions can be introduced to mitigate their impact. Social psychologist Walter Stephan has identified several affective, cognitive, and behavioral processes at work in intergroup reconciliation that should be anticipated since they are relatively identifiable; interventions to counter them can be introduced by a mediator as part of the reconciliation process. However, both the cognitive and behavioral processes that he references have already been discussed and will not be repeated.

There are several types of affective processes; they include anxiety and feeling threatened, both of which can lead to an out-group being perceived negatively. Often these anxieties stem from learned associations linking objects and emotions to traits or stereotypes of the out-group. Appropriate face-to-face contact and the giving of accurate information about the out-group have been shown to be salutary. Emotional empathy, the ability to share vicariously in the suffering of the out-group, has been shown to be relevant in the reconciliation process by limiting victim-blaming. Emotional empathy can also be stimulated by educating the in-group on the travails of the out-group. Another affective response that can benefit from exposure is awareness of the hypocrisy that conflicted groups engage in as their practice fails to live up to their stated values. This renewed awareness of discrepancies could lead to either reform or recalcitrance, but an effective mediator can enable individuals to see how their discomfort and dissonance can be minimized.[76]

---

[76] Nadler, et al., 382-84.

Also associated with the affective processes of reconciliation is collective guilt of the in-group for possible culpability for the plight of the out-group. Despite the fact that emotions can be volatile and resistance to mutual responsibility problematic, both can be countered by a constructive dialogue (or information from credible sources) about the suffering experienced by the out-group at the hands of the in-group. Akin to emotional empathy is cognitive empathy in which the in-group takes an out-group perspective of the world as a means of prejudice reduction. This perspective-taking could result in both the in-group and out-group learning to view each other as not as significantly different as previously thought, limiting polarization. What should be apparent at this stage is how complex it is to engage in any form of reconciliation, given the subtleties of culture, race, gender, religion, and social status, not to mention the disparity brought about by interethnic hostilities in the past and present. When such complexities are compounded with these three psychological processes (cognition, affect and behavior), it makes reconciliation a daunting, multilayered and, by necessity a multidisciplinary problem-solving process. Few academic disciplines should be excluded from this multivalent approach to reconciliation, chief among which should be the SCPC field with its porous boundaries that allow input from other disciplines. Such a multivalent approach to racial reconciliation is evident in the work of Eric Yamamoto, the subject of the next segment.

Adaptation of Yamamoto's "Interracial Justice" Model as an
SCPC Approach for Racial Reconciliation
    In addition to social-psychological approaches to understanding and resolving ethnic conflicts, scholars and practitioners of peacebuilding have applied themselves to the thorny issue of racial reconciliation. Notably, the work of law professor Eric K. Yamamoto will be appropriated to form the basis of an SCPC methodology for attempting racial reconciliation, what he calls "Interracial Justice." His four "Rs" of interracial justice are Recognition, Responsibility, Reconstruction, and Reparation. When synchronized with Clebsch and Jaekle's formulation of reconciling as forgiveness (confession and repentance) and discipline, along with other ethical, theological, and SCPC insights, these can point the way towards an effective strategy of racial reconciliation. Underlying

217

Yamamoto's notion of "interracial justice" is his "Race Praxis," an overcoming of the paralysis of analysis to achieve real-world outcomes relative to racial justice.

Race praxis is a loose amalgam of various theories including critical race theory, feminist, and theological reflections which are guided by four lines of inquiry. The first aspect of analysis is the *"conceptual,"* which is a "sociolegal" assessment with implications for the legality of the conflict and grievances arising from it. The second is the *"performative,"* involving what realistic approaches will address the obvious and the opaque claims of the aggrieved, and who should act on them. *"Material"* is the third aspect of race praxis and perhaps the most important, for it addresses change to social and representational structures that reinforce racial oppression. Fourth is the *"reflective,"* which urges vigilance among lawyers, activists, and theorists to establish a feedback loop in which practice impacts theory.[77] Given his profession, it is understandable that Yamamoto's race praxis is weighted towards judicial activism to address political, economic and legal disparity and subordination.

Notwithstanding the legal dimensions of his approach, which is geared towards upending embedded structures as well as interpersonal dimensions of interracial conflicts, it remains a viable option among many. Its viability is enhanced by Yamamoto's multidisciplinary approach to healing, engaging as he does his own field of law, which can at best achieve indirect healing; theology with its freedom narratives; social psychology with its ability to address the emotional content of conflict and healing to achieve a cathartic release; political theory with its focus on righting wrongs through democratic means; and indigenous healing practices like the Hawaiian *ho'oponopono* or the Navajo peacemaking practice of *hozhooji naat' aanii*.[78] This eclectic approach to racial reconciliation enables Yamamoto to reflect both the subtleties and the spiritual import of racial reconciliation. In so doing, Yamamoto avoids one of the misconceptions of reconciliation pointed out by Schreiter: that it is often viewed as little more than a managed process, typical of conflict mediation.

---

[77] Yamamoto, 129-32.
[78] Yamamoto, 154-67.

Yamamoto is commended by critics for raising significant concerns regarding race relations beyond the black/white paradigm so that people of all colors can have their justice claims addressed, not just legally but therapeutically. One such critic, James R. Hackney, Jr., writes of "having a visceral response to Yamamoto's enterprise," particularly regarding the first chapter entitled 'Can We All Get Along?' Hackney contends that the plea by Rodney King from the Los Angeles riot of 1992 was "both heartfelt and empty" since he believes that Rodney King, who made the appeal for togetherness, was unrealistic.[79] Hackney finds Yamamoto reparation approach similarly unrealistic since it is central to his reconciliation approach, yet Yamamoto fails to champion it "as a tool for redistribution."[80] Further, Hackney argues that reparations as a "mechanism to heal relationships," from Yamamoto's perspective, reveals a blind spot, namely that "beneficiaries of reparations frequently have a different agenda."[81] Despite his criticism, Hackney is sensitive to the goals of Yamamoto's enterprise but believes that there are material constraints to agency and that these constraints "hinder any efforts towards true reconciliation."[82]

Further criticism has come from Kathleen. S. Yep of UC Berkeley, who observes two areas of challenge for Yamamoto's interracial justice, namely "implementation and a limiting single axis analysis."[83] Despite laying out a theoretical framework for healing cross-racial hostility, Yep is unclear as to how the concepts translate into reality. Particularly of concern is the haziness of how the four R's organically integrate at the community level. Secondly, Yep believes that Yamamoto unintentionally diminishes the issue of "color-on-color hostility to race" at the expense of a more thorough

---

[79] James R. Hackney, Jr., Review of *Interracial Justice: Conflict and Reconciliation in Post-Civil Rights America* by Eric K. Yamamoto, *Social and Legal Studies* 10.2 (2001): 279.

[80] Hackney.

[81] Hackney.

[82] Hackney, 280.

[83] Kathleen S. Yep, "Book Review: *Interracial Justice: Conflict and Reconciliation in Post-Civil Rights America*," *Journal of Asian American Studies* 4.2 (2001): 186-90; http://muse.jhu.edu.ezproxy.libraries.claremont.edu/journals/journal_of_asian_american_studies/toc/jaas4.2.html (accessed 12/12/10).

analysis of gender and class.[84] Yet, Yamamoto's work is not adversely impacted by these criticisms for three reasons, writes Yep: 1) the pivot from the black/white paradigm to relations between people of color; 2) the analysis of why color-on color conflicts endure and how to address them; and 3) the fact that he rethinks the intent of justice to include religious healing and reconciliation.[85]

While a Christian approach to reconciliation includes an array of contributions from several disciplines, it encompasses much more. Since God is the reconciler and the initiator of reconciliation, God must be paramount in any Christian reconciliation approach. Also, Christian reconciliation is less a skill to be taught, what Schreiter calls a "technical rationality," than it is an art to be discovered and developed – a spiritual practice that is the outgrowth of God's grace in the life of the believer. Additionally, Christian reconciliation is more "spirituality than strategy," for it allows for a more individualized cultural expression than simply a Western cultural perspective.[86] The spiritual nature of reconciliation also affords it the potential to address issues of volition and agency, for the gospel wills and empowers conflicted groups to view each other as part of a whole–the family of God. Given our interconnectedness inherent at creation and in the cross, the basis for restorative metanarrative is not only possible but necessary. Furthermore, our common humanity comes under the canopy of Christ's words of forgiveness, "Father, forgive them, for they do not know what they are doing," (Luke 23:34, NIV). And in the Lord's Prayer, the believer's response to divine pardon is "forgive us our debts, as we also have forgiven our debtors" (Matt 6:9, NIV).

Recognition and Confession

As with the first steps in recovering from a substance addiction, Yamamoto's first dimension of racial reconciliation begins with "recognition," of which there are three components. One component is the empathetic acknowledgement of the aspirations and anger of communities of resistance whose collective narrative of oppression and collective memory of suffering should stimulate

---

[84] Yep.
[85] Yep.
[86] Schreiter, 25-27.

inquiry into the personal and societal perceptions of the meaning of their experience. Assigning meaning is critical to a group which has experienced physical and psychic suffering as such experiences tend to be framed from the standpoint of their oppressors (e.g., "If they had only assimilated sooner," or "They had it coming to them"). In addition to meaning-making is the need for an honest appraisal of the historic context of the suffering and disparity caused by the conflict, which is now at the heart of the present grievance. The capacity to achieve this level of empathetic awareness is what Yamamoto calls, "Seeing into the Woundedness of the 'Other.'"[87] A further task of the recognition stage is examining the veracity of "stock stories," narratives that are largely revisionistic in nature, ones that present the group using them in the most favorable light, as a means of mitigating culpability.[88] An example of a stock story from some white Adventist perspective is the belief that black preaching and worship is too emotional and lacking in depth, while some black Adventists hold the view that white preaching and worship is dull and uninspiring. As a consequence, the separation of blacks and whites in church worship is reinforced.

Although Yamamoto's assessment of stock stories can serve to unearth issues of denial and indifference, it lacks specificity in coping with a common feature of the TRC, namely maximum buy-in and meaningful participation by most whites and some blacks who felt the process was rigged against them. Just as recognition is the beginning of any recovery process, denial is its scourge, for it keeps the individual or group deluded and disengaged from present reality and the reason for the suffering of others, making emotional empathy difficult to muster. In this respect, Yamamoto's model fails to address this common dilemma of generating empathy by simple force of will. However, recognition in the form of confession can serve to challenge the believer to engage as a requirement of his or her faith. Historically, the nexus between confession and repentance has been difficult to distinguish, with the latter considered a subset of the former. Confession is rooted in the notion of speaking with or affirming a reality. It is the admission of culpability as a means to

---

[87] Yamamoto, 176.
[88] Yamamoto, 181.

restoring relationships. Whereas, repentance is a deep sorrow for wrongdoing and a strong commitment to desist.

In the context of healing, whether physical, spiritual or psychic, the apostle James urged believers to confess their sins and personal failings to each other, as a means of affecting healing (James 5:15-17, NIV). This spiritual practice remains meritorious as a means of enhancing and restoring fractured relationships since it is premised on a mutual vulnerability to acknowledge past failings without overreaction or denial. Confession is an antidote to isolation, which is often enforced by the social distance resulting from conflict. Since most white and some black church leaders are discomforted by the current racial divide inherent in separate conferences and the isolation attributed to them, it is hoped that an appeal for the adherence to the spiritual practice of confession would be favorably considered. In his reflections on the nexus between confession and community, Bonhoeffer is emphatic: "In confession the break-through to community takes place. Sin demands to have a man by himself. It withdraws him from his community. The more isolated a person is, the more destructive will be the power of sin over him, and the more deeply he becomes involved in it, the more disastrous is his isolation."[89] Viewed from this perspective, confession is an invaluable spiritual discipline for the believer. Underutilization of confession has serious consequences for the very essence of the individual's or group's spiritual life and resources. Given the deleterious consequences of resisting or being indifferent to confession, it could be argued that the spurned invitations

---

[89] The benefits of confession extend beyond a breakthrough community, notes Bonhoeffer; it also is a breakthrough to the cross, to new life, and to certainty. Bonhoeffer, *Life Together* (New York: Harpers & Brother, Publishers, 1954), 112-113. Elsewhere, Bonhoeffer connects recognition and a reluctance to admit guilt with a state of isolation. "Recognizing that we are guilty makes us solitary before God; we begin to recognize what has been the case objectively, namely that we are in a state of isolation. With this recognition the old community-of-God, whose norm and constituting power is the law, is broken up. The law does not establish community but solitude—as a consequence of human sin." Dietrich Bonhoeffer, *Sanctorum Communio: A Theological Study of the Sociology of the Church* (tr. Reinhard Krauss and Nancy Lukens; Minneapolis: Fortress Press, 1998), 149.

described in the parable of the Great Banquet and the mandated invitations to all and sundry reveal a Gospel of compulsion: "Compel them to come in!" (Luke 14:23-24, NIV). Does confession come with a similar mandate? Since God is the initiator of reconciliation, an affirmative response could be in order. Finally, notwithstanding the potential for exploitation, confession remains a divinely inspired gateway to relational health.

Other features of this stage of recognition as confession include issues of suspicion, which could be reduced by the groups' willingness to engage in mutual self-disclosure. Battling suspicions through self-disclosure is never easy since such sharing involves the discloser being significantly vulnerable. The fact that addressing suspicions through self-disclosure is difficult does not mean that it should not be attempted. Another aspect of recognition is the constructing from the individual narratives a collective narrative as a broader context for the conflict and its concomitant suffering. Finding commonality through the groups' shared interests and values is yet another. The stories of suffering, oppression, and revenge combine with the stories of privilege, insensitivity, and guilt, combine to form one collective narrative of the conflict, with the cross at its center, argues Yamamoto. He concludes that the process of racial reconciliation can transition to the next stage of interracial justice, even while confession is ongoing.

Responsibility and Repentance

Just as confession and repentance are linked, so too are recognition and responsibility; for responsibility solicits the reflections of conflicted groups to explore agency and admit blame for causing undue harm to the out-group, reminiscent of Yancey's notion of mutual responsibility. Indeed, much of the literature reviewed in this text argues for this approach to any reconciliation process. What is not often emphasized is that responsibility for conflicts is not always equally distributed; one group often must bear the larger share of blame for their role. This desire for mutual responsibility was at the heart of resistance by the ANC during the TRC, since they did not equate being a part of a resistance community as comparable to their perpetrators' actions, in the repressive system of apartheid. I remain unconvinced that mutual responsibility is comparable to equal responsibility as outlined by many of the reconciliation authors. This lack of distinction could inadvertently augment the very trauma symptoms and reactive responses that the process of reconciliation is designed to address. Furthermore, if mutual responsibility is likened to equal responsibility, then one could contend that the issue of reparations is a moot point; since everyone is equally to blame, then one cannot be more liable than the other.

Yamamoto does, however, acknowledge that there is often a clear distinction between victims and perpetrators, making analysis of group agency over personal responsibility necessary. This evaluation of agency vs. responsibility is to include how one group derives power over another through economic advancement, public propaganda, and institutional structures, shaping them for oppression. This abuse of power over another group, which advantages some and disadvantages others, essentially impairs both groups, and it is this dynamic that is at the core of the responsibility stage, observes Yamamoto. Psychic wounds and moral injuries are the unseen scars of subjugation and exclusion, causing almost irreparable damage to the soul, but for God's gracious intervention. Yamamoto must be commended for reckoning with the fundamental self-inflicted impairment on perpetrators for their own egregious actions of denigration, what could be called "otherness-making" of the out-group in order to oppress them.[90]

Systematic theologian Miroslav Volf deals at length with the phenomenon of exclusion, connecting it to a perversion of the differentiation process inherent in creation, which connotes "separating and binding." Volf argues that exclusion accomplishes two things. First, it curtails the bonding of one to another, which leads to one's removal from the realms of interdependence to an apparently superior position of independence — a position much in vogue in the late 20th century, with seepage into this new century. Second, exclusion negates the process of creation by failing to acknowledge the other as belonging to the interdependence sphere.[91] To summarize, Volf writes, "Exclusion takes place when the violence of expulsion, assimilation, or subjugation and the indifference of abandonment replace the dynamics of taking in and keeping out as

---

[90] Yamamoto, 185-87.
[91] Volf, 65-66.

well as the mutuality of giving and receiving."[92] This awareness of the destructive nature of exclusion thus becomes the target of the responsibility stage, as a more ethical approach to being, creates connectivity between agency and responsibility.

The process of racial reconciliation thus advances beyond mere recognition of the inequality and suffering of an ethnic group. It goes beyond the assuming of responsibility by beneficiaries of a structural hierarchy that advances their economic, political and social interests. In fact, racial reconciliation rises toward a level of advancement that does not denigrate the other, though to be sure, this mutual advancement will remain elusive without engagement with the two latter stages of the interracial justice process. Importantly, Yamamoto detects an obvious hurdle to the full embrace of collective responsibility, namely, the individualized nature of contemporary society, including the law's support for individual rights. Predictably, perpetrators shun responsibility for the harm they have caused others for many reasons. These include acting as a defense mechanism, in which there is a lack of conscious awareness or an unwillingness to show weakness, like an act of disarmament. One response to this level of resistance is to expand the perimeter of responsibility for redressing the racial wounds of the afflicted group to include those who may not have been adversely impacted so that it is not the offending group alone that must bear this burden.[93]

Attempting to motivate and trigger the taking of responsibility is a difficult task in the reconciliation process, hence the need for repentance. The biblical view of repentance — a turning away from the old and familiar to the new and unknown — may provide for interethnic conflicts between believers a mandate to do that which is appropriate. Repentance speaks to an inner, conscious, change dynamic, an attitudinal adjustment that precipitates external realignments, some of which are fundamental in nature (2 Cor. 7:10). In repentance, contrition and a desire to take corrective action to right a wrong is emphasized, and at the heart of this drive for moral

---

[92] Volf, 67. Bonhoeffer expresses similar sentiments of the need for all to be acknowledged as individuals and not as the "other." Bonhoeffer, *Sanctorum Communio*, 50f.

[93] Yamamoto, 188-90.

rectitude is the divine initiative (Acts 11:18) made possible by the cross of Christ. SCPC can appeal to the believers' changed attitudes as a means of engaging them in taking responsibility and acting in a responsible manner as it relates to racial conflict. Even if the individual or group was not party to the original violation but have nevertheless benefited from it (e.g., privilege), they may be able to assume vicariously the faults of their forebears, in addition to taking responsibility for their own culpability. This vicarious form of repentance as a means to strengthening community is attested to by Bonhoeffer.[94] Issues that are ripe for repentance may flow from the individual narratives that, when processed, can begin to create a metanarrative of the reconciling groups. Issues can be framed as mutually solvable, and the use of effective communications skills can facilitate a solution. It is possible that a successful outcome to this stage of responsibility as repentance, could adequately address grievances and promote racial healing without advancement to the third stage.

Reconstruction and Accountability

Overlapping the responsibility stage is reconstruction, a performance-based act of establishing physical, psychic, social, and material healing. The demands of this stage are that perpetrators apologize for contributing to historic and ongoing injuries, that forgiveness of the perpetrators by the victims occurs when appropriate, and that a reframing of the combined narratives of the conflicting groups assumes an intergroup relational quality.[95] In his acclaimed sociological study on apology and reconciliation, sociologist Nicholas Tavuchis demonstrates that the elements of a satisfactory apology reside in successfully staunching the effects of the conflict through forgiveness and restoring intergroup relations. He rightly views the maintenance of group affiliation as predicated

---

[94] Bonhoeffer observes that "In the church, as in any other community, people repent both for their own sin and for that of the collective person of the community." Bonhoeffer, *Sanctorum Communio*, 145. Further he writes, "One person bears the other in active love, intercession, and forgiveness of sins, acting completely vicariously." Bonhoeffer, *Sanctorum Communio*, 191.

[95] Yamamoto, 175, 190f.

on acknowledging, accepting, and conforming to universal norms. This includes the moral commitment to apologize for wrongs both past and present. How can mutual trust and the dignity of all be preserved without wrongs being acknowledged and repented of, thus giving the relationship a chance to recalibrate?

Instructively then, Tavuchis envisions an apology as expressing:

> ...itself as the exigency of a painful re-membering, literally of being mindful again, of what we were and had as members and, at the same time, what we have jeopardized or lost by virtue of our offensive speech or action. And it is only by personally acknowledging ultimate responsibility, expressing genuine sorrow and regret, and pledging henceforth (implicitly or explicitly) to abide by the rules, that the offender simultaneously recalls and is re-called to that which binds. As shared mementos, apologies require much more than admission of confession of the unadorned facts of wrongdoing or deviance. They constitute–in their most responsible, authentic, and hence, vulnerable expression–a form of self-punishment that cuts deeply because we are obligated to retell, relive, and seek forgiveness for sorrowful events that have rendered our claims to membership on a moral community suspect or defeasible.[96]

This description serves to highlight the regenerative nature of an apology, in its ability to engage both the offended and the offender in a constructive act of recollection without defensiveness or equivocation, setting the stage for the all-important act of forgiveness. As a precursor to forgiveness, an effective apology is designed to disarm and disengage mutually exclusive traits in the offender and the offended. The offender is obligated to surrender self-righteousness and thirst for power, while the offended is to jettison resentment and victimhood.[97] I believe that neither can effectively be achieved without some form of bilateral deactivation

---

[96] Tavuchis, 8. The author also observes that the one apologizing "stands naked. No excuses, appeal to circumstances, etc., can elicit that which alone can release, eradicate, and renew: forgiveness and, hence, redemption." Tavuchis, 18.

[97] Yamamoto, 192-95.

effort. The incentive for such an effort can be based on the community-oriented nature of the relationship that the conflicting groups are seeking to reestablish.

Should this approach to achieving an effective apology be pursued, it is necessary to view this process as a means to an end — that end being forgiveness and beyond to reparations. Forgiveness has routinely been viewed as the first and often only step in the righting of wrongs. Even within the Christian tradition, there is often an undue haste placed on conflicted parties to arrive at a point of forgiveness prematurely. This is perhaps bequeathed to many of us from childhood quarrels in which children are told to "kiss, and makeup" or both are simply urged to say "sorry" to each other without due consideration of the facts. However, the Bible challenges this perception in Luke 17:3-4 (NIV): "If your brother or sister sins against you, rebuke them; and if they repent, forgive them." As coeditor of the volume *Violence Against Women and Children*, pastoral theologian Marie M. Fortune writes of this flawed perspective by asserting that

> Because of the obligation to forgive, which is taught in Christian formation, persons who are victims of family violence often feel that they must forgive their offender immediately... For many victims or survivors of family violence, the longing or obligation to forgive is superseded by the subjective sense of not feeling forgiving."[98]

Even the Clebsch and Jaekle model of reconciling falls prey to this hasty approach to forgiveness since forgiveness is the first of two stages. Fortunately, in Yamamoto's Interracial Justice model, forgiveness is predicated on an appropriate apology in the third stage, and even then, forgiveness is to occur at an appropriate time. Yet he affirms that forgiveness is not unilateral, random, exoneration

---

[98] Marie M. Fortune, "Forgiveness: The Last Step," *Violence Against Women and Children: A Christian Theological Sourcebook* (eds. Carol J. Adams and Marie M. Fortune; New York: Continuum, 1995), 201. She latter writes that the forgiveness preconditions include justice, repentance and justice-making or restitution. The justice dispensed by the wider community, says Fortune, are: 1) acknowledging the harm done to victims; 2) breaking the silence; 3) reconstructing the entire offense narrative; 4) safeguarding the welfare of victims. Fortune, "Forgiveness: The Last Step," 203.

but a transactional agreement between the conflicted parties. The power of this transaction is in mutually unearthing painful legacies and establishing a shared narrative of liberation. A corrective process of removing distortions without redacting unpleasantries serves to release painful affective, cognitive and behavioral components of conflict, deepening and enriching the bonds between the conflicted groups. Since a significant aspect of racism and racial disparity is intertwined with the denigration of the black psyche through the process of "otherness-making," any reconstruction would of necessity have to include healing of these psychological wounds, which requires the re-storying of destructive narratives.[99] Sociology and psychology have come closest to providing a rationale for racism with an array of theorists and theories.[100] These psychosocial insights will enhance any attempt at restoring personhood by means of the group narratives and the overarching metanarrative that the conflicting groups construct.

In addressing the intrapsychic woundedness caused by offenders, one model by two educational psychologists may have some usefulness, though it has been rightly called an intrapsychic model of forgiveness and not an interpersonal model, as Clendenen

---

[99] Yamamoto, 197-199.

[100] One theorist has made the case thus: Freud considered that individuals were aroused by a "sense of the uncanny." The defense mechanisms of projection and repression have been seen as the most fruitful concepts in the examination of racism and exclusion. Stephen Frosh uses Lacan to attribute racism to fears around the safety of the psyche. Frantz Fanon drew on the psychological work of Freud, Jacques Lacan, and Jean-Paul Sartre to explain the position of the blacks in a dominant white world. Melanie Klein's theory of object relations, with its world of good and bad objects has been viewed as a basis of the making of the "other" through a process of projections and introjections, and the notion of the "phantasy." For Zygmunt Bauman, xenophobia is explained in his concept of the "familiar stranger," one who is neither friend nor foe, who must be watched. This psychological manifestation is a projection and internalization of our fear of difference, of being polluted, of being psychologically invaded by otherness. There is also Slavoj Zizek's idea of the "Theft of Enjoyment," in which the bond which holds a given community together is a shared relationship to a "Thing—to our enjoyment incarnate." Cited in Simon Clark, *Social Theory, Psychoanalysis and Racism* (Hampshire, UK: Palgrave, Macmillan, 2003), 1-27.

and Martin have labeled it.[101]   This model of forgiveness defines forgiveness solely in terms of its affective and cognitive components, suggesting that the offender is not even needed for forgiveness to take place.   Forgiveness is attained as the offended learns to overcome the negative affect and cognition that the offender generates within him or her as a result of the offense. Its four stages of forgiveness begin with the awareness and processing by the offended of his or her emotional hurt arising from the offense.   This awareness leads to a "Decision" that to end these hurt feelings the offender is to be forgiven. During the "Work Phase," the offended is challenged to empathize with the offender by gaining his or her perspective on the context for the cause of the hurt and to agreeing not to continue a cycle of hurt. Finally, the "Outcome Phase" has the offended experience affective relief by forgiving the offender and, as a result, psychic healing transpires.[102]

Clendenen and Martin's interpersonal model of forgiveness for alleviating trauma-like symptoms and in re-establishing personhood are noteworthy.   However, the issue of justice, the exoneration of the offender since he or she is not confronted to relive the offense — and questions about the rebuilding of community following   the   offense   remain   unaddressed.   Despite   this shortcoming, Clendenen and Martin's model of forgiveness can act as a complement to Yamamoto's "Reconstruction" stage, as it has potential to address the "otherness" denigration that is a core feature of   racial   prejudice   and   racial   disparity.   Since   face-to-face

---

[101] Avis Clendenen and Troy Martin, *Forgiveness: Finding Freedom Through Reconciliation* (New York: A Crossroad Book, 2002), 17-18.

[102] Clendenen and Martin, 17-18. Clendenen and Martin are not alone in defining forgiveness in terms of an affect response. Enright and Gassin offer this definition: "Forgiveness is the overcoming of negative affect and judgment toward the offender, not by denying ourselves the right to such affect and judgment, but by endeavoring to view the offender with compassion, benevolence, and love while recognizing that he or she has abandoned the right to them." Robert D. Enright and Elizabeth A. Gassin, "Forgiveness: A Developmental View," *Journal of Moral Education* 21.2 (1992): 99-114: http://web.ebscohost.com/ehost/detail?hid=119 &sid=1493175c-264e-4ccb-b628-555e5ebfa170%40sessionmgr111&vid=3& bdata=JnNpdGU9ZWhvc3QtbGl2ZQ%3d%3d#db=aph&AN=9604291600 (accessed 12/12/10).

confrontation to resolve past grievances are not always possible, the interpersonal (intrapsychic) model provides the offended with the only option left to address their own intrapsychic discomfort when the offender refuses to reconcile – a practice that was both prescribed and practiced by Christ. In Matt. 18:15-20, Christ indicates the importance of interpersonal relationships within the Christian community by offering how interpersonal conflicts are to be resolved. Christ frames violations as a breach within the community of believers, which must be accounted for in order that the offender can be restored back to full community membership, once the violation is acknowledged and repentance is offered. The offender is expelled from the community when he or she refuses to engage in the work of recognition, assuming responsibility, and seeking forgiveness. Christ often challenged and confronted offenders throughout his ministry with the expressed purpose of restoring their community fellowship. Confrontation as a method of restoring offenders through forgiveness is an expression of what Reinhold Niebuhr calls "the final form of love."[103]

Reparation that is Transformative

As the fourth dimension of interracial justice, reparation is, and continues to be, the most contentious for reasons that will become apparent. "Repair" is the essence of reparation, restoring material conditions of racial disparity and restoring injured psyches so that the oppressed live not *in* history but *with* history. The very act of engaging in reparations is a critique of exploitation while assenting to justice. In this regard, reparation completes the reconciliation cycle by addressing justice grievances. Yamamoto provides three examples of inadequate or nonexistent reparation efforts: failures to compensate black slaves at the end of the U.S. Civil War; Native Hawaiians' partial redress for cultural wounds, restored land rights, and governance structure changes; half-measures by the Japanese government to accept responsibility for World War II crimes and to compensate victims. These were in contrast to the German government's monetary contributions, legislative policies, a war museum, and Holocaust remembrances to

---

[103] Reinhold Niebuhr, *The Irony of American History* (New York: Charles Scribner's Sons, 1954), 63.

Jewish survivors. Such efforts, however, are costly and mean the loss of advantage to the already advantaged.[104]

There are many social, economic and political objections to reparation with critics charging that "it will just reopen old wounds," "the country cannot afford it," "that was then, but this is now," and "this is a hot potato which could ruin a political career." Yamamoto distills these concerns into one overarching question, "Will reparation help heal intergroup wounds and establish or restore right relationships? ...or will it create further victimization of the oppressed group?"[105] Since very little was done for blacks beyond Reconstruction, it is not surprising that in every category measurable by statistics, blacks compare significantly less favorable to whites in this country.

One study estimated that if blacks were to be compensated for slavery and labor force discrimination, the combined total, including interest, would consume the combined wealth of the United States citizenry.[106] It is not surprising that most whites and some blacks balk at this notion of reparation, given the sheer size of the debt owed the black community. However, lawyer and activist Randall Robinson argues for a more achievable target–though he does not specify the amount–in the form of an educational and economic trust fund that should be used to educate at least two successive generations of black children "K-through-college" and to provide residential housing for black children at risk.[107] Whether such ambitious plans materialize is indeed questionable. What is not questionable are studies supporting the positive psychosocial impact of reparations on the mental health of those who have benefitted from such efforts, notwithstanding the backlash from societal forces seeking to retain the structural advantages embedded in the

---

[104] Yamamoto, 203-05.

[105] Yamamoto, 206.

[106] Mills, 39.

[107] Randall Robinson, *The Debt: What America Owes To Blacks* (New York: A Dutton Book, 2000), 244-46. An additional resource on the subject of reparation is Ronald W. Walters' book, in which he explores the reparation movement as a liberatory narrative. Ronald W. Walters, *The Price of Racial Reconciliation* (Ann Arbor, MI: University of Michigan Press, 2009), 162-88.

system.[108] Indeed, Boyd and Bohler have observed a retrenchment occurring in progress made by blacks to gain institutional access. The result of this retrenchment, they argue, is that "African American institutions may experience a new vitality as blacks do not spend their energies trying to transform white institutions but redouble their efforts to maintain and strengthen their own institutions."[109]

Within the context of the Christian church, reparations could focus on collective redistribution of resources by denominations to upgrade, build, or even relocate houses of worship within the black community. Other areas of consideration could be the redistribution of administrative positions to establish a form of parity among all ethnic groups within the denomination. From an SDA perspective, this issue of reparations was, not surprisingly, addressed by Ellen White in 1896 though one would not think this was the case, given some of the challenges that continue to face the church. White presents a moral argument in defense of reparation, stating that all have an ultimate duty to love God and one's neighbor. She continues:

> The American nation owes a debt of love to the colored race, and God has ordained that they should make restitution for the wrong they have done them in the past. Those who have taken no active part on enforcing slavery upon the colored people are not relieved from the responsibility of making special efforts to remove, as far as possible, the sure result of their enslavement.[110]

Importantly, White responds to an oft-repeated refrain made by some whites that they were not alive at the time of slavery nor are they to blame. She asserts the central argument against white privilege: that, while not responsible for establishing the "invisible knapsack," they nevertheless benefit from its results.[111] This attack on the structural nature of racism and its legacy is designed, contends White, "to remove from this race [blacks] the degradation

---

[108] Yamamoto, 208.
[109] Boyd and Bohler, 207.
[110] White, *The Southern Work*, 54
[111] McIntosh.

233

that has been brought upon them."[112] Not losing sight of the transformative nature of the work of reparations and the communal nature of the Gospel, White declares that "the white people who embrace the truth in the Southern field, if converted to God, will discern the fact that the plan of redemption embraces every soul that God has created. The walls of sectarianism and caste and race will fall down when the true missionary spirit enters the hearts of men."[113] A heartfelt conversion is, in the end, the essential motivation for engagement in the reconciliation process. Given the complexity of this practice, there must first develop in the soul of the believer a God-ordained hunger for acting justly, loving mercy, and walking humbly with the divine (Micah 6:8, NIV).

Summary

This chapter has attempted to establish an SCPC paradigm for engaging in racial reconciliation. Such a model could also serve as a template for the SDA Church in its engagement in the ministry of reconciliation. Observing how Adventists engaged in such a ministry through the Race Summit would suggest that a more thorough approach in which truth-telling and collective responsibility were essential features may resonate more effectively. Similarly, any effort to mitigate social distance and thereby engender mutual trust and acceptance, as outlined by contact theory, could also prove salutary. The commonly held beliefs and practices of Adventists could serve as the basis for eliminating latent suspicion and distrust, as outlined in the Recategorization model. Since the SDA Church epitomizes diversity with an array of ethnicities represented in churches in the United States, there is merit in maximizing this range of opinions and perspectives to achieve greater cultural awareness and interaction, given the research evidenced presented. As all groups within the church are honored and respected, this can only enhance the level of belonging, commitment, and investment each group is likely to render for their church.

As outlined, reconciliation as a spiritual practice is not only confirmed in the Apostle Paul's theological position, but also in

---

112 White, *The Southern Work*, 54.
113 White, *The Southern Work*, 55.

SCPC literature, and the work of many theologians in general. Collectively, the message is one of centering reconciliation within the Christian tradition, from which it has occasionally been absent, particularly around the thorny subject of race relations. The relationality of God forms the basis for the Christian Church's ministry of reconciliation, with its key objective being the movement from disunion to union. This drive for community, a "unity in community" ethic, so to speak, has the benefit of achieving not only interpersonal restoration, but also intrapsychic repair. For as communal bonds are strengthened, creating more secure attachments, inner healing is permitted to occur in the safety of community, leading to the recovery of lost humanity. The loss of humanness, as in the racial oppression and violence of the South African Apartheid system, and the path to recovery from such devastating loss through the TRC, is a helpful lesson for the Christian community. For despite clear inadequacies, the future that is daily emerging in that once troubled nation can buoy the spirits of Idealists and Pragmatists alike, who ultimately seek a church at peace with itself.

The Christian community can also glean inspiration from the peacemaking efforts of nonreligious entities, which seek to create peaceful coexistence in places of violent conflicts. While all their peacemaking strategies may not be applicable to racial reconciliation in the SDA church, given the lack (in general) of violent tensions, some of the problem-solving and decision-making approaches are worthy of emulation. Of particular benefit is the fourfold Interracial Justice model of Yamamoto, given the eclectic nature of the model, spanning philosophy, psychology, ethics, religion, and law. Yamamoto's narrative approach, similar to some extent to the TRC, goes beyond Clebsch and Jaekle's two-stage approach (forgiveness and correction) to healing. He illustrates the healing power of individual stories and re-storying these individual stories into a metanarrative so that abuse histories are both reckoned with, and accountability assumed. The desired outcome of a transformed interethnic conflict is achieved as both conflicted parties realize the justice of the cause and remedy it through reparations. Despite the fact that this stage is the most difficult, given the opposition to many forms of redress, if achieved, the conflicted parties can be content in knowing that the triumph of right brings healing that no amount of financial resources can secure, yet without such resources, healing is often stymied.

An Approach to Racial Reconciliation
for the SDA Church in the United States

...reconciliation must be at the heart of our practices of care. It
is the practical aim or our commitment to people who suffer
historical injuries.[1]

In a rare article on the SDA Church and racial reconciliation,
black SDA Church Administrator Ricardo B. Graham laments the
fact that the denomination has been conspicuously inaudible on the
issue of racial reconciliation. Writing in 1996, prior to the NAD Race
Summit, Graham made this ominous assertion: "One lingering
challenge that will continue to cast a shadow upon the Adventist
denomination in the twenty-first century is the phenomenon of
racism. In an attempt to be authentic biblical Christians, Black
Adventists must summon the courage to confront racism in society
and in the church, to strive for racial reconciliation."[2] "Black
Adventists" are referenced as agents in racial reconciliation, perhaps
for two reasons: first, they are the target audience of the essay;
second, as has been noted, it is often the oppressed that must
demand redress. Graham leaves little doubt regarding the
implication of this long-term silence in which both black and white
Adventists have been "co-conspirators." An invisible wall of
separation remains between blacks and whites, he argues, and it is a
divide that results in "a weakened church with a weakened witness
to a sick and dying world."[3] These are challenging words, forming
as they do an indictment on the church he serves as the current
president of the Pacific Union Conferences.

As has already been observed, relative silence on social issues
has been a legacy of both the SDA Church's historicist
premillennialism roots and Ellen White's cautious approach to

---

[1] Thornton, 148.

[2] Rock, *Perspectives*, 127.

[3] Rock, *Perspectives*.

provocative issues.[4] Yet, this approach is counterproductive, particularly on matters of racism and white privilege since it reinforces oppressive attitudes, behaviors, and structures. In this regard, silence is never "golden." On the contrary, silence on any matter of oppression is complicity. Perhaps a positive aspect of the current debate is the fact that, while the issues of racism and racial disparity may be considered peripheral to the discussion by some, they will never be far from the surface. Indeed, one can only hope that what is now superficial will gain currency as the debate and the clamor for resolution continues.

To ensure that matters of racism, racial disparity, white privilege, and the need for interethnic healing through racial reconciliation gain ascendancy within the SDA Church, a revisioning of reconciliation is required. Reconciliation, as articulated in the *Handbook of Seventh-day Adventist Theology,* is the restoration of a fractured relationship triggered by sin. Because of God's unfailing love, God initiates and achieves reconciliation for humanity through the cross of Christ. As reconciliation is accomplished between God and the individual, the reconciled individual is to reciprocate by reconciling with others and leading the estranged to reconciliation.[5] However, in the Handbook and in practice, this ministry of reconciliation receives minimal attention, particularly as it relates to white privilege and the racial discrimination and disparity experienced by black members. The ministry of reconciliation must be placed at the heart of Adventist theology and practice, and along with it racial reconciliation, for only such a profile can restore the sense of God's disdain for racism in its myriad forms, and the manner in which it dehumanizes offenders and offended alike.

One place the SDA Church could start in re-centering the ministry of reconciliation is to update it's 1985 "A Statement on

---

[4] Ellen G. White's cautious stance and its lingering legacy are often repeated by Bull and Lockhart, as in this quote: "The prophetess's vision of Adventists appeared to be an unobtrusive people who avoided undue conflict." Bull and Lockhart, [2007], 193.

[5] Raoul Dederen, Nancy J. Vyhmeister, and George W. Reid, eds., *Handbook of Seventh-day Adventist Theology* vol. 12, *Commentary Reference Series* (Hagerstown, MD: Review and Herald Publishing Association, 2000), 181-82.

Racism." I understand that this is a statement and not an official apology; nevertheless, it appears to be written as if the SDA Church stands unsoiled by "one of the odious evils of our day."[6] The statement is eloquently expressed and linguistically crafted with all the appropriate sentiments being referenced, including this phrase: "racism is really a heresy and in essence a form of idolatry, for it limits the fatherhood of God by denying the brotherhood of all mankind and by exalting the superiority of one's own race."[7] It is difficult to disagree with this compelling statement. However, missing from this high-minded rhetoric is any collective responsibility for at least past infractions to this ideal. Rhetoric without remorse is deficient at best. Particularly troubling is the fact that, while adamant about adhering to the Commandments of God, the church is also holding fast to human traditions (Mark 7:8). Without racial reconciliation, SDA leaders' complicity remains in the human devising of racism with its structures, privileges, attitudes, and behaviors as well as in the social construction of race from which such categorization has led to the minimization and dehumanization of persons of color the world over.

An Adventist Model of Racial Reconciliation

As I have attempted to argue in this book, reconciliation, and with it, racial reconciliation, is not an optional extra to placate a guilty conscience, appease one's Christian sensibilities, or assuage the clamor of the offended for "doing the right thing." Rather, racial reconciliation is a part of the continued ministry of Christ on earth, of healing the broken, freeing the captives, and releasing the oppressed as well as the oppressor (Luke 4:18). I fully embrace Thornton's formulation of reconciliation as practice, a practice which lies at the heart of the passion of Christ.[8] This is the Christian's mandate, and this is the Gospel message from which there are no exemptions or waivers, even for "The Remnant Church." To this end, a model of racial reconciliation structured around Eric Yamamoto's Interracial Justice model is being recommended as one of many that can be considered by the SDA Church, should it deem

---

[6] The SDA Church's "A Statement on Racism."
[7] The SDA Church's "A Statement on Racism."
[8] Thornton, 147

this process necessary. It will be essential to have a preliminary stage of preparation, establishing the parameters of any racial reconciliation process: who should be in attendance, the scale of the event and its publicity, its duration and possible follow-up as well as a decided focus on the future. However, the church may choose to reflect on what preconditions are adopted since those from the 1999 Race Summit may have served to diminish the chances of a more consequential outcome.

The executive officers of the NAD have the authority to initiate this preliminary process, perhaps cajoled by the black members of the administrative committee and possibly by the largely white Adventist academic community. It is possible to activate elements of this academic community particularly those on the liberal and conservative wings of the church. On the left of the academic spectrum is the Association of Adventist Forums (AAF) established in 1968; and on the right, is Adventists Affirm (AA) organized in 1987 and the Adventist Theological Society (ATS) founded in 1988. The AAF emerged out of a desire expressed by the GC to have an educational system able to rival that of the secular society.[9] The main organ of the AAF is the quarterly journal *Spectrum* which promotes academic freedom with the objective of looking "without prejudice at all sides of a subject."[10] Both the AA and ATS were reactionary in origin with the former resisting liberal influences on Adventist beliefs and practice including being anti-women's ordination and the latter promoting conservative SDA scholarship among academics.[11] I believe that both sides could be persuaded to see a common interest in promoting racial reconciliation since they have previously addressed the issue of race relations in the NAD.[12]

---

[9] Bull and Lockhart, [2007], 322.

[10] *Spectrum*, "About Us": http://spectrummagazine.org/about_us (accessed 12/9/11).

[11] Bull and Lockhart, [2007], 270, 326.

[12] Just a few examples of their publications on the issue of race: The entire issue of *Spectrum* 2.2 (Spring, 1970); Alexander Carpenter, "Between a Rock and a Hard Race Question," *Spectrum* (July 2008): http://www.spectrummagazine.org/blog/2008/07/27/between_rock_and_hard_race_question (accessed 8/18/10); the longtime director of AAF Samuel Koranteng-Pipim addressed the issue in his book, *Must We Be*

An essential precursor to any racial reconciliation process would have to be an official action of the NAD Executive Committee to recognize the unfinished but urgent business of racial reconciliation and to vote to approve the commencement of such a process. Leading from the front, the president of the NAD could make such a recommendation to his executive committee, or he may act in response to lobbying from ethnically diverse leaders from subordinate institutions. Motivation for the president's actions could come from the need to be congruous in beliefs and practice, particularly the assertions made in the church's racism statement of wanting "to be faithful to the reconciling ministry assigned to the Christian church... [and the SDA Church's desire] to witness to and exhibit in her own ranks the unity and love that transcends racial differences and overcome past alienation."[13] It is possible that additional lobbying from the liberal and conservative theological wings of the SDA Church could be efficacious since both would have a vested in a positive outcome. The liberals should see progress on race relations as possibly leading to progress on women's ordination, while the conservatives may welcome closure on the church's racial past as evidence of conformity to the love-unity ethic. Having any discussion on racism is difficult enough, but to encourage the NAD Executive Committee, composed largely of white people, to initiate and formulate a meaningful resolution on the way forward will require the entire committee to struggle with issues of racism, privilege, and prejudice. Coping with additional discomforts including, guilt, shame, pain, and emotional sensibilities around issues of ethnicity, will likely necessitate adequate preparation for deliberations on racial reconciliation. It is therefore recommended that the committee is provided with cultural competence and antiracism training. In particular, the Office of Human Relations at the NAD can be empowered by the executive committee to lead out in providing this training. Psychologist Paul

---

Silent: Issues Dividing Our Church; and for the ATS, Trevor O'Reggio, "Slavery, Prophecy, and the American Nation as Seen by the Adventist Pioneers, 1854-1865," *Journal of Adventist Theological Society*, 17.2 (Fall, 2006): 135-58; and Pipim, "Saved by Grace and Living by Race: The Religion Called Racism," *Journal of Adventist Theological Society* 5.2 (Fall, 1994): 37-78.

[13] The SDA Church's "A Statement on Racism."

Pedersen offers five strategies that should be included in such training: 1) be aware of the history of racism as a social phenomenon; 2) know the importance of power difference in promoting racism; 3) recognize that not all racist behaviors are intentional; 4) challenge the racist assumptions that encapsulate us; 5) identify racist behaviors in the cultural contexts where they were learned and displayed.[14] Capitalizing on the church's tradition of tolerance, forgiveness, and renewal, committee members could be encouraged to acknowledge their own prejudices. Efforts could also be made to avoid further delay in achieving racial reconciliation by reemphasizing the Scripture's mandate of a ministry of reconciliation and its compatibility with the church's belief in the brother and sisterhood of humanity.

Furthermore, truth-telling and collective responsibility should be made to seem as more favorable than continued silence on such a hot button topic. Since a NAD president, had issued an apology in 2000, the current president could build on this apology by inviting self-disclosure in his administration on their experience with racism, or awareness of white privilege and its consequence. The power of this acknowledgment by national leaders of the church would have significant repercussion throughout the church. The SDA Church is a hierarchical organization, in which church leaders generally receive support, though this support is by no means universal. Consequently, action taken by the NAD president and the executive committee regarding racial reconciliation should have wide-spread appeal at all levels of the church. This general allegiance to leadership by church members should make it easier for these leaders to implement a top-down reconciliation process, with their leading from the front strategy ensuring significant membership participation.

The NAD Executive Committee could then approve a resolution outlining a roadmap for racial reconciliation. Central to any such roadmap would of necessity be a sober review of the issue of racism and the Adventists church's role in fostering and maintaining vestiges of a racialized society. Such a review could

---

[14] Paul Pedersen, "Five Antiracism Strategies," *Addressing Racism: Facilitating Cultural Competence in Mental Health and Educational Settings*, 235-50.

take the form of a Symposium on Race, in which an interdisciplinary approach to the SDA Church's past and present dealings with its black members in particular, and members of color, in general, can be explored. A range of perspectives can be offered with the help of the following suggested disciplines: history, philosophy, ethics, theology, psychology, sociology, social psychology, pastoral care and counseling, organizational behavior theory, and law. Specialists in these fields, especially white Adventists in those fields, could pose critical questions and explore workable solutions by presenting papers at a two-or-three-day symposium. Delegates to this symposium could number 500, with an equitable distribution reflecting the ethnic diversity of the membership of the eight U.S. unions within the NAD. The structure of the symposium could incorporate the Yamamoto model of racial reconciliation with different disciplines approaching their work with one or more of the stages in mind (e.g., historians and theologians could frame their presentation around recognition; social psychologists, ethicists and philosophers around responsibility; pastoral theologians and psychologists around reconstruction; legal scholars and sociologists around reparations).

The academic papers presented at this Symposium on Race could then be published in full and available to all, along with a compendium that is more accessible to all church members. The solutions offered in this publication could then form the basis for an action by the NAD Executive Committee to recommend that the GC host a Race Summit on the magnitude of a GC Session. This Summit could cover other areas of past and ongoing conflicts that may benefit from racial, ethnic, and cultural reconciliation. In addition, the NAD could commission a survey of its membership to gauge attitudes and alternatives to the existing administrative structure. Whatever process the NAD adopts to address racial reconciliation, it should be open, honest and widely publicized both within and outside of the church. This kind of media blitz could be salutary by giving voice to a critical social justice issue. It could spark a renewed interest in the SDA Church and its beliefs, possibly leading to the potential for additional converts. Further, media and other public attention may ensure that taking short-cuts to resolution is minimized.

Additionally, a sense of commonality can be reinforced, similar to the Recategorization process, if the GC scheduled a Sabbath School Quarterly (a daily Bible study guide used worldwide by members) on the theme of cultural awareness, ethnic difference and diversity and sensitivity training. Importantly, care must be taken to ensure that the graphic design of the Quarterly reflects a plurality of individuals and includes visual images expressing antiracism sentiments as a means of decreasing prejudice.[15] Being deliberate about exposing members to a wide range of ethnicities and cultures in literature published by the church, and presenting arguments advancing diversity is vital since current research also confirms that attitudes can be changed with such explicit messaging. Relevant to the study of the quarterly (notwithstanding it does suffer from an underwhelming use in certain parts of the United States), research suggests that to the extent in which individuals are able to "articulate and rehearse their own idiosyncratic thoughts to the information presented," persuasion can occur.[16] The under- whelming use of the Quarterly can be addressed by the NAD stressing the importance of this particular issue, and church leaders at every level of the church prioritizing attendance in Sabbath School for that quarter. Given the discussion format of most Sabbath School classes in which the weekly study is presented, there is scope for attitude changes within the memberships on matters of difference.

With a symposium and summit to address racial reconciliation occurring at the macro level of the church, the NAD could encourage its respective unions, conferences, and local churches to engage in reconciliation efforts at the micro level. All

---

[15] Simple pictorial antiracism advertisements with a picture and caption have been used with mixed results by Britain's Commission for Racial Equality leading to the conclusion that "the antiracism advert- isements increased prejudice among ambivalent participants, but decreased prejudice among nonambivalent participants." Gregory R. Maio, Geoffrey Haddock, Susan E. Watt, and Miles Hewstone, "Implicit Measures in Applied Contexts: An Illustrative Examination of Antiracism Advertising," *Attitudes: Insights from the New Implicit Measures* (ed. Richard E. Petty, Russell H. Fazio, and Pablo Briñol: New York: Psychology Press, 2009), 343.

[16] Pablo Briñol, Richard E. Petty, and Michael J. McCaslin, "Changing Attitudes on Implicit Versus Explicit Measures: What Is the Difference?" *Attitudes: Insights from the New Implicit Measures*, 286.

affiliated institutions of the NAD should also participate in some form of antiracism training as they strive for cultural competence.[17] This more localized effort could emphasize fellowship and accountability in crossing ethnic and cultural barriers in a true spirit of Christian brother and sisterhood. Pulpit exchanges could be a prerequisite between different ethnic and cultural groups within the same locality, and even distant homogenous churches should find a way to participate in this exchange. To further mitigate the social distance common in Adventism, churches with different ethnic and cultural backgrounds should hold joint services regularly (perhaps once a quarter–perhaps for the Communion Service) as a means of minimizing suspicion and distrust. Also, helpful in this regard are seminars conducted both at the local church level and conference-wide cities rallies, in which calls for inclusion and brother-sisterhood can be invoked, our common humanity can be affirmed, problem-solving and effective decision-making can occur at the local level, and experiences of meaningful racial and ethnic harmony and healing can be created. Of course, these suggestions can also be used in later stages of the reconciliation process.

During the Recognition and Confession stage, the essential focus is on exploring empathetic acknowledgments of accurately relayed narratives, avoiding revisionism, creating meaning from these narratives of estrangement, and prompting repentance and confession. Church leaders may wish to have historical, theological,

---

[17] One pastoral theologian suggests that cultural competence in religious communities would result in them being able to: 1) Know the difference between race, ethnicity, and culture; 2) Get in touch with issues of prejudice and stereotypes; 3) Challenge the myth of 'colorblindness,' and be aware of the reality of 'color consciousness' as it pertains to race; 4) Understand that race, ethnicity, gender, economic class, sexual identity, age, ability, religion, nationality, immigration status, and so forth are organizing principles for good or ill in everything we do; 5) Recognize there are multiple centers of truth, whose legitimacy is often determined by the amount of power any given perspective may have in a particular context; 6) Develop a rich symbolic life; and 7) Cultivate spiritual stamina. Sheryl A. Kujawa-Holbrook, "Love and Power: Antiracist Pastoral Care," *Injustice and the Care of Souls: Taking Oppression Seriously in Pastoral Care* (ed. Sheryl A. Kujawa-Holbrook and Karen B. Montagno; Minneapolis: Fortress Press, 2009), 24-26.

and psychological presentations on matters of race and its enduring legacy, relative to the church. Particularly beneficial would be insights on white privilege and interethnic conflict by white Adventists who are experts in the field. But of paramount importance is establishing the connection between the work of storying the church's past and recommitting to community building, through a process of confession. A clinical intervention that could be useful during this stage is the narrative therapy concept of externalization.[18] The use of externalization (or objectification) is designed to take the painful and disturbing memory and project it outward so that it can be examined without reference to the individual. Consequently, the affective element of the problem eventually disappears, as the individual learns new ways and gains a fresh perspective on the reconstruction of his or her narrative.

The advantage of this approach is that none should feel exclusively blamed or personally responsible for past oppression. It should also be easier for all participants — Pragmatists, Idealists, and Adventists in general — to shoulder collective responsibility for the church's past conduct towards its black members. In this regard, blacks would be able to confess to blacks, whites to whites, whites to blacks, blacks to whites, and all others in-between. As I have previously noted, it is the black-white dynamic that is the focus of this study. However, all other ethnic groups will have a vital role to play in the construction of the metanarrative in the Reconstruction phase, since some of their own narratives may also reveal elements

---

[18] Though time does not permit a fuller examination of narrative therapy, it must suffice to state that this modality is the creation of Michael White and David Epson in the 1980s, and it has gained currency within the pastoral care tradition. Narrative therapy focuses on the personal stories of individuals, since lives are framed through narratives. Yet these narratives must be viewed through a cultural, social and politically-constructed lens. During a process of collaboration, the therapist and client are able to reframe and gain new meaning from the challenging narrative, leading to the construction of a new healing narrative. As a postmodern therapy, its view of truth is relative, and it affirms that interpretation is in the eye of the beholder. Narrative therapy can be encapsulated in the phrase, "people are not the problem, the problem is the problem itself." Michael White and David Epston, *Narrative Means to Therapeutic Ends* (New York: W. W. Norton, 1990).

of oppression, exclusion, and embrace that require a hearing. It is hoped that the collective interest of the SDA Church to maintain its theological integrity would override any inhibition to engage in reconciliation, including constructing a shared narrative, but impetus will have to come from church leaders who will have to lead and not simply manage. Furthermore, if the theological anthropology advocated by Justes is appealed too, steps away from distortions and division should lead to recognition of our oneness as humanity and a greater sense of intimacy.[19]

As the process moves to the Responsibility and Repentance stage, the individual narratives will need to be corralled into a wider narrative of the SDA Church's evolution and expansion in the south during the 1890s and the ad hoc strategies that were devised until the church arrived at a position based on the minimizing of offense in order to evangelize whites. One possible intervention to achieve this wider narrative is to remind Adventists of the oft quoted words of Ellen White: "We have nothing to fear for the future, except as we forget the way the Lord has led us and His teachings in our past history."[20] Linking the past with the future, Ellen White admonishes that anxiety over the way ahead can be ameliorated by rehearsing God's past guidance and provision, despite historical failures. Hence, the totality of Adventist history, including its racial injustices, should be considered in a wider narrative of the church's progress from its fledgling cult status to a mainstream, international, multiethnic denomination. The embracing of this broader multiethnic narrative could serve to illustrate the past, present and future challenge of harmonious coexistence. I believe that the solidarity engendered through this collective storytelling process and the vulnerability that it should evoke could produce a new vision for relatedness between the ethnic groups within the S.D.A

---

[19] Justes writes, "Greater intimacy can develop when we are not bound by patterns that divide us from one another… When we cling to a dividing status that creates classes of helper and helpee, we work against the development of intimacy. A willingness to become more intimate can mean that we will be drawn away from making too much or our differences." Justes, "We Belong Together," 149.

[20] White, *Life Sketches* (Mountain View, CA: Pacific Press Publishing Association, 1915), 196.

Church. In this regard, Thornton correctly observes that a "New vision emerges when memory is honored."[21] An additional benefit in the construction of this metanarrative within the reconciliation process and mediated through the cross is that individual, as well as, communal wholeness and restoration may be realized.

The history of racism in U.S. history and the power of white privilege are also useful additions to a wider narrative. While mutual responsibility may ultimately be a worthwhile goal, it should not be achieved at the expense of black Adventists who were — and, along with other ethnic groups continue to be — negatively affected by their treatment in the church. Exploring how blacks have experienced "otherness" and the psychic injuries that are being inflicted is a part of our "brother-sister keeperliness" and must not be ignored. This process of reflection on the injury of blacks, and the white privilege that sustains such injuries, can be a vital ingredient in establishing vicarious repentance, as well as personal repentance, leading to a mutually solvable stance and a more authentic community. Butler observes that community life, which at its core is spiritual, "expresses the functional nature of the African American religious experience as the force of its collective identity."[22] Religious organizations like the Adventist Church should be obligated to achieving a degree of community, which enables blacks, as well as all other ethnic groups to find wholeness and healing.

The key element of the Reconstruction and Accountability stage would be the creation of a metanarrative that encompasses all narratives from each ethnic group. Given the multiethnic composition of Adventists today, constructing the divergent stories of the different ethnicities could be accomplished with assistance from the conference and union leaders with responsibilities for the respective ethnic groups. These leaders could solicit short stories from those with experience of oppression, and with them, create a collective narrative that could best articulate the particular experience of that ethnic group. These distilled stories of each ethnic

---

[21] Thornton, 135.

[22] Butler further states that "Individual identification with the community and the articulation of individual hopes became community hopes... The individual and the community live the same reality simultaneously." Butler, 152.

group can then become the foundation for the metanarrative. Once constructed, this metanarrative can serve as the basis for an official apology and forgiveness process, setting the stage for restoration in intergroup relations. These restored relationships must transcend mere professional contact. Active and intentional effort must be made for all members of the denomination to become a family. This could be facilitated by mutual interethnic exchanges to churches and homes, and combined community outreach efforts.

Since Ellen White has articulated the rightness of Reparations, I will simply reflect on the reality of any reparations effort. The current leadership structures of the church in the United States are largely white and male, though modest changes have been made recently. For example, despite the fact that blacks comprise more than 40 percent of the membership of the NAD, they are under-represented in the NAD executive committee with even less representation for all other ethnic minorities. It will require some magnanimity on the part of white church leaders or demographic shifts, which will occur in time if this reality is to change. Since white church leaders are overrepresented in positions of power, some will need to relinquish their positions in order that other ethnicities can be better represented within the church hierarchy. As Holbrook reminds us, one obstacle to genuine reconciliation is the lack of awareness by the dominant culture of the power disparity of the marginalized.[23] Without a more diffusive interethnic leadership structure at all levels of the church hierarchy, including healthcare, education, and media, the visible face of a truly multiethnic denomination will remain monochromatic.

One must always remain hopeful that the SDA Church in the United States will eventually engage in or adopt some formula for racial reconciliation. Should this occur, the process will invariably warrant church leaders, who are mostly white, to assume responsibility for the church's racially discriminatory practices as well as having to contend with a power realignment based on a just ethnic distribution. It is possible that the largely white Adventist academic community could provide some leadership in championing the cause of racial reconciliation. These academics

---

[23] Holbrook, "Love and Power: Antiracist Pastoral Care," *Injustice and the Care of Souls*, 13.

would certainly benefit from the previously mentioned insights of Nancy Ramsay in her personal journey in navigating racial difference.[24] Overcoming the potency of white privilege will also be a major hurdle for these white church leaders who are increasingly seeing their shrinking majority erased by demographic shifts, which could result in a knee-jerk clutch to hold on to power. Yet, as belief in the transformative power of the Gospel beckons optimism, so too do the winds of change, which is inspiring a generation within and outside of the church, who are more tolerant of difference and who, around the world are successfully challenging the old order. As St. Francis of Assisi wisely observed, "Start by doing what's necessary; then do what's possible; and suddenly you are doing the impossible."[25]

In admonishing believers to emulate a member who sought out another to express his sincere regret and to seek forgiveness, Ellen White penned these words:

> Do not let anything interpose between you and your brethren. If there is anything that you can do by sacrifice to clear away the rubbish of suspicion, do it. God wants us to love one another as brethren...Do we expect to meet our brethren in heaven? If we can live with them here in peace and harmony we could live with them there...Those who are following a course of action that separates them from their brethren and brings in discord and dissension, need a thorough conversion. We shall pass through this world but once. Shall we not strive to leave on those with whom we associate the impress of the character of Christ?[26]

White's admonition is a challenge to resist estrangement in favor of reconciliation, to move from a default position of suspicion to one of trustworthiness. For in such a move lies earthly community and heavenly communion, but outside of it lies disjuncture from diversity and disengagement from the divine. White urges that in our interaction with others, our goal is to ensure

---

[24] Ramsay, "Navigating Racial Differences as a White Pastoral Theologian," 24.

[25] "Possibility Quotes," http://www.motivational-well-being.com/possibility-quotes.html (accessed 1/12/11).

[26] White, *Testimonies for the Church*, 9:193.

that an untarnished image of Christ's character is replicated in the exchange. This image is in essence composed of the characteristics exhibited by Christ while here on the Earth, including self-sacrificing love, compassion, patience, and hopefulness, to name but a few. The ultimate price for believers failing to engage in reconciliation and renewal, White postulates, is the forfeiting of eternal life. As the Bible admonishes: "For whoever does not love their brother and sister, whom they have seen, cannot love God, whom they have not seen" (1 John 4:20, NIV).

Reconciliation in the Quarrel Narrative of Abraham and Lot

The Bible is replete with conflict and reconciliation narratives. One such quarrel narrative is the experience of Abraham (Abram at the time) and his paternal nephew Lot, recorded in Genesis 13:1-13. The two traveling companions and their entourages had experienced many challenges in their quest for the land promised them by God. Yet ironically, it was their economic gains, as a result of God's blessing, that triggered a competitive, conflicted, and aggressive exchange between their workers. Their exploding animal husbandry enterprise as well as unfriendly nationals–the Canaanites and Perizzites – constricted their territorial expansion. The expanding business and the diminishing pastoral lands to accommodate that business led to an inevitable clash between the employees of Abraham and of Lot. The tensions revealed that any solution would involve some form of separation. Following *recognition* of the ongoing tensions and his inadvertent role in it, Abraham, as the senior partner in this enterprise, assumes *responsibility* to problem-solve, ensuring a mutually beneficial outcome. By confronting the conflict head-on, Abraham seeks to mitigate the need for any deterioration in his relationship with his nephew, necessitating a *reconstruction* phase.

With Lot initially being a passive participant in this reconciliatory effort, Abraham proposes a *reparatory* solution by appealing to what they had in common–their consanguinity and faith tradition. Premier OT scholar Claus Westermann contends that on display in this pericope was more than Abraham's conciliatory and gracious nature. At stake was the escalation of a dispute that threatened the survival of both camps.[27] To prevent a bloodbath leading to a blood feud, Abraham abandons patriarchal privilege by offering Lot a share of the Promised Land. Abraham magnanimously allows Lot to choose first where he desires to live; the Edenic beauty of the fertile Jordan plain arrests his attention and influences his decision. Abraham's conduct in this incident triggered the following pertinent insights from Ellen White:

> Here the noble, unselfish spirit of Abraham was displayed. How many under similar circumstances would, at all hazards, cling to their individual rights and preferences! How many households have thus been rent asunder! How many churches have been divided, making the cause of truth a byword and a reproach among the wicked! 'Let there be no strife between me and thee,' said Abraham, 'for we be brethren;' not only by natural relationship, but as worshipers of the true God. The children of God the world over are one family, and the same spirit of love and conciliation should govern them.[28]

The pertinence of White's remarks is in its direct challenge to self-interest when the ministry of reconciliation, based on our common humanity in Christ, is required to resolve conflicts. From her perspective, the rightness of the cause or the justice of one's position should never be a deterrence to peacemaking.

A final but fundamental lesson conveyed by this quarrel narrative is its message of separation in community. The sheer volume of the livestock and the land required to maintain them made it evident that separation was to be among a limited range of options available to Abraham and Lot. However, the basis for this separation was not lingering hostilities or discriminatory actions but economic necessity. For one NT scholar, this encounter illustrates an important Biblical principle that "when peaceful community is

---

[27] Westermann's historical analysis leads him to conclude that "the significance of this narrative becomes comprehensible only when it is realized that small nomadic groups cannot wage war; the quarrel, therefore, takes the place of war in which the larger unions, from tribes on, engage." Claus Westermann, *Genesis 12-36: A Commentary* (tr. John J. Scullion; Minneapolis: Augsburg Publishing House, 1985), 176.

[28] Ellen G. White, *The Story of Patriarchs and Prophets* (Mountain View, CA: Pacific Press Publishing Association, 1958), 132.

impossible, Scripture prefers amicable separation (Acts 15:39; 1 Cor. 7:12-15)."[29] This approach is also implied in the words of the Apostle Paul in Romans12:18, where he argues that peaceful coexistence should always be the goal, but it is not always achievable.

However, it is important to remember that the amicable nature of the separation between Abraham and Lot meant that when either of them was in need of assistance, such help should be immediate and selfless. This selfless display of solidarity and support occurs in the next chapter of Genesis in which Abraham rescues Lot and other prisoners of war from foreign captors (Gen. 14). In the case of Abraham and Lot, their separation was mutual but without malice. Consequently, Abraham was able to offer selfless solidarity and support to his distressed nephew without hesitation. Given the challenge in both personal attitudes towards Regional Conferences by Idealists and Pragmatists, as well as the entrenched nature of these administrative structures, it may be too optimistic to expect their dissolution as an outcome of a racial reconciliation process. I believe that this quarrel narrative offers a Biblical warrant for an outcome to a reconciliation process that leaves the existing separate conference structures intact as harmonious coexistence. But for harmonious coexistence to be anything more than what exists currently, the interplay between cultural difference and church unity would have to come into sharper focus. Hence Austern's useful concept of practical solidarity with its emphasis on gaining perspective on one's own social location relative to others could be meaningful.[30] In the event that Regional Conferences remain, this pastoral perspective could assist the Adventist Church in addressing exclusion by advocating deliberate individual pilgrimages between the parallel conferences, ensuring that the kind of solidarity and support offered to Lot by Abraham is available to either conference system constituencies.

---

[29] Gordon J. Wenham, *Genesis 1-15; Word Biblical Commentary* (gen. ed., David A. Hubbard and Glenn W. Barker; Waco, Texas: Word Books Publisher, 1987), 1: 299.

[30] Austern, 35.

Motivating Change

Confucius reportedly made this compelling statement, "When it is obvious that the goals cannot be reached, don't adjust the goals, adjust the action steps."[31] Action beyond the current rhetoric of the debate over Regional Conferences is now needed. Action in the direction of a meaningful racial reconciliation process could provide the SDA Church in the United States with the impetus to address a host of needed administrative changes. In his international bestselling book on change, John P. Kotter devised an eight-stage process that he argues leads to transformational change, of which the first stage is establishing a sense of urgency.[32] What would be required for the SDA Church to engage in racial reconciliation, based on what is being recommended in this book, is uncertain? It is true, however, that the denomination has in the past, in at least four instances, responded to the "fierce urgency of now" message of Martin Luther King, Jr. on matters of race: the death of Lucy Byard triggered the creation of Regional Conferences; the withholding of tithe by prominent black churches in London triggered the Pierson package and racial redress in the BUC; the fight for Regional Unions appeared to trigger the elections of the first black president of the NAD; and finally, the meeting of religious leaders with Adventist representation, called by President Clinton, appears to have triggered the Race Summit the following year.

These incidences would suggest a reactive mentality at work within Adventism so that events dictate change by creating urgency. It is highly possible that the demographic shifts in the United States, which will impact the SDA Church, likely leading to fewer whites and more minority members, will trigger a corresponding decrease in white church leaders, and perhaps then, a desire for racial reconciliation. Or maybe, as one black church administrator suggested in a private conversation, racial reconciliation will be a moot point, as the next generation with their more global perspective, growing up as they did with the likes of Jordan, Kobe, Shaq, and Michael Jackson, will, at last, fulfill King's dream of a day

---

[31]"Motivation Quotes," http://thinkexist.com/quotations/motivation /3. html (accessed 2/15/11).

[32] John P. Kotter, *Leading Change* (Boston, MA: Harvard Business School Press, 1996), 21.

when "they will not be judged by the color of their skin but by the content of their character."[33] Yet such optimism about the next generation and their desire to move away from past racial conflicts should be tempered with the insight that "The past is never dead. It's not even past."[34]

Conclusion

Reconciliation is a never-ending journey with no clear terminus, but its route leads through the necessary terrain of trust, compassion, and fairness. Racial reconciliation, in particular, is an even more challenging and invidious process with outcomes not amenable to hasty resolutions. Yet these facts should not so perplex us that we become bereft of dreaming of a more noble future. I believe that beyond the obvious success of the SDA Church in the United States it has a blind spot that places limits on its future attainments. This book has attempted to challenge the church on the issue of racial reconciliation so that it can live up to its affirmative statement on race to "exhibit in her own ranks the unity and love that transcend racial differences and overcome past alienation."[35] This study has led me to the conclusion that far from being merely a pastoral function, reconciliation is a spiritual practice grounded in the passion of Christ, and creating the prospects of a more just humanity. Through reconciliation, the SDA Church can be at the vanguard of liberation, setting captives free, including freedom from racism, particularly as it manifests itself in the form of privilege.

Intentionality must be at the heart of any racial reconciliation effort undertaken by the SDA Church, so motivating it to be intentional about racial reconciliation could begin with an appeal to the church's laudable statement on racism. Other drivers of racial reconciliation could be the Idealists and the Pragmatist who are already invested in the debate about the future of Regional Conferences. The Adventist academic community represents a further driver for a racial reconciliation effort, as well as leaders of

---

[33] Martin Luther King, Jr., "I Have a Dream," http://www. americanrhetoric.com/speeches/mlkihaveadream.htm (accessed 1/12/11).

[34] William Faulkner, *Requiem for A Nun* (New York: Random House, 1951), 92.

[35] The SDA Church's "A Statement on Racism."

all the conferences and unions within the NAD. It is hoped that a possible publication of an abbreviated form of this book, as well as widely distributed articles in Adventists publications, could trigger a reconciliation debate. Assuming that the need for racial reconciliation is accepted by NAD administrators, they could follow the suggested outline in this chapter.

As the field of SCPC and the TRC have illustrated, the restoration of human dignity is central to racial reconciliation; and the most effective way of achieving this goal is the liberating nature of storytelling. Adventist Church leaders should embrace this medium as a means of revisiting the church's intolerant past. This past could be explored in detail with a Symposium on Race using as a framework Yamamoto's Interracial Justice model. Findings from this symposium could then be the basis of action at a race summit, where strategies for the practical aspects of racial reconciliation can be agreed upon and implemented. A significant challenge would be how to implement a top-down racial reconciliation process, but as previously noted, church members are often ready to follow where their leaders direct them.

Since the SDA Church routinely schedules worldwide days of prayer, engaging in a national day or week of prayer and fasting, repentance and confession around the issue of racial reconciliation should not be difficult to organize, once a campaign to generate national interest is promoted. Finally, efforts at how to achieve some form of reparations, and what such efforts would look like can commence. It is here that discussion about the future of the administrative structures of the SDA Church can then be addressed, including the status of Regional Conferences. I am not naïve enough to believe that any particular outcome which satisfies all can be achieved even after a reconciliation process; consequently, mutual separation without malice may have to suffice. As previously stated, my expectations and perspective have changed as I have undertaken this research. I have fluctuated from being an ardent Idealist to a lukewarm Pragmatist, to now an optimistic realist. I am optimistic that given the rightness of the cause of racial reconciliation, some form of it may one day occur within the SDA Church. But given the nature of human self-interest, I am equally realistic that such a day may yet be in the distance, since those who currently set the agenda of the church, may not be invested in such a self-reflective process.

Consequently, one area for future research can be an exploration of motivation within religious communities to act out of the interest of others and not simply self-interest.

Appendix A

A Statement on Racism by the SDA Church

One of the odious evils of our day is racism, the belief or practice that views or treats certain racial groups as inferior and therefore justifiably the object of domination, discrimination, and segregation.

While the sin of racism is an age-old phenomenon based on ignorance, fear, estrangement, and false pride, some of its ugliest manifestations have taken place in our time. Racism and irrational prejudices operate in a vicious circle. Racism is among the worst of ingrained prejudices that characterize sinful human beings. Its consequences are generally more devastating because racism easily becomes permanently institutionalized and legalized and in its extreme manifestations can lead to systematic persecution and even genocide.

The Seventh-day Adventist Church deplores all forms of racism, including the political policy of apartheid with its enforced segregation and legalized discrimination.

Seventh-day Adventists want to be faithful to the reconciling ministry assigned to the Christian church. As a worldwide community of faith, the Seventh-day Adventist Church wishes to witness to and exhibit in her own ranks the unity and love that transcend racial differences and overcome past alienation between races.

Scripture plainly teaches that every person was created in the image of God, who "made of one blood all nations of men for to dwell on all the face of the earth" (Acts 17:26). Racial discrimination is an offense against our fellow human beings, who were created in God's image. In Christ "there is neither Jew nor Greek" (Gal. 3:28). Therefore, racism is really a heresy and in essence a form of idolatry, for it limits the fatherhood of God by denying the brotherhood of all mankind and by exalting the superiority of one's own race.

The standard for Seventh-day Adventist Christians is acknowledged in the church's Bible-based Fundamental Belief No. 13, "Unity in the Body of Christ." Here it is pointed out: "In Christ we are a new creation; distinctions of race, culture, learning, and nationality, and differences between high and low, rich and poor, male and female, must not be divisive among us. We are all equal in Christ, who by one Spirit has bonded us into one fellowship with Him and with one another; we are to serve and be served without partiality or reservation."

Any other approach destroys the heart of the Christian gospel.

This public statement was released by the General Conference president, Neal C. Wilson, after consultation with the 16 world vice presidents of the Seventh-day Adventist Church, on June 27, 1985, at the General Conference session in New Orleans, Louisiana.

http://www.adventist.org/beliefs/statements/main-stat18.html (accessed 2/20/10).

Appendix B

Charles M. Kinney's 12-Point Plan — Oct. 2, 1889

I wish to present twelve propositions, which, to my mind, would be a complete or perfect solution to the difficulty:

1. A frank understanding between the two races on all questions affecting each. This would avoid much trouble that would otherwise occur.
2. That colored laborers shall have no special desire to labor among white people, except an occasional invitation where to accept would cause no trouble.
3. That the colored brethren do not interfere with the outside interest among the white people; the minister in charge of such work to be judge of such interference.
4. Where the two races cannot meet together without limitation in the church, it is better to separate.
5. That missions be established among them, thus raising up separate churches. White laborers giving their time exclusively to this work.
   I realize the difficulty of white laborers attempting to labor for both classes in the South, for if they labor for the colored people they will lose their influence among the white people, but in laboring among the colored people exclusively that difficulty is obviated.
6. That in view of the outside feeling on the race question, and the hindrance it makes in accomplishing the work desired among the whites, the attendance of the colored brethren at the general meetings should not be encouraged, yet not positively forbidden. If they do attend let there be a private, mutual understanding as to the position they should assume on every phase of the meeting.
   I would say in this connection that in my judgment a separate meeting for the colored people to be held in connection with the general meetings, or a clear-cut distinction, by having them

occupy the back seats etc., would not meet with as much favor from my people as a total separation. I am willing, however, to abide by whatever the General Conference may recommend in the matter, and advise my people to do the same.

7. In those churches where there are two or more let them remain until an effort can be made to raise up a church among them; then have them to unite with it.

8. Until there is enough to form a conference of colored people, let the colored churches, companies or individuals pay their tithes and other contributions to the regular state officers, and be considered a part of the state conference.

9. That the General Conference do what it can in educating worthy colored laborers to engage in various branches of the work among them, when such can be found.

10. That Christian feeling between the two races be zealously inculcated everywhere, so that the cause of separation may not be because of the existence of prejudice within, but because of those on the outside whom you hope to reach.

11. That when colored conferences are formed they bear the same relation to the General Conference that white conferences do.

12. That these principles be applied only where this prejudice exists to the injury of the cause.

Telling The Story: An Anthology on the Development of the Black SDA Work. Complied by Delbert W. Baker, Ph.D. Loma Linda University Printing Services, Loma Linda, CA, 1996 (2nd printing, March), pages 2/8 to 2/9 .

Appendix C

"The Sixteen Point Proposal" — April 16, 1970

Regional Conferences and Human Relations—

1. Seventh-day Adventist churches open their doors to any would-be worshipper or prospective member regardless of race or color and welcome such with brotherly love and concern. Where it is felt that this principle is violated it is the duty of the next higher organization to investigate and recommend effective measures to correct.

2. The following additions to the baptismal vow and Church Manual are being recommended to the General Conference session:

   "6. All who enter the kingdom of heaven must have experienced conversion, or the new birth, through which man receives a new heart and becomes a new creature. Thus, regardless of ethnic or social background, he becomes a member of 'the whole family in heaven and earth.' (Matt. 18:3; John 3:3; 2 Cor. 5:17; Eze. 36:26, 27; Heb. 8:10-12; 1 Peter 1:23; 2:2; Eph. 3:15; Acts 17:26.)" [This paragraph is in the section dealing basic instruction and indoctrination of baptismal candidates.]

   "13. Do you believe that the Seventh-day Adventist Church is the remnant church of prophecy into which people of every nation, race, and language are invited and accepted, and do you desire membership in its fellowship?" This paragraph is a part of the baptismal vow that is presented to a candidate prior to administering the rite of baptism. At an appropriate time during this session in Atlantic City a forthright statement should be made by the leadership of the church dealing with and giving support to the position of the church on race relations.

3. Conferences selecting qualified spiritual leaders as pastors shall not be limited by race or color. Should some black pastors be appointed to white churches and some white pastors to black churches, a very desirable example of church fellowship and understanding would result; therefore programs to this end should be undertaken with the support and guidance of unions.

4. In order to make our public ministry more effective and to help members and potential members realize the importance of this brotherhood, conference administrators are urged to make clear to pastors and evangelists that it is their duty to teach these principles as a part of the gospel and our special message for the world. We further recommend that prospective members be so instructed either in the baptismal class or in personal Bible studies.

5. Special emphasis should be given to human-relations workshops to implement resolutions, which unless carried out are useless. These workshops should include all workers — field, educational, and institutional, and leading laymen from both black and white conferences and churches. It is recommended that union and/or conference-wide human-relations workshops be conducted in every union in North America before the 1971 Autumn Council.

6. Where normal entrance requirements are met, all Seventh-day Adventist schools from the elementary to the university level shall admit Seventh-day Adventist youth to the school of their choice without regard to race or color. Where a church-supported school fails to follow the counsel of the church as stated on this point, it is the duty of the next higher organization to investigate and recommend corrective measures.

7. A bi-racial commission of not more than seven members shall be appointed in the North American Division to deal with complaints of discrimination or exclusion and other problems that arise in the area of race relations that may be appealed to it for help. This commission in cooperation and in counsel with the union conferences and/or the local conference and/or the institution shall have authority to act immediately, making a thorough investigation and seeking solutions to these problems.

8. On the union conference level positive steps should be taken to open doors in the area of administrative and departmental leadership for those who have demonstrated their ability and qualifications to serve all segments of the church. In unions where there are Regional conferences or where there is an organized Regional department, the administrative officer level should include black leadership.

9. Black personnel shall be selected to serve in our publishing houses, hospitals, academies, colleges, universities, and other denominational institutions on the staff and/or administrative levels. Where it seems advisable, institutions should institute training programs for the development of black personnel in technical and administrative skills.

10. There is a missionary magazine dedicated to the black community in North America. The circulation of this journal is primarily the responsibility of the Regional churches. The Autumn Council of 1967 voted to help finance an associate circulation manager for The Message Magazine. We reaffirm that recommendation on the basis of the 1967 agreement on union participation and ask that this be implemented in the immediate future.

11. At the time of the annual North American union conference presidents' meetings one or more black administrators on the union level will be invited to participate, as well as representation from the Regional Department of the General Conference.

12. In order to provide opportunity for the presidents of Regional conferences (including the secretary of the Regional department of the Pacific Union) to consult together regarding problems distinctive to their work, Autumn Councils will schedule two meetings of this group each year, under North American Division leadership, in conjunction with other regularly called meetings. When additional meetings are required such would be arranged by the North American Division administration.

13. The next edition of the *Ministers' Manual* should include as a part of the ministerial candidate's examination before ordination questions regarding the candidate's attitude toward human relations.

14. We recommend that the General Conference lay plans to provide literature that would be useful in operating human relations workshops, setting forth standards, guidelines, and procedures in this area.
15. We recommend that the General Conference officers develop some plan whereby reports of progress in human relations may be publicized throughout the constituency in North America on local, as well as general, levels.
16. We recommend the adoption in principle of the following plan of increased financial relationships involving Regional work.

http://www.adventistarchives.org/docs/RH/RH19700604-V147-23__B.pdf#view=fit (accessed 2/22/10).

Appendix D

The Pierson Package's Nine Recommendations

The "Pierson Package" was outlined in a letter to ministers in the South England Conference dated 15 March, 1978.

1. The early employment of black office secretaries in the Union and South England Conference offices:
2. The election at each of the ensuing South England and North British Conference sessions of one black officer (with departmental responsibilities).
3. The election, not later than the next British Union Conference session, of a black officer and at least one black departmental director for the BUC.
4. The election at each of the imminent SEC and NBC sessions of one black departmental director.
5. The early placement with the General Conference and the Inter-American Division of regular calls for experienced, top-drawer black pastors with leadership potential.
6. The Union committee, in consultation with the Division Education Department, to structure a five-ten-year plan for the opening and operation of new Church schools, especially in the great metropolitan areas such as London, Birmingham and Manchester.
7. The SEC committee, in close consultation with the Union administration, to plan for the provision of a social, evangelistic, educational centre for black youth in London.
8. The prompt arrangement for measurable increased promotion of the seven-year Deed of Covenant Plan among all church members.
9. To request the General Conference through NEWAD, for generous additional financial assistance, in order to make possible the above programme of integrated fellowship and evangelism for the masses of Great Britain.

http://www.adventisthistory.org.uk/documents/souvenirmesseng er1902-1992.pdf).

Appendix E

Goals, Desired Outcomes, and
Recommendations of the 1999 SDA Race Summit

Goals
1. To identify racial barriers within the church that contribute to distrust and disunity.
2. To identify Christian methods of resolving racial conflict and preventing cultural tension through education, love, and diplomacy.
3. To identify specific manifestations of racism in the church (personally, culturally, and institutionally).
4. To recommend specific strategies for dismantling racism through consciousness raising, education, advocacy, or activism.
5. To recommend a replicable methodology for social change with specific, manageable, and realistic goals that will encourage a new level of unity within the North American Division.
6. To recommend ongoing strategies for improving race relations within the Seventh-day Adventist Church.

Desired Outcomes
1. To identify initiatives that the North American Division needs to develop and promote to better model the ministry of Christ and achieve racial harmony in the church in the new millennium.
2. To identify the impediments that need to be overcome in energizing congregational and individual action.
3. To recommend strategies for motivating and translating the initiatives to North American Division conferences, institutions, and other entities.
4. To recommend strategies for translating the initiatives to the congregational level.

Recommendation from the Delegates
WHEREAS the North American Division has recognized the need for a frank and open discussion on race relations within the

church at every level, and has responded by convening the Race Relations Summit in October 1999, and

WHEREAS the powerful presentations and discussions have demonstrated the necessity of developing a broad strategic plan of desegregation and harmony based on our Lord's prayer for "oneness" in His body, it is

RECOMMENDED that the North American Division appoint a committee, in which all members will meet on an equal footing to:

Plan a second Race Relations Summit in the year 2001,

Create a vision for the future of our church based on values so its public and internal image will be one of integration and racial harmony,

Create a strategic plan with measurable objectives and identify persons to achieve that vision,

Build on the moral imperative of Jesus for unity that will lead to a true diversity that incorporates culture, race, gender, and disability,

Create a strategic plan for the church to achieve that vision, in

a. The ecclesiastical structure, with measurable objectives for diversity, that will include seeking potential leaders and mentoring them, and

b. Congregations, to develop approaches to increase sensitivity to each other's history, personal experience, dreams for the future, and the utilization of their spiritual gifts, and the intentional cooperation and exchange of the members of diverse congregations, and

c. Education addressing the five voted key issues, utilizing all the media of the church, reaching all levels of the church and the education system, K-16, presenting practical pathways to inclusivity, so the Holy Spirit may have full say in the community of faith, preparing us on earth for the fellowship of heaven, where all forms of diversity will be affirmed and celebrated forever.

http://www.adventistreview.org/9948/story1-3.htm (accessed 2/22/10).

Bibliography

"A Statement on Racism." *The Official Site of the Seventh-day Adventist Church* (June 27, 1985): http://www.adventist.org/beliefs/statements/main-stat18.html (accessed 12/12/10).

Abu-Nimer, Mohammed, ed. *Reconciliation, Justice and Coexistence: Theory and Practice*. Lanham, MD: Lexington Books, 2001.

Aden, Leroy. "Comfort/Sustaining." *Dictionary of Pastoral Care and Counseling*, 193-195. General Editor Rodney J. Hunter, 193-195. Nashville: Abingdon Press, 1990.

Aden, Leroy, and J. Harold Ellens, eds. *Turning Points in Pastoral Care: The Legacy of Anton Boisen and Seward Hiltner*. Grand Rapids, MI: Baker Book House, 1990.

Ali, Carroll A. Watkins. *Survival and Liberation: Pastoral Theology in African American Context*. St. Louis, MO: Chalice Press, 1999.

Allen, Gregory J. "Reconciliation in the Pauline Tradition: Its Occasions, Meaning, and Functions." Ph.D. Diss. Boston University, 1995.

Allport, Gordon. *The Nature of Prejudice*. New York: Doubleday, 1954.

Anderson, Alan A. "Should the Church Organize Black Unions in North America?" *Review and Herald* 155.36 (September 7, 1978): http://www.adventistarchives.org/docs/RH/RH19780907-V155-36__B/index.djvu (accessed 11/28/10).

Appleby, R. Scott. *The Ambivalence of the Sacred: Religion, Violence, and Reconciliation*. Lanham, MD: Rowman & Littlefield Publishers, 2000.

Asante, Molefi Kete. *Afrocentricity*. New revised edition. Trenton, NJ: Africa World Press, 1991.

Ashby, Homer U., Jr. *Our Home Is Over Jordan: A Black Pastoral Theology*. St. Louis, MO: Chalice Press, 2003.

Baker, Delbert. *Make Us One: Celebrating Spiritual Unity in the Midst of Cultural Diversity: Removing Barriers, Building Bridges*. Boise, ID: Pacific Press Publishing, 1995.

_____. "Regional Conferences: 50 Years of Progress." *Adventist Review* 96 (November 2, 1995): 11-15.

_____. *The Unknown Prophet*. Washington, DC: Review and Herald Publishing, 1987.

Baker, Houston A., Jr. *Betrayal: How Black Intellectuals Have Abandoned the Ideals of the Civil Rights Era*. New York: Columbia University Press, 2008.

Baldwin, Lewis, with Rufus Burrow, Jr., Barbara A. Holmes, and Susan Holmes Winfield. *The Legacy of Martin Luther King, Jr.: The Boundaries of Law, Politics, and Religion*. Notre Dame, IN: University of Notre Dame Press, 2002.

Bar-Siman-Tov, Yaacov, ed. *From Conflict Resolution to Reconciliation*. New York: Oxford University Press, 2004.

Barham, Nigel Garth. "The Progress of the Seventh-day Adventist Church in Great Britain, 1878-1974." Ph.D. Diss. University of Michigan, 1976.

Battalora, Jacqueline. "Whiteness: The Workings of an Ideology in American Society and Culture." *Gender, Ethnicity, and Religion: Views from the Other Side*, 3-23. Edited by Rosemary Radford Ruether. Minneapolis: Fortress Press, 2002.

Battle, Michael. *Reconciliation: The Ubuntu Theology of Desmond Tutu*. Cleveland: Pilgrim Press, 1997.

Baum, Gregory, and Harold Wells. *The Reconciliation of Peoples: Challenges to the Churches*. Geneva: WCC Publications, 1997.

Bauman, Zygmunt. *Modernity and Ambivalence*. Cambridge: Polity Press, 1991.

_____. *Thinking Sociologically*. Oxford: Blackwell, 1990.

Beasley-Murray, George R. John. *Word Biblical Commentary*, 36. Waco, TX: Word Books, 1987.

Beckford, James A. *The Trumpet of Prophecy: A Sociological Study of Jehovah's Witnesses*. New York: John Wiley & Sons, 1975.

Beckley, Harlan. *Passion for Justice: Retrieving the Legacies of Walter Rauschenbusch, John A. Ryan, and Reinhold Niebuhr*. Louisville, KY: Westminster/John Knox Press, 1992.

Bell, Derrick J., Jr. *Race, Racism and American Law*. 2nd Edition. Boston: Little Brown, 1980.

Blight, David W. *Race and Reunion: The Civil War in American Memory*. Cambridge: Harvard University Press, 2001.

Blum, Edward J. *Reforging the White Republic: Race, Region, and American Nationalism, 1865-1898.* Baton Rouge: Louisiana State University Press, 2005.

Blumberg, Herbert H., A. Paul Hare, and Anna Costin. *Peace Psychology: A Comprehensive Introduction.* Cambridge: Cambridge University Press, 2006.

Boisen, Anton T. *The Exploration of the Inner World: A Study of Mental Disorder and Religious Experience.* New York: Harper & Bros., 1936.

Bonhoeffer, Dietrich. *The Cost of Discipleship.* Translated by R. H. Fuller. London: SCM Press, 1948.

_____. *Ethics.* Translated by Neville Horton Smith. New York: Touchstone Book by Simon and Schuster, 1955.

_____. *Life Together.* Translated by John W. Doberstein. New York: Harpers & Bros., 1954.

_____. *Sanctorum Communio: A Theological Study of the Sociology of the Church.* Translation by Reinhard Krauss and Nancy Lukens. Minneapolis: Fortress Press, 1998.

Bowers, Laurene Beth. *Becoming a Multicultural Church.* Cleveland: Pilgrim Press, 2006.

Boyd, Marsha Foster and Carolyn Stahl Bohler. "Womanist-Feminist Alliances: Meeting on the Bridge." *Feminist and Womanist Pastoral Theology,* 189-209. Edited by Bonnie J. Miller-McLemore and Brita L. Gill-Austern. Nashville: Abingdon Press, 1999.

Branson, Roy. "Ellen G. White, Racist or Champion of Equality." *Review and Herald* 147.15 (April 9, 1970): http://www.adventistarchives.org/docs/RH/RH19700409-V147-15__B/index.djvu (accessed 9/27/10).

_____. "Ellen G. White, Racist or Champion of Equality: Slavery and Prophecy." *Review* 147.16 (April 16, 1970): http://www.adventistarchives.org/docs/RH/RH19700416-V147-16__B/index.djvu (accessed 9/27/10).

_____. "Ellen G. White, Racist or Champion of Equality: Slavery and Prophecy: The Crisis of the Nineties." *Review* 147.17 (April 23, 1970): http://www.adventistarchives.org/docs/RH/RH19700423-V147-17__B/index.djvu (accessed 9/27/10).

Bringhurst, Newell G. *Saints, Slaves and Blacks: The Changing Place of Black People within Mormonism*. Westport, CT: Greenwood Press, 1981.

Briñol, Pablo, Richard E. Petty, and Michael J. McCaslin. "Changing Attitudes on Implicit Versus Explicit Measures: What Is the Difference?" *Attitudes: Insights from the New Implicit Measures*, 285-326. Edited by Richard E. Petty, Russell H. Fazio, and Pablo Briñol. New York: Psychology Press, 2009.

Bromiley, Geoffrey W. "Reconcile, Reconciliation." *The International Standard Bible Encyclopedia*, 4: 55-57. Edited by Geoffrey W. Bromiley. Grand Rapids, MI: W. B. Eerdmans, 1988.

Brown, Amy Benson, and Karen M. Poremski, eds. *Roads to Reconciliation: Conflict and Dialogue in the Twenty-First Century*. Armonk, NY: M.E. Sharpe, 2005.

Brown, Charles C. *Niebuhr and His Age: Reinhold Niebuhr's Prophetic Role and Legacy*. New Edition. Harrisburg, PA: Trinity Press International, 2002.

Brown, Colin, and Herwart. Vorländer. "Reconciliation, Restoration, Propitiation, Atonement." *The New International Dictionary of New Testament Theology* 3: 145-176. Edited by Colin Brown. Exeter: Paternoster Press, 1978.

Brown, Jeffery, and Pattiejean Brown. *A Guide to Parenting: On the Winning Team with Your Children*. Grantham, England: Stanborough Press, 2003.

Brownstein, Ronald. "White Flight." *The National Journal* online edition: http://nationaljournal.com/magazine/in-2012-obama-may-need-a-new-coalition-20110105?page=1 (accessed 1/7/11).

Brooks, Roy L. *Racial Justice in the Age of Obama*. Princeton: Princeton University Press, 2009.

Brueggemann, Walter. *The Prophetic Imagination*. Second ed. Minneapolis: Fortress Press, 2001.

Buber, Martin. *Between Man and Man*. New York: Macmillan, 1968.

Büchsel, Hermann M. F. "*katallasso*." *Theological Dictionary of the New Testament*, 1: 254-259. Edited by Gerhard Kittel. Grand Rapids, MI: W. B. Eerdmans, 1977.

Bull, Malcolm, and Keith Lockhart. *Seeking a Sanctuary: Seventh-day Adventism and the American Dream*. Second ed. Bloomington: Indiana University Press, 2007.

Bull, Malcolm, and Keith Lockhart. *Seeking a Sanctuary: Seventh-day Adventism and the American Dream.* San Francisco: Harper & Row, 1989.

Bush, Lester E., Jr., and Armand L. Mauss, eds. *Neither White Nor Black: Mormon Scholars Confront the Race Issue in a Universal Church.* Midvale: Signature Books, 1984.

Bush, Melanie. E. L. *Breaking the Code of Good Intentions: Everyday Forms of Whiteness.* Lanham, MD: Rowman and Littlefield, 2004.

Bushman, Richard L. *Mormonism: A Very Short Introduction.* New York: Oxford University Press, 2008.

Butler, Jon, Grant Wacker, and Randall Balmer. *Religion in American Life: A Short History.* Oxford: Oxford University Press, 2003.

Bulter, Lee H. Jr. *Liberating Our Dignity, Saving Our Souls.* St. Louis, MO: Chalice Press, 2006.

Campolo, Tony, and Michael Battle. *The Church Enslaved: A Spirituality of Racial Reconciliation.* Minneapolis: Fortress Press, 2005.

Carpenter, Alexander. "Between a Rock and a Hard Race Question." *Spectrum* (July 27, 2008): http://www.spectrummagazine.org/blog/2008/07/27/between_rock_and_hard_race_question (accessed 8/18/10).

Carson, Clayborne, ed. *The Autobiography of Martin Luther King, Jr., by Martin Luther King, Jr.* New York: Intellectual Properties Management in association with Warner Books, 1998.

Carson, Clayborne, Tenisha H. Armstrong, Susan A. Carson, Erin K. Cook, and Susan Englander. *The Martin Luther King, Jr., Encyclopedia.* Westport, CT: Greenwood Press, 2008.

Carson, D. A. *Christ and Culture Revisited.* Grand Rapids, MI: William B. Eerdmans Publishing, 2008.

Carter, Craig A. *Rethinking Christ and Culture: A Post-Christendom Perspective.* Grand Rapids, MI: Brazos Press, 2006.

Carter, J. Kameron. *Race: A Theological Account.* Oxford: Oxford University Press, 2008.

Cash, W. J. *The Mind of the South.* Garden City, NY: Doubleday/Anchor Books, 1954.

Cassidy, Laurie M., and Alex M. Mikulich, eds. *Interrupting White Privilege: Catholic Theologians Break the Silence.* Maryknoll, NY: Orbis Books, 2007.

Chapman, Audrey R, and Hugo van der Merwe, eds. *Truth and Reconciliation in South Africa: Did the TRC Deliver?* Philadelphia: University of Pennsylvania Press, 2008.

Chinula, Donald M. *Building King's Beloved Community: Foundations for Pastoral Care and Counseling with the Oppressed.* Cleveland: United Church Press, 1997.

Christerson, Brad, Korie L. Edwards, and Michael O. Emerson. *Against All Odds: The Struggle for Racial Integration in Religious Organizations.* New York: New York University Press, 2005.

Christie, Daniel J., Richard V. Wagner, and Deborah Du Nann Winter, eds. *Peace, Conflict, and Violence: Peace Psychology for the 21st Century.* Upper Saddle River, NJ: Prentice Hall, 2001.

Clark, Clifford E., Jr. *Henry Ward Beecher: Spokesman for a Middle-class America.* Chicago: University of Illinois Press, 1978.

Clarke, Simon. *Social Theory, Psychoanalysis, and Racism.* Houndmills, Basingstoke, Hampshire: Palgrave Macmillan, 2003.

Clebsch, William A., and Charles R. Jaekle. *Pastoral Care in Historical Perspective: An Essay with Exhibits.* Englewood Cliff, NJ: Prentice-Hall, 1964.

Clendenen, Avis, and Troy Martin. *Forgiveness: Finding Freedom Through Reconciliation.* New York: Crossroad Publishing, 2002.

Cleveland, E. Earl. "Regional Union Conferences." *Spectrum* 2.2 (Spring 1970): 41-46.

Clinebell, Howard J., Jr. *Basic Types of Pastoral Care and Counseling: Resources for the Ministry of Healing and Growth.* Rev. and enlarged ed. Nashville: Abingdon Press, 1992.

Constantine, Madonna G, and Derald Wing Sue, eds. *Addressing Racism: Facilitating Cultural Competence in Mental Health and Educational Settings.* Hoboken, NJ: John Wiley & Sons, 2006.

Cooper-White, Pamela. *The Cry of Tamar: Violence Against Women and the Church's Response.* Minneapolis: Fortress Press, 1995.

Couture, Pamela D, and Rodney J. Hunter, eds. *Pastoral Care and Social Conflict.* Nashville: Abingdon Press, 1995.

Cross, William E., Jr. *Shades of Black: Diversity in African-American Identity.* Philadelphia: Temple University Press, 1991.

Cross, William E., Jr., Thomas A. Parham, and Janet Helms. "The Stages of Black Identity Development: Nigrescence Models." *Black Psychology*, 3rd ed. 319-38. Edited by Reginald L. Jones. Berkeley, CA: Cobb & Henry Publishers, 1991.

Daly, Erin, and Jeremy Sarkin. *Reconciliation in Divided Societies: Finding Common Ground*. Philadelphia: University of Pennsylvania Press, 2007.

Davies, Susan E, and Sister Paul Teresa Hennessee, eds. *Ending Racism in the Church*. Cleveland: United Church Press, 1998.

Dederen, Raoul, ed. *Handbook of Seventh-day Adventist Theology*, 12. Commentary Reference Series. Hagerstown, MD: Review and Herald Publishing Association, 2000.

De Gruchy, John W. *Reconciliation: Restoring Justice*. Minneapolis: Fortress Press, 2002.

Dei, Sefa, George J. Leeno, Luke Karumanchery, and Nisha Karumanchery-Luik. *Playing the Race Card: Exposing White Power and Privilege*. New York: Peter Lang, 2004.

De La Torre, Miguel A. *Liberating Jonah: Forming an Ethics of Reconciliation*. Maryknoll, NY: Orbis Books, 2007.

Denney, James. *The Christian Doctrine of Reconciliation*. New York: George H. Doran Co., 1918.

Deutsch, Morton, Peter T. Coleman, and Eric C. Marcus, eds. *The Handbook of Conflict Resolution: Theory and Practice*. 2nd ed. San Francisco: Jossey-Bass, 2006.

Deymaz, Mark. *Building A Healthy Multi-Ethnic Church: Mandate, Commitments, and Practices of a Diverse Congregation*. San Francisco: John Wiley & Sons, 2007.

DeYoung, Curtiss Paul, Michael O. Emerson, George Yancey, and Karen Chai Kim. *United By Faith: The Multiracial Congregation as an Answer to the Problem of Race*. Oxford: Oxford University Press, 2003.

Donnelly, Denise A, Kimberley J. Cook, Debra van Ausdale, and Lara Foley. "White Privilege, Color Blindness, and Services to Battered Women." *Violence against Women*, 11.6 (2005): 6-37.

Douglass, Fredrick. "The Color Question." *The Fredrick Douglass Papers at the Library of Congress*: http://memory.loc.gov/cgi-bin/ampage?collId=mfd&fileName=23/23001/23001page.db&recNum=0&itemLink=/ammem/doughtml/dougFolder5.html&linkText=7 (accessed 2/9/10).

277

Du Bois, W. E. B. *Black Reconstruction in America: An Essay toward a History of the Part Which Black Folk Played in the Attempt to Reconstruct Democracy in America, 1860-1880.* New York: Russell and Russell, 1966.

———. *The Souls of Black Folk.* New York: New American Library, 1969.

Eagles, Charles W., ed. *The Mind of the South: Fifty Years Later.* Jackson: University Press of Mississippi, 1992.

Embry, Jessie L. *Black Saints in a White Church: Contemporary African American Mormons.* Salt Lake City: Signature Books, 1994.

Emerson, Michael O, and Christian Smith. *Divided by Faith: Evangelical Religion and the Problem of Race in America.* Oxford: Oxford University Press, 2000.

Emerson, Michael O., with Rodney M. Woo. *People of the Dream: Multiracial Congregations in the United States.* Princeton: Princeton University Press, 2006.

Enright, Robert D, and Elizabeth A. Gassin. "Forgiveness: A Developmental View." *Journal of Moral Education* 21.2 (1992): 99-114.

Erskine, Noel Leo. *King among the Theologians.* Cleveland: Pilgrim Press, 1994.

Faber, Heije. "The Prophetic Role in Pastoral Care." *Pastoral Psychology* 29.3 (1981): 191-202.

Fanon, Frantz. *Black Skin, White Masks.* Translated by Charles Lam Markmann. New York: Grove Press, 1991.

———. *The Wretched of the Earth.* New York: Grove, 1963.

Feagin, Joe R., and Eileen O'Brien. *White Men on Race: Power, Privilege, and the Shaping of Cultural Consciousness.* Boston: Beacon Press, 2003.

Ferguson, Andrew. "The Boy from Yazoo City." *Weekly Standard* 16.15 (December 2010): http://www.weeklystandard.com/articles/boy-yazoo-city_523551.html (accessed 12/28/10).

Findlay, James F., Jr. *Dwight L. Moody: American Evangelist 1837-1899.* Chicago: University of Chicago Press, 1969.

Fordham, W.W. *Righteous Rebel: The Unforgettable Legacy of a Fearless Advocate for Change.* Washington, DC: Review and Herald P Publishing Association, 1990.

Fortune, Marie M. "Forgiveness: The Last Step." *Violence Against Women and Children: A Christian Theological Sourcebook*, 201-06. Edited by Carol J. Adams and Marie M. Fortune. New York: Continuum, 1995.

Foster, Brian G. "The Global and the Local: Black Britain and Globalization." Ph.D. Diss. Claremont Graduate University, 2010.

Fryer, Peter. *Staying Power: The History of Black People in Britain.* London: Pluto Press, 1984.

Galtung, Johan. "After Violence, Reconstruction, Reconciliation, and Resolution: Coping with Visible and Invisible Effects of War and Violence." *Reconciliation, Justice, and Coexistence: Theory and Practice, 3-24. Edited by Mohammed Abu-Nimer.* Lanham, MD: Lexington Books, 2001.

Garfield, Sol L. *The Practice of Brief Psychotherapy.* 2nd ed. New York: John Wiley & Sons, 1998.

"GC president A. G. Daniell in his speech to the GC session." *Advent Review and Sabbath Herald.* 86.23 (June 10, 1909): 13. *http://www.adventistarchives.org/docs/RH/RH19090610-V86-23__B/index.djvu* (accessed 9/27/10).

Gerkin, Charles V. "On the Art of Caring." *Journal of Pastoral Care* 45.4 (1991): 399-408.

_____. *Prophetic Pastoral Practice: A Christian Vision of Life Together.* Nashville: Abingdon Press, 1991.

_____. *Widening the Horizons: Pastoral Responses to a Fragmented Society.* Philadelphia: Westminster Press, 1986.

Gerloff, Roswith I. H. *A Plea for British Black Theologies: The Black Church Movement in Britain: The Black Church Movement in Britain in Its Transatlantic Cultural and Theological Interaction with Special Reference to the Pentecostal Oneness (Apostolic) and Sabbatarian Movements.* Frankfurt am Main: Peter Lang, 1992.

Gill-Austern, Brita L. "Engaging Diversity and Difference: From Practices of Exclusion to Practices of Practical Solidarity." *Injustice and the Care of Souls: Taking Oppression Seriously in Pastoral Care, 13-27.* Edited by Sheryl Kujawa-Holbrook and Karen B. Montagno. Minneapolis: Fortress Press, 2009.

"Goals and Recommendations." *Adventist Review.* December 2, 2000: http://www.adventistreview.org/9948/story1-3.htm (accessed 12/20/10).

Graham, Larry K. "Healing." *Dictionary of Pastoral Care and Counseling*, 497-501. General Editor Rodney J. Hunter. Nashville: Abingdon Press, 1990.

Graybill, Lyn S. *Truth and Reconciliation in South Africa: Miracle or Model?* Boulder, CO: Lynne Rienner Publishers, 2002.

Graybill, Ronald D. E. G. *White and Church Race Relations.* Washington, DC: Review and Herald Publishing Association, 1970.

_____. *Mission to Black America: The True Story of Edson White and the Riverboat Morning Star.* Mountain View, CA: Pacific Press Publishing Association, 1971.

Greene, Alfonzo Jr. "[Black] Regional Conferences in the Seventh-day Adventist Church (SDA) Compared with United Methodist [Black] Central Jurisdiction/Annual Conferences with White SDA Conferences, from 1940-2001." Ph.D. Diss. Loyola University Chicago, 2009.

Greider, Kathleen J. *Reckoning with Aggression: Theology, Violence, and Vitality.* Louisville, KY: Westminster John Knox Press, 1997

_____. "'Too Militant'? Aggression, Gender, and the Construction of Justice." *Through the Eyes of Women: Insights for Pastoral Care*, 123-42. Edited by Jeanne Stevenson-Moessner. Minneapolis: Fortress Press, 1996.

Griffiths, Herbert. "The Impact of African Caribbean Settlers on the Seventh-day Adventist Church in Britain, 1952-2001." Ph.D. Diss. University of Leeds, 2002.

Grillo, Trina, and Stephanie M. Wildman. "Obscuring the Importance of Race: The Implication of Making Comparisons between Racism and Sexism (or Other Isms)." *Privilege Revealed: How Invisible Preference Undermines America*, 85-102. Edited by Stephanie M. Wildman. New York: New York University Press, 1996.

Hackney, James R, Jr. Review of *Interracial Justice: Conflict and Reconciliation in Post-Civil Rights America*, by Eric K. Yamamoto. *Social and Legal Studies* 10.2. (2001): 278-80.

Hale, Frank, W., Jr. "Commitment vs. Capitulation." *Spectrum* 2.2 (Spring 1970): 31-40.

_____. *Out of the Trash Came Truth: The 45th Anniversary of the 1962 Challenge of the People, and for the People Against Racism in the Seventh-day Adventist Church.* Columbus, OH: F. W. Hale, 2007.

Hale, Frank Jr., ed. *What Makes Racial Diversity Work in Higher Education: Academic Leaders Present Successful Policies and Strategies.* Sterling, VA: Stylus Publishing, 2004.

Harrison, Barbara Grizzuti. *Visions of Glory: A History and a Memory of Jehovah's Witnesses.* New York: Simon Schuster, 1978.

Harris, Paula, and Doug Schaupp. *Being White: Finding Our Place in a Multiethnic World.* Downers Grove, IL: InterVarsity Press, 2004.

Hatch, John B. *Race and Reconciliation: Redressing Wounds of Injury.* Lanham, MD: Lexington Books, 2008.

Haynes, Stephen R. *Noah's Curse: The Biblical Justification for American Slavery.* Oxford: Oxford University Press, 2002.

Hays, Danica G, and Catherine Y. Chang. "White Privilege, Oppression, and Racial Identity Development: Implications for Supervision." *Counselor Education and Supervision,* 43 (Dec. 2003): 134-145.

Heltzel, Peter Goodwin. *Jesus and Justice: Evangelicals, Race, and American Politics.* New Haven: Yale University Press, 2009.

Helms, Janet E. *A Race is a Nice Thing to Have: A Guide to Being a White Person or Understanding the White Person in Your Life.* Topeka, KS: Content Communications, 1992.

Herman, Judith. *Trauma and Recovery.* New York: BasicBooks, 1992.

Heyse, Amy L, and Ebony A. Uley. "Barack Obama's (Im)Perfect Union: An Analysis of the Strategic Success and Failures of His Speech on Race." *Western Journal of Black Studies* 33.3 (2009): 153-163.

Hill, Johnny Bernard. *The Theology of Martin Luther King, Jr. and Desmond Mpilo Tutu.* New York: Palgrave Macmillan, 2007.

Hiltner, Seward. *Preface to Pastoral Theology.* New York: Abingdon Press, 1958.

Hines, Samuel George, and Curtiss Paul DeYoung. *Beyond Rhetoric: Reconciliation as a Way of Life.* Valley Forge: Judson Press, 2000.

Hoekema, Anthony A. *Jehovah's Witnesses.* Grand Rapids, MI: William B. Eerdmans Publishing, 1963.

Holifield, E. Brooks. *A History of Pastoral Care in America: From Salvation to Self-Realization.* Nashville: Abingdon Press, 1983.

Hutchinson, Brian. G. E. *Moore's Ethical Theory: Resistance and Reconciliation.* Cambridge: Cambridge University Press, 2001.

Ings, William, "Missionary Work in England." Review and Herald. (July 11, 1878): 19: http://www.adventistarchives.org/docs/ RH/RH18780711-V52-03__B/index.djvu (accessed 11/4/10).

Jackson, Jennifer V., and Mary E. Cothran. "Black Versus Black: The Relationship among African, African American, and African Caribbean Persons." *Journal of Black Studies* 33.5 (May 2003): 576-604.

Jackson, Walter C., III. "The Oates Agenda for Pastoral Care." *Spiritual Dimensions of Pastoral Care: Witness to the Ministry of Wayne E. Oates*, 119-42. Edited by Gerald L. Borchert and Andrew D. Lester. Philadelphia: Westminster Press, 1985.

Jacobson, Cardell K., John P. Hoffmann, and Tim B. Heaton, eds. *Revisiting Thomas F. O'Dea's "The Mormons": Contemporary Perspectives.* Salt Lake City: University of Utah Press, 2008.

Jacobson, Matthew Frye. *Whiteness of a Different Color: European Immigrants and the Alchemy of Race.* Cambridge: Harvard University Press, 1998.

Jensen, Robert. *The Heart of Whiteness: Confronting Race, Racism, and White Privilege.* San Francisco: City Lights, 2005.

Jeong, Ho-Won. *Peacebuilding in Postconflict Societies: Strategy and Process.* Boulder, CO: Lynne Rienner Publishers, 2005.

Johnson, Allan G. *Privilege, Power, and Difference.* Boston: McGraw Hill, 2001.

Johnson, Lee M., Rehan Mullick, and Charles Mulford. "General Versus Specific Victim Blaming." *Journal of Social Psychology* 142.2 (2002): 249-63.

Johnsson, William G. "Four Big Questions." *Adventist Review* (May 25, 2006): http://www.adventistreview.org/issue.php?Issue= 2006-1515&page=8 (accessed 8/17/10).

Jones, R. Clifford. *James K. Humphrey and the Sabbath-Day Adventists.* Jackson, MI: University Press of Mississippi, 2006.

Jones, William R. *Is God a White Racist? A Preamble to Black Theology.* Boston: Beacon Press, 1998.

Jordan, Winthrop D. *The White Man's Burden: Historical Origins of Racism in the United States.* London: Oxford University Press, 1974.

Justes, Emma J. "We Belong Together: Toward an Inclusive." *The Treasure of Earthen Vessels: Exploration in Theological Anthropology in Honor of James N. Lapsley*, 137-50. Edited by Brian H. Childs and David W. Waanders. Louisville, KY: Westminster John Knox Press, 1994.

Kendall, Frances E. *Understanding White Privilege: Creating Pathways to Authentic Relationships across Race.* New York: Routledge, 2006.

Kibble, Alvin M. "When Silence is Not Golden." *Adventist Review* (January 15, 2008): http://www.adventistreview.org/ article.php?id=2360 (accessed 11/22/10).

Kimmel, Michael S, and Abby L. Ferber, eds. *Privilege: A Reader.* Boulder, CO: Westview Press, 2003.

King, Martin Luther, Jr. *Strength to Love.* Philadelphia: Fortress Press, 1981.

_____. *Stride Toward Freedom: The Montgomery Story.* New York: Harper & Bros, 1958.

_____. *Where Do We Go from Here: Chaos or Community?* New York: Harper & Row, 1967.

_____. *Why We Can't Wait.* New York: New American Library, 1964.

Kinney, Charles M. "Statement on the Concept of Regional Conferences." (October 2, 1889). *Telling the Story: An Anthology on the Development of the Black SDA Work,* 2/8 – 2/9. Edited by Delbert Baker: http://www.blacksdahistory.org/files/ 39717569.PDF (accessed 9/27/10).

Knight, George R. *Organizing to Beat the Devil: The Development of Adventist Church Structure.* Edited by Gerald Wheeler. Hagerstown, MD: Review and Herald Publishing Association, 2001.

Koranteng-Pipim, Samuel. *Must We Be Silent? Issues Dividing Our Church.* Ann Harbor, MI: Berean Books, 2001.

Kornfeld, Margaret Zipse. *Cultivating Wholeness: A Guide to Care and Counseling in Faith Communities.* New York: Continuum, 2000.

Kotter, John P. *Leading Change.* Boston: Harvard Business School Press, 1996.

Kubo, Sakae. *The God of Relationships: How the Gospel Helps to Reach Across Barriers Such as Race, Culture and Gender.* Hagerstown, MD: Review and Herald Publishing Association, 1993.

Kujawa-Holbrook, Sheryl A. "Love and Power: Antiracist Pastoral Care." *Injustice and the Care of Souls: Taking Oppression Seriously in Pastoral Care*, 13-27. Edited by Sheryl Kujawa-Holbrook and Karen B. Montagno. Minneapolis: Fortress Press, 2009.

Küng, Hans. *The Church*. Trans. Ray and Rosaleen Ockenden. London: Burns & Oates, 1968.

Lake, Judson S. *A Nation in God's Hands: Ellen White and the Civil War*. Nampa, ID: Pacific Press Publishing Association, 2017.

Land, Gary, ed. *The World of Ellen G. White*. Washington, DC: Review and Herald Publishing Association, 1987.

Lartey, Emmanuel Y. *Pastoral Theology in an Intercultural World*. Cleveland: Pilgrim Press, 2006.

Lederach, John Paul. *Building Peace: Sustainable Reconciliation in Divided Societies*. Washington, DC: United States Institute of Peace Press, 1997.

"Let Talk Encore: D.C. Young Professionals Talk Change with Adventist Church President." *Adventist News Network* (September 29, 2009): http://news.adventist.org/2009/09/lets-talk-encore-dc.html (accessed 8/25/10).

Lewis, David Levering, ed. *W. E. B. Du Bois: A Reader*. New York: Henry Holt and Co, 1995.

Lincoln, C. Eric, and Lawrence H. Mamiya. *The Black Church in the African American Experience*. Durham: Duke University Press, 1990.

Lipsitz, George. *The Possessive Investment in Whiteness: How White People Profit from Identity Politics*. Revised and expanded ed. Philadelphia: Temple University Press, 2006.

Lochman, Jan Milič. *Reconciliation and Liberation: Challenging a One-Dimensional View of Salvation*. Translated by David Lewis. Philadelphia: Fortress Press, 1980.

London, Samuel Gene. "From Conservatism to Activism: The Evolution of Seventh-day Adventist Participation in Civil Rights politics." Ph.D. Diss. Purdue University, 2006.

Lund, Carole L., and Scipio A. J. Colin, III., eds. *White Privilege and Racism: Perceptions and Actions*. San Francisco: Jossey-Bass, 2010.

MacMullan, Terrance. *Habits of Whiteness: A Pragmatist Reconstruction*. Bloomington: Indiana University Press, 2009.

Maio, Gregory R, Geoffrey Haddock, Susan E. Watt, and Miles Hewstone. "Implicit Measures in Applied Contexts: An Illustrative Examination of Antiracism Advertising." *Attitudes: Insights from the New Implicit Measures*, 327-57. Edited by Richard E. Petty, Russell H. Fazio, and Pablo Briñol. New York: Psychology Press, 2009.

Makapela, Alven. *The Problem with Africanity in the Seventh-day Adventist Church*. Lewiston, NY: E. Mellen Press, 1996.

Marshall, David N, ed. *A Century of Adventism in the British Isles*. Grantham, England: Stanborough Park, 2000: http://www.adventisthistory.org.uk/documents/CenturyofAdventism.pdf (accessed 11/4/10).

Martin, Ralph P. *Reconciliation: A Study of Paul's Theology*. Atlanta: John Knox Press, 1981.

Matsuoka, Fumitaka. *The Color of Faith: Building Community in a Multiracial Society*. Cleveland: United Church Press, 1998.

McClure, Alfred C. "An Expression of Sorrow and Apology." *Adventist Review* (December 2, 2000): http://www.adventistreview.org/9948/story1-4.htm (accessed 12/20/10).

McIntosh, Peggy. "White Privilege: Unpacking the Invisible Knapsack." http://www.case.edu/president/aaction/unpackingTheKnapsack.pdf (accessed 7/6/10).

McNeill, T. John. *A History of the Cure of Souls*. New York: Harper & Bros., 1951.

Meredith, Martin. *Coming to Terms: South Africa's Search for Truth*. New York: Public Affairs, 1999.

Metzler, Christopher J. "Barack Obama's Faustian Bargain and the Fight for America's Racial Soul." *Journal of Black Studies* 40.3 (January 2010): 395-410.

Miles, Norman K. "Tensions between the Races." *The World of Ellen G. White*, 47-60. Edited by Gary Land. Washington, DC: Review and Herald Publishing, 1987.

Miller, E. M. "Victimization." *Dictionary of Pastoral Care and Counseling*, 1301. General ed. Rodney J. Hunter. Nashville: Abingdon Press, 1990.

Miller, William Robert. "Dynamics of Reconciliation." *Pastoral Psychology* 18.8 (1967): 25-32.

Mills, Charles W. *The Racial Contract*. Ithaca: Cornell University Press, 1997.

Ministerial Association of Seventh-day Adventists. *Seventh-day Adventists Believe: A Biblical Exposition of 27 Fundamental Doctrines.* Hagerstown, Maryland: Review and Herald Publishing Association, 1988.

Mitchell, K. R. "Guidance, Pastoral." *Dictionary of Pastoral Care and Counseling,* 486-487. General ed. Rodney J. Hunter. Nashville: Abingdon Press, 1990.

Morgan, Douglas. *Adventism and the Republic: The Public Involvement of a Major Apocalyptic Movement.* Knoxville: University of Tennessee Press, 2001.

_____. *Lewis C. Sheafe: Apostle to Black America.* Hagerstown, MD: Review and Herald Publishing, 2010.

Mulford, Charles L., Motoko Y. Lee, and Stephen C. Sapp. "Victim-Blaming and Society-Blaming Scales for Social Problems." *Journal of Applied Social Psychology* 26.15 (1996): 1324-336.

Murray, Peter C. *Methodists and the Crucible of Race, 1930-1975.* Columbia: University of Missouri Press, 2004.

Myrdal, Gunnar. *An American Dilemma: The Negro Problems and Modern Democracy.* New York: Harper and Bros., 1944.

Nadler, Arie, Thomas E. Malloy, and Jeffrey D. Fisher, eds. *The Social Psychology of Intergroup Reconciliation.* New York: Oxford University Press, 2008.

Nelson, Dwight K. *The Eleventh Commandment: A Fresh Look at Loving Your Neighbor as Yourself.* Nampa, ID: Pacific Press Publishing Association, 2001.

_____. "The Truth in Black and White." Pioneer Memorial SDA Church. http://www.pmchurch.tv/article.php?id=30 (accessed 9/6/10).

Newport, Kenneth G. C. *Apocalypse and Millennium: Studies in Biblical Eisegesis.* Cambridge: Cambridge University Press, 2000.

Niebuhr, H. Richard, and Daniel D. Williams, eds. *The Ministry in Historical Perspectives.* New York: Harpers & Bros., 1956.

Niebuhr, H. Richard. *Christ and Culture.* York: Harper & Row Publishers, 1951.

_____. *The Kingdom of God in America.* Hamden, CT: Shoe String Press, 1956.

_____. *The Responsible Self: An Essay in Christian Moral Philosophy.* New York: Harper & Row, 1963.

_____. *The Social Sources of Denominationalism.* New York: Meridian Books, 1957.

Niebuhr, Reinhold. *The Children of Light and the Children of Darkness: A Vindication of Democracy and a Critique of its Traditional Defense.* New York: Charles Scribner's Sons, 1944.

_____. "The Gospel in Future America." *Christian Century* 75 (June 18, 1958): 714-16.

_____. *The Irony of American History.* New York: Charles Scribner's Sons, 1954.

_____. *Moral Man and Immoral Society: A Study in Ethics and Politics.* vol. 1. New York: Charles Scribner's Sons, 1932.

_____. *Moral Man and Immoral Society: A Study in Ethics and Politics.* Louisville: Westminster/John Knox Press, 2001.

"1998: Apartheid Report Accuses SA Leaders." *BBC, On This Day.* (October 29, 1998): http://newsbbc.co.uk/onthisday/hi/dates/stories/october/29/newssid_2468000/2468007.stm (accessed 1/12/11).

Nissim-Sabat, Marilyn. *Neither Victim nor Survivor: Thinking Towards a New Humanity.* Lanham, MD: Lexington Books, 2009.

Oates, Wayne. *The Christian Pastor.* 3rd ed. Philadelphia: Westminster Press, 1982.

_____. *Pastoral Counseling.* Philadelphia: Westminster Press, 1974.

_____. *Pastoral Counseling in Social Problems: Extremism, Race, Sex, Divorce.* Philadelphia: Westminster Press, 1966.

O'Dea, Thomas F. *The Mormons.* Chicago: University of Chicago Press, 1957.

Office of Human Relations [the official North American Division website]. "Race Relations Committee." http://www.nadadventist.org/humanrelations/about/racecom.html (accessed 5/2/03).

Oglesby, E. Hammond. *O Lord, Move This Mountain: Racism and Christian Ethics.* St. Louis, MO: Chalice Press, 1998.

Okholm, Dennis L., ed. *The Gospel in Black and White: Theological Resources for Racial Reconciliation.* Downers Grove, IL: InterVarsity Press, 1997.

Omi, Michael, and Howard Winant. *Racial Formation in the United States: From the 1960s to the 1990s.* 2nd ed. New York: Routledge, 1994.

"Oration of Frederick Douglass." *American Missionary* 39.6 (June 1885): http://digital.library.cornell.edu/cgi/t/text/pageviewer-idx?c=amis;cc=amis;rgn=full%20text;idno=amis0039-6;didno=amis0039-6;view=image;seq=0177;node=amis0039-6%3A10 (accessed 9/21/10).

Osborn, Richard. "Floppy Disc Event or Revolutionary Summit." *Adventist Review* (December 2, 2000): http://www.adventist review.org/9948/story1-2.htm (accessed 1/3/10).

Oskamp, Stuart, ed. *Reducing Prejudice and Discrimination.* Mahwah, NJ: Lawrence Erbuam Associates, 2000.

Padilla, Amado M, and William Perez. "Acculturation, Social Identity, and Social Cognition: A New Perspective." *Hispanic Journal of Behavioral Sciences* 25.1 (February 2003): 35-55.

Page, Scott E. *The Difference: How the Power of Diversity Creates Better Groups, Firms, Schools, and Societies.* Princeton: Princeton University Press, 2007.

Pattison, E. Mansell. "Defense and Coping Theory." *Dictionary of Pastoral Care and Counseling,* 267-269. General ed. Rodney J. Hunter. Nashville: Abingdon Press, 1990.

Pearson, Michael. *Millennial Dreams and Moral Dilemmas: Seventh-day Adventism and Contemporary Ethics.* Cambridge: Cambridge University Press, 1990.

Peart, Norman Anthony. *Separate No More: Understanding and Developing Racial Reconciliation in Your Church.* Grand Rapids, MI: Baker Books, 2000.

Penno, David K. "An Investigation of the Perceptions of Clergy and Laity on Race-Based Organizational Segregation in the Southern Union Conference of Seventh-day Adventists." Ph.D. Diss. Andrews University, 2009.

Perkins, Spencer, and Chris Rice. *More than Equals: Racial Healing for the Sake of the Gospel.* Downers Grove, IL: InterVarsity Press, 1993.

Perkinson, James W. *White Theology: Outing Supremacy in Modernity.* New York: Palgrave Macmillan, 2004.

Pew. "Blacks Upbeat about Black Progress, Prospects." The Pew Research Center (January 12, 2010): http://pewsocial trends.org/2010/01/12/blacks-upbeat-about-black-progress-prospects/ (accessed 12/28/10).

Pewewardy, Nocona and Margaret Severson. "A Threat to Liberty: White Privilege and Disproportionate Minority Incarceration." *Journal of Progressive Human Services* 14.2 (2003): 53-74.

Phillips, Mike, and Trevor Phillips. *Windrush: The Irresistible Rise of Multi-Racial Britain*. London: HarperCollins Publishers, 1998.

Pinterits, E. Janie, Lisa B. Spanierman, and V. Paul Poteat. "The White Privilege Attitudes Scale: Development and Initial Validation." *Journal of Counseling Psychology* 56.3 (2009): 417-429.

Plantak, Zdravko. *The Silent Church: Human Rights and Adventist Social Ethics*. Basingstoke, Hampshire: Macmillan, 1998.

Poling, James N. *Deliver Us from Evil: Resisting Racial and Gender Oppression*. Minneapolis: Fortress Press, 1996.

Pollard, Leslie. "The Cross-Culture: Challenging a Church as It Begins a New Millennium." *Adventist Review* (February 2000): 20-24.

_____. "What Do We Do With Differences?" *Adventist Review* (November 2, 2000): http://www.adventistreview.org/2000-1549/story1.html (accessed 8/17/10).

Porter, Dennis. S. *A Century of Adventism in the British Isles*. Grantham, England: Stanborough Press, 1974.

"Possibility Quotes." http://www.motivational-well-being.com/possibility-quotes.html (accessed 1/12/11).

Putnam, Robert D. "E Pluribus Unum: Diversity and Community in the Twenty-first Century." *The 2006 Johan Skytte Prize Lecture*. http://www3.interscience.wiley.com/cgi-bin/fulltext/118510920/PDFSTART (accessed 7/22/10).

Quille, Marta Martinelli. "A Response to Recent Critiques of Conflict Resolution: Is Critical Theory the Answer?" *Copenhagen Peace Research Institute* (August 2000). http://www.ciaonet.org/wps/qum01/(accessed 12/12/10).

"Racial and Ethnic Reconciliation in the Seventh-day Adventist Church." http://www.thepetitionsite.com/1/race-reconciliation-in-the-seventh-day-adventist-church (accessed 7/23/10).

Ramsay, Nancy J. "Navigating Racial Difference as a White Pastoral Theologian." *Journal of Pastoral Theology* 12.2 (2002): 11-27.

_____., ed. *Pastoral Care and Counseling: Redefining the Paradigms*. Nashville: Abingdon Press, 2004.

_____. *Pastoral Diagnosis: A Resource for Ministries of Care and Counseling*. Minneapolis: Fortress Press, 1998.

"Readers Respond to Four Big Questions." http://www.adventist review.org/ issue/php?=660%action=print (accessed 8/6/ 10).

"Regional Voice Founder Passes." *Regional Voice* [Magazine]. 2010 Special General Conference Issue, 6-7.

Reynolds, Louis B. *We Have Tomorrow: The Story of American Seventh-day Adventists with an African Heritage.* Washington, DC: Review and Herald Publishing Association, 1984.

Richardson, Tina Q., Angela R. Bethea, Charlayne C. Hayling, and Claudette Williamson-Taylor. "African and Afro-Caribbean American Identity Development: Theory and Practice." *Handbook of Multicultural Counseling,* 227-39. Edited by Joseph G. Ponterotto, J. Manuel Casas, Lisa A. Suzuki, and Charlene M. Alexander. Thousand Oaks, CA: Sage Publications, 2010.

Rivera, Lourdes M. "Acculturation: Theories, Measurement, and Research." *Handbook of Multicultural Counseling,* 331-42. Edited by Joseph G. Ponterotto, J. Manuel Casas, Lisa A. Suzuki, and Charlene M. Alexander. Thousand Oaks, CA: Sage Publications, 2010.

"Robert M. Kilgore." *Review and Herald* (October 29, 1889): 683.

Roberts, Samuel K. *African American Christian Ethics.* Cleveland: Pilgrim Press, 2001.

Robinson, Randall. *The Debt: What America Owes to Blacks.* New York: Dutton, 2000.

Rock, Calvin B. "Adventist Review: Readers Respond to Four Big Questions." *Adventist Review* (August 10, 2006): http://www.adventistreview.org/issue.php?issue=2006-1522&page=13 (accessed 8/17/10).

_____. "Cultural Pluralism (A Sociological Reality) and Black Unions." D.Min. Thesis, Vanderbilt University, 1978.

_____. "Institutional Loyalty Versus Racial Freedom: The Dilemma of Black Seventh-day Adventist Leadership." Ph.D. Diss. Vanderbilt University, 1984.

_____, ed. *Perspectives: Black Seventh-day Adventists Face the Twenty-first Century.* Hagerstown, MD: Review and Herald Publishing Association, 1996.

_____. "Revisiting 'The Obama Message." *Adventist Review* (July 24, 2008): http://www.adventistreview.org/issue.php?issue=2008-1505&page=1991 (accessed 8/18/10).

_____. "Regional Conferences: An Exhibition of Unity in Diversity." *Regional Voice* [Magazine], Special General Conference Issue, 2010, 8.

Rodríquez, Rubén Rosario. *Racism and God-Talk: A Latino/a Perspective.* New York: New York University Press, 2008.

Roediger, David R. *The Wages of Whiteness: Race and the Making of the American Working Class.* Revised ed. London: Verso, 1999.

Rothenberg, Paula S, ed. *White Privilege: Essential Readings on the Other Side of Racism.* New York: Worth Publishers, 2008.

Rosado, Caleb. *Broken Walls.* Boise, ID: Pacific Press Publishing Association, 1990.

Rothstein, Robert L., ed. *After the Peace: Resistance and Reconciliation.* Boulder, CO: Lynne Rienner Publishers, 1999.

Russell, Fredrick A. "The Obama Message." *Adventist Review* (February 21, 2008): http://www.adventistreview.org/issue.php?issue=2008-1505&page=17 (accessed 8/18/10).

Ryan, William. *Blaming The Victim.* New York: Pantheon Books, 1971.

Sandeen, Ernest R. *The Origins of Fundamentalism: Toward a Historical Interpretation.* Philadelphia: Fortress Press, 1968.

Scheurich, James J. "Toward a Discourse on White Racism." *Educational Researcher* 22.5 (1993): 5-10.

Scheurich, James J. and Michelle D. Young. "Coloring Epistemologies: Are Our Research Epistemologies Racially Biased?" *Educational Researcher* 26.4 (1997): 4-16.

Schreiter, Robert J. *Reconciliation: Mission and Ministry in a Changing Social Order.* Maryknoll, NY: Orbis Books, 1992.

Schuman, Howard, Charlotte Steeh, Lawrence Bobo, and Maria Krysan. *Racial Attitudes in America: Trends and Interpretations.* Revised ed. Cambridge: Harvard University Press, 1997.

Schwarz, Richard W., and Floyd Greenleaf. *Light Bearers: A History of the Seventh-day Adventist Church.* Nampa ID: Pacific Press Publishing Association, 2000.

Seifert, H. "Prophetic/Pastoral Tension in Ministry." *Dictionary of Pastoral Care and Counseling*, 963-66. General ed. Rodney J. Hunter. Nashville: Abingdon Press, 1990.

Seventh-day Adventist. GC Committee meeting (July 11, 1890): http://www.adventistarchives.org/docs/GCC/GCC1890/index.djvu (accessed 9/27/10).

Seventh-day Adventist. "Annual Statistical report for 1974." http://www.adventistarchives.org/docs/ASR/ASR1974_B/ index.djvu (accessed 11/4/10).

Seventh-day Adventist. "Annual Statistical Report for 1902." http://www.adventistarchives.org/docs/ASR/ASR1902_B/ index.djvu (accessed 11/4/10).

Seshadri-Crooks, Kalpana. *Desiring Whiteness: A Lacanian Analysis of Race.* London: Routledge, 2000.

Shelp, Earl E, and Ronald H. Sunderland. *The Pastor as Prophet.* New York: Pilgrim Press, 1985.

Smith, Archie, Jr. *Navigating the Deep River: Spirituality in African American Families.* Cleveland: United Church Press, 1997.

Smith, Kenneth L., and Ira G. Zepp, Jr. *Search for the Beloved Community: The Thinking of Martin Luther King, Jr.* Valley Forge, PA: Judson Press, 1998.

South Africa. *Truth and Reconciliation Commission of South Africa Report.* London: Macmillan, 1998.

"Southampton, England." *Review and Herald* (January 22, 1880): 60.

Spalding, Arthur W. *Origin and History of Seventh-day Adventists.* 4 vols. Washington, DC: Review and Herald Publishing Association, 1962.

Stassen, Glen H., D. M. Yeager, and John Howard Yoder. *Authentic Transformation: A New Vision of Christ and Culture.* Nashville: Abingdon Press, 1996.

Stäuble, Estheranna. "Nonviolent Direct Action, Conflict Transformation, and the Global Justice Movement: The Aubonne Bridge Case." M.A. Thesis. University of Bradford, 2004.

Stephan Walter G, and Cookie White Stephan. *Intergroup Relations.* Boulder, CO: Westview Press, 1996.

Stott, John. *The Contemporary Christian: An Urgent Plea for Double Listening.* Leicester, UK: Inter-Varsity Press, 1992.

Sue, Derald Wing. *Overcoming Our Racism: The Journey to Liberation.* Hoboken: John Wiley & Sons, 2003.

Sullivan, Shannon. *Revealing Whiteness: The Unconscious Habits of Racial Privilege.* Bloomington: Indiana University Press, 2006.

Swim, Janet K., and Charles Stangor, eds. *Prejudice: The Target's Perspective.* San Diego, CA: Academic Press, 1998.

Taggart, Stephen. *Mormonism's Negro Policy: Social and Historical Origins.* Salt Lake City: University of Utah Press, 1970.

Tatum, Beverly Daniel. *Can We Talk About Race? And Other Conversations in an Era of School Resegregation*. Beacon: Boston Press, 2007.

_____. *"Why are all the Black Kids Sitting Together in the Cafeteria?" and Other Conversations about Race*. New York: BasicBooks, 1997.

Tavuchis, Nicholas. *Mea Culpa: A Sociology of Apology and Reconciliation*. Stanford: Stanford University Press, 1991.

Taylor, Vincent. *Forgiveness and Reconciliation: A Study in New Testament Theology*. London: MacMillan, 1941.

Teel, Charles W. Jr., ed. *Remnant and Republic: Adventist Themes for Personal and Social Ethics*. Loma Linda, CA: Loma Linda University, Center for Christian Bioethics, 1995.

"The sixteen-point proposal." http://www.adventistarchives.org /docs/NAD/NAD1970-04/index.djvu (accessed 11/4/10).

"The Adventist Desegregation Coalition." Facebook (February 1, 2009): http://www.facebook.com/group.php?gid=537347 49401 (accessed 11/22/10); "Racial and Ethnic Reconciliation in the Seventh-day Adventist Church." Care 2: petitionsite (May 26, 2010): http://www.thepetitionsite.com/1/race-reconciliation-in-the-seventh-day-adventist-church/ (accessed 8/20/10).

Thandeka. *Learning to be White: Money, Race, and God in America*. New York: Continuum, 1999.

Theobald, Robin. "The Politicization of a Religious Movement: British Adventism under the Impact of West Indian Immigration." *British Journal of Sociology* 32.2 (June 1981): 203-23.

Theobald, Robin C. "The Seventh-day Adventist Movement: A Sociological Study with Particular Reference to Great Britain." Ph.D. Diss. University of London, 1979.

Thompson, Damian. *The End of Time: Faith and Fear in the Shadow of the Millennium*. Hanover, NH: University Press of New England, 1997.

Thornton, Sharon G. *Broken Yet Beloved: A Pastoral Theology of the Cross*. St. Louis, MO: Chalice Press, 2002.

Tillich, Paul. *Love, Power, and Justice: Ontological Analyses and Ethical Applications*. London: Oxford University Press, 1954.

Townes, Emilie. *In a Blaze of Glory: Womanist Spirituality as Social Witness*. Nashville: Abingdon Press, 1995.

Underwood, Grant. *The Millenarian World of Early Mormonism*. Urbana: University of Illinois Press, 1993.

Valley, Clinton A. *Help! I'm Being Followed: What to Do When You've Been Called to Lead*. Hagerstown, MD: Autumn House Publishing, 2008.

Van Biema, David. "The Color of Faith." *Time* (January 11, 2010): http://www.time.com/time/printout/0,8816,1950943,00.html (accessed 1/3/10).

Van der Merwe, Hugo. "Reconciliation and Justice in South Africa." *Reconciliation, Justice and Coexistence: Theory and Practice*, 187-207. Edited by Mohammed Abu-Nimer. Lanham, MD: Lexington Books, 2001.

Vickerman, Milton. "The Responses of West Indians to African-Americans: Distancing and Identification." *Research in Race and Ethnic Relations*, 7:83-128. Edited by Rutledge M. Dennis. Greenwich, CT: JAI Press, 1994.

Villa-Vicencio, Charles, and Wilhelm Verwoerd, eds. *Looking Back, Reaching Forward: Reflections on the Truth and Reconciliation Commission of South Africa*. Cape Town: University of Cape Town Press, 2000.

Vine, Richard D., ed. "A Century of Adventism in the British Isles: Brief History of the British Union Conference of Seventh-day Adventists." *Messenger: Centennial Historical Special*. Grantham, England: Stanborough Park, 1974.

Volf, Miroslav. *Exclusion and Embrace: A Theological Exploration of Identity, Otherness, and Reconciliation*. Nashville: Abingdon Press, 1996

Vyhmeister, Nancy, ed. *Women in Ministry: Biblical and Historical Perspectives*. Berrien Springs, MI: Andrews University Press, 1998.

Walters, Ronald W. *The Price of Racial Reconciliation*. Ann Arbor, MI: The University of Michigan Press, 2008.

Warren, Mervyn A. *Oakwood! A Vision Splendid: 1896-1996*. [Huntsville, AL]: Oakwood College, 1996.

Washington, Booker T., and W. E. B. Du Bois. *The Negro in the South: His Economic Progress in Relation to His Moral and Religious Development*. Philadelphia: George W. Jacobs & Co, 1907.

Washington, James Melvin, ed. *A Testament of Hope: The Essential Writings of Martin Luther King, Jr.* San Francisco: Harper & Row, 1986.

Wenham, Gordon J. *Genesis 1-15.* Word Biblical Commentary 36. Waco, Texas: Word Books, 1987.

West, Russell W. "That His People May Be One: An Interpretative Study of the Pentecostal Leadership's Quest for Racial Unity." Ph.D. Diss. Regent University, Virginia Beach, VA, 1997.

"What is Trauma-Focused Cognitive Behavioral Therapy (TF-CBT)?" http://academicdepartments.musc.edu/projectbest/tfcbt/tfcbt.htm (accessed 1/23/11); and http://tfcbt.musc.edu/ (accessed 1/23/11).

White, Ellen G. *The Desire of Ages.* Mountain View, CA: Pacific Press Publishing Association, 1940.

_____. *Life Sketches of Ellen G. White.* Mountain View, CA: Pacific Press Publishing Association, 1915.

_____. *The Southern Work.* Washington, D. C.: Review and Herald Publishing Association, 1966.

_____. *Testimonies for the Church.* Vol. 1. Mountain View, CA: Pacific Press Publishing Association, 1948.

_____. *Testimonies for the Church.* Vol. 9. Mountain View, CA: Pacific Press Publishing Association, 1948.

White, Terry, ed. *Blacks and Whites Meeting in America: Eighteen Essays on Race.* Jefferson, NC: McFarland & Co., 2003.

Wildman, Stephanie M. *Privilege Revealed: How Invisible Preference Undermines America.* New York: New York University Press, 1996.

Williams, David R. "The Right Thing to Do: A Divided Church and What to Do about It." *Adventist Review* (February 20, 1997).

Williams, Jarvis J. *One New Man: The Cross and Racial Reconciliation in Pauline Theology.* Nashville: B & H Academic, 2010.

Williams, Linda F. *The Constraint of Race: Legacies of White Skin Privilege in America.* University Park: Pennsylvania State University Press, 2003.

Williams, Preston N. "The Social Gospel and Race Relations: A Case Study of a Social Movement." *Toward a Discipline of Social Ethics: Essays in Honor of Walter George Muelder*, 232-55. Edited by Paul Deats. Boston: Boston University Press, 1972.

Williamson, Joel. *The Crucible of Race: Black/White Relations in the American South since Emancipation.* New York: Oxford University Press, 1984.

Wilson, Neal C. "Recent Developments in the Field of Human Relations in North America." Review and Herald (June 4, 1970): 147.

Wimberly, Edward P. *African American Pastoral Care.* Revised ed. Nashville: Abingdon Press, 2008.

_____. *Relational Refugees: Alienation and Reincorporation in African American Churches and Communities.* Nashville: Abingdon Press, 2000.

Wimmer, Andreas, Richard J. Goldstone, Donald L. Horowitz, Ulrike Joras, and Conrad Schetter, eds. *Facing Ethnic Conflicts: Toward a New Realism.* Lanham, MD: Rowman & Littlefield, 2004.

Wise, Tim. *White Like Me: Reflections on Race from a Privileged Son.* Revised and updated ed. Brooklyn, NY: Soft Skull Press, 2008.

_____. *Between Barack and a Hard Place: Racism and White Denial in the Age of Obama.* San Francisco: City Lights Books, 2009.

Woolford, Orville. "The 70s Struggle: A Black Perspective." "A Century of Adventism in The British Isles: Brief History of the British Union Conference of Seventh-day Adventists." *Messenger: Centennial Historical Special.* Edited by Richard D. Grantham. England: Stanborough Park, 1974.

Worthington, Everett L, Jr. *Forgiveness and Reconciliation: Theory and Application.* New York: Routledge, 2006.

Yamamoto, Eric K. *Interracial Justice: Conflict and Reconciliation in Post-Civil Rights America.* New York: New York University Press, 1999.

Yancey, George A. *Beyond Black and White: Reflections on Racial Reconciliation.* Grand Rapids, MI: Baker Books, 1996.

_____. *Beyond Racial Gridlock: Embracing Mutual Responsibility.* Downers Grove, IL: InterVarsity Press, 2006.

Yep, Kathleen S. "Book Review: *Interracial Justice: Conflict and Reconciliation in Post-Civil Rights America.*" *Journal of Asian American Studies* 4.2 (2001): 186-190.

Zizek, Slavoj. *Tarrying with the Negative: Kant, Hegel, and the Critique of Ideology.* Durham: Duke University Press, 1993.

Index

297

298

Printed in Poland
by Amazon Fulfillment
Poland Sp. z o.o., Wrocław

52501442R00190